THE ADOLESCENT MOLESTER

ABOUT THE AUTHOR

William Breer is a Board Certified Diplomate in Clinical Social Work. He is in full-time private practice specializing in male victims of sexual assault and child and adolescent perpetrators of sexual assault. Professional affiliations include the Society for Clinical Social Work, the American Group Psychotherapy Association, and the Adolescent Perpetrator Network of the C. Henry Kempe Center. He is a former board member of the California Coalition on Sex Offending. He is also the author of *The Diagnosis and Treatment of the Young Male Victim of Sexual Abuse.*

THE ADOLESCENT MOLESTER

Second Edition

By

WILLIAM BREER, M.S.W.

CHARLES C THOMAS • PUBLISHER
Springfield • Illinois • U.S.A.

Published and Distributed Throughout the World by

CHARLES C THOMAS • PUBLISHER
2600 South First Street
Springfield, Illinois 62794-9265

© *1996 by* CHARLES C THOMAS • PUBLISHER
ISBN 0-398-06571-3 (cloth)
ISBN 0-398-06572-1 (paper)

Library of Congress Catalog Card Number: 95-47296

First Edition, 1987

Second Edition, 1996

With THOMAS BOOKS *careful attention is given to all details of manufacturing
and design. It is the Publisher's desire to present books that are satisfactory as to their
physical qualities and artistic possibilities and appropriate for their particular use.*
THOMAS BOOKS *will be true to those laws of quality that assure a good name
and good will.*

Printed in the United States of America
SC-R-3

Library of Congress Cataloging-in-Publication Data

Breer, William.
    The adolescent molester / by William Breer. — 2nd ed.
       p.   cm.
    Includes bibliographical references and index.
    ISBN 0-398-06571-3 (cloth). — ISBN 0-398-06572-1 (paper)
    1. Teenage child molesters.   2. Child analysis.   3. Adolescent
psychotherapy.   I. Title.
RJ506.C48B74   1996
616.85'836—dc20
                                                                    95-47296
                                                                      CIP

PREFACE

The realm of those who work with adolescent molesters has changed a great deal since 1987 when I wrote the original edition of this work. Since that time, there has been an explosion of publication and professional interest in this area. A national task force has drawn recommendations for the treatment of adolescent molesters. Organizations of those who treat this population have grown and the number of conferences held worldwide has increased. I, too, have grown in knowledge and experience with this population since that time. Since the publication of the original book, I have had eight more years to work among and study this population. Inevitably, this has lead to new and deeper understandings on my part.

The idea for this revision was the publisher's. I initially did not wish to do it, realizing that it would be an immense task to do so. The book would, indeed, need to be almost totally rewritten. Too many weekends and holidays spent at the word processor instead of more pleasant activities. I changed my mind. I have learned much since the 1987 edition of this work. I decided that it was worth the sacrifices to assemble this experience and information in one place in the hope that it will challenge and stimulate those who will treat this population long after I retire.

In 1987, there was not the body of literature on adolescent molesters that exists now. Nor was I as familiar with it. This work begins with an attempt to review the significant literature on the psychodiagnosis and treatment of adolescent molesters. Such a survey is a necessary foundation to my attempt to offer an integration of research, theory, and practice which constitutes the rest of this book.

Theory has always been important to me. In 1987, I was strongly influenced by the Ego Psychologists, and particularly by Otto Kernberg and the syntheses published by Gertrude and Ruben Blanck. Since that time, I have discovered and delved more deeply into the work of the self-psychologists, most notably Heinz Kohut and Arnold Goldberg. I first used this perspective in my 1992 book on male victims. Here I have used these understandings to help throw light on the special problems of boys who molest others. In the 1987 edition much use is made of dreams. Since that time, I have discovered the works of dream theorists who are trying to integrate modern neurobiology and dream theory. A new model of dream interpretation based on this model is offered here.

The reviews of my 1987 book focused on two defects. The first was a lack of integration of the existing literature into the corpus of the work. The second and related critique was that the book was a kind of a case notebook, simply describing the clinical experience of one author. Those criticisms had much validity. I have worked very hard to correct those defects in this work. I do not, however, expect that it will make it less controversial. I expect this book to be more controversial. I have departed in several significant ways from the recommendations made by the National Task Force on Treatment of Adolescent Sex Offenders (1988, 1992). How and why I have done this will be more clearly explained in following chapters. I can only say here that I feel that I treat a population somewhat different than that worked with by most of the people publishing in this field. I work mostly with outpatients whom I have selected as suitable for community treatment. I routinely refer the more seriously criminal molesters for residential treatment. I do not accept rapists in my outpatient practice.

From time to time, I work on a contractual basis with residential programs who, indeed, treat molesters much like those described in the literature. When I do that, I incorporate much more from the standard model recommended by The National Task Force on Adolescent Sex Offending. None of the existing literature gives any specific attention to the kind of sex offender that is a central focus here. This kind of adolescent sex offender has committed the more minor offenses. He still has some ability to form a therapeutic alliance with a skilled clinician. Many of the sex offenders treated in residential settings are most properly diagnosed as antisocial personality, borderline personality, and other severe personality disorders, or covert, or not so covert, psychosis. These populations are extremely refractory to treatment. I believe that this fact has caused most of the people working with such offenders to retreat into a cluster of behavioral cognitive techniques which, though limited in aim and scope, are effective with that population. For such sex offenders, I have no quarrel with the statement that the behavioral-cognitive model is the best approach.

Techniques such as masturbatory satiation and plethysmography are, however, difficult to use in an outpatient setting. They are usually perceived as intrusive and therefore run the risk of disrupting the therapeutic alliance. Nationwide, hundreds, perhaps thousands, of therapists treat adolescent sex offenders in the community. Some have specialized backgrounds. Others treat this population as part of a generic practice. This book will be most useful to those practitioners. If a therapist who sees adolescent sex offenders goes to the literature for help, he or she will find an almost unanimous recommendation to use behavioral-cognitive techniques. These techniques are often accompanied by a style which is more correctional than therapeutic. This simply will not fly in most communities. Attorneys, judges, and administrators of major community agencies will often not support the use of these techniques. Use of the plythysmograph is particularly risky. A therapist in Phoenix, Arizona got in a dilemma of this sort in 1992. His work with behavioral-cognitive techniques and the plethysmograph came to the attention of *The Arizona Republic*'s reporter Allison Young (see Bibliography). She ran a series of articles on this therapist and his practice. The publicity was most unfavorable with some of those interviewed calling the practices child abuse. The ACLU became involved in this case and the Arizona legislature was considering mandating limits on the use of at least the plethysmograph with adolescents. Last but not least is the risk of lawsuits which intrusive techniques inevitably invite in litigious America.

If I believed that the behavioral-cognitive techniques were the best way to treat the boys I work with, I would advocate defying this community pressure and doing what is best for the patient. I believe, however, that for those adolescent molesters who should stay in the community, the standard model of treatment recommended by The National Task Force on Adolescent Sex Offending (1988, 1992) is not the treatment of choice. Some of its elements may benefit some or all of an outpatient population, but the pure form was designed for and best serves a severely disturbed and sexually damaged population that is usually and desirably treated in institutions. The standard model and its advocates do not mention such therapeutic techniques as the use of transference, empathy, and the therapeutic alliance. Those who attend professional conferences will find that for most presenters such ideas are anathema. They are considered outdated concepts that either do not affect the behavior of sex offenders or make them worse. I am advocating specifically that we make a sincere effort to identify youth who can benefit from a more traditional mental health approach which emphasizes empathy and the therapeutic alliance. These techniques are the ones which in my judgment are most likely to result in long-term and enduring personality change.

Much of this book is devoted to an attempt to understand why adolescent molesters molest. This problem is viewed here from the point of psychodynamic theory, most frequently and specifically self psychology, as well as material drawn from several other clinical and theoretical disciplines. An equally important component of the book are recommendations for treatment, particularly of outpatient and less severe populations of adolescent sex offenders. I believe the book will be of interest to those who treat the more severe cases, but that interest will be largely in its theoretical and psychodiagnostic sections. Anyone who deals with adolescent molesters in a community setting will find here an approach for treating that population which will allow them to practice effectively in the community and also pose the possibility of genuine personality change and long-term correction of underlying problems. The reader is invited to explore the rest of this work with an open but critical mind.

WILLIAM BREER

CONTENTS

THE ADOLESCENT MOLESTER

Chapter One

INTRODUCTION

Those familiar with the 1987 edition will find that much has been changed and much added in this edition. In part, this is a function of how much has been learned about adolescent and other molesters since 1987. The literature has expanded almost exponentially. In 1987, this was the only book-length treatment of the issue of boys who molest. Now there are at least four others. Each passing year sees the addition of several new journal articles on this population.

The structure available to those who treat adolescent molesters has also been greatly enhanced. By 1987, a group of pioneers had laid the foundation for an organized discipline for those treating teenage molesters. Their works have borne fruit. There is now an identifiable and coherent discipline embracing those who treat adolescent molesters. It has largely emerged in the years since 1987. It is also a much larger discipline. Each year several professional conferences deal with the issues posed by adolescent sex offenders. This gives those working in the field a chance to meet, share ideas, and grow professionally.

The pioneers spent much time pondering what works with this population and what does not. A National Task Force on Sexual Offending sponsored by the National Adolescent Perpetrator Network spent countless hours reviewing literature and sharing clinical experience. The result was a series of positions about how to treat adolescent molesters. These conclusions were published first in 1988 and most recently in 1993. I have called these positions the standard model throughout this work. Although I have reservations about the model as applicable to segments of the molester population, I cannot but applaud the hard work and sincerity of the effort.

Even before the publication of the reports of The National Task Force, the idea was emerging that a behavioral-cognitive model was the best way to treat adolescent molesters. For extremists, this became the only ethical way to treat adolescent sex offenders. The publication of the Task Force's reports congealed the orthodoxy that molesters respond best to behavioral-cognitive approaches. I will spend much time challenging that in this work. I feel the standard model works well with the most disturbed and dangerous of the molester population, but is not well adapted to the needs of the kind of boy who is typically seen in outpatient settings. Others have recently begun to challenge the universal suitability of the standard model. Their views will be detailed in the literature review.

The earliest stage of the emergence of a discipline is often chaotic. Typically chaos is followed by attempts at standardization. Standardization is in turn followed by qualification and modification of the new standards. The adolescent sex offender discipline seems to be currently at this last stage, the beginning of a critique of a newly emerged orthodoxy.

Perhaps a more alarming trend since 1987 is that those who treat sexual abuse are now viewed with some suspicion by both the American public and a significant cohort of their fellow professionals. For a while, sex abuse was at the crest of public and professional awareness. The findings of those working in the developing field acquired an unquestioning acceptance from fellow professionals and the literate public. Those who work with adolescent molesters are in most ways a part of the broader movement to deal with sexual abuse in society. By treating perpetrators we hope to prevent the abuse of others in the future. Many of our patients are also victims of sexual abuse in their own right.

Much of the public and professional reassessment of sexual abuse has been brought upon the discipline by its own irresponsible practices. Most of the scandal has been in the victim rather than the perpetrator field. There, some overzealous therapists have given all professionals who work with sexual abuse a black eye by hyping "recovered" memory, multiple personality, and other difficult to prove sequelae of sexual abuse. There may be truly repressed memories and real multiple personalities, but they have been grossly overdiagnosed. In some cases false memories have been produced by hypnosis, psychoactive drugs, and indirect or direct therapist suggestion. We have all read about the lawsuits, court battles, and public skepticism about those who treat victims of sexual abuse.

Nor is the house of those who treat perpetrators totally without blemish. In 1992, we got some very bad press in the *Arizona Republic.* This paper ran a series of articles on a sex offender treatment program in that state. An unlicensed Arizona therapist was using the plethysmograph on boys as young as 12. The paper called it "tax supported child abuse." There are obvious lessons in this. If we are to survive as a discipline, we must conduct ourselves at the highest professional standards. Practitioners need to keep up on the literature. We need to consult with each other and with those in related disciplines that impinge upon our work. We need to constantly reflect on what we are doing. Does it help the patient? Does it help society? Does it protect future victims? Does it conform to the dictates of reason? One of the primary purposes of this book is to suggest careful thought about what we are doing and why we are doing it.

Probably as a direct outgrowth of the self-inflicted wounds of those treating victims, courts are returning to a more permissive handling of juvenile sex offenders. More adolescent molesters are being left at home. Those who administer residential programs are complaining that they are getting either fewer or more disturbed referrals. Some of this is budget-driven. Every level of government wants to spend less. Removing adolescent sex offenders from their homes and sending them to residential facilities is costly. Managed care certainly does not want to pay from programs that may last years.

Whatever the reasons, courts all over the country will probably be asking therapists who treat adolescent molesters as outpatients to take on more and more difficult patients. If a judge is making such a choice because he or she believes that professionals have distorted the nature of the problem to suit their professional needs, they will not be very supportive of the intrusive techniques of the standard model. Even if the real reason for leaving a molester at home is fiscal, the courts are likely to justify it by convincing themselves that it is in the best interest of the molester and his family. Such courts are unlikely to support a therapist if families complain that some crazy therapist wants to hook their child up to some machine that measures his penis or to have him masturbate to verbalized fantasies on an audiotape.

My principal reason for preferring to avoid much of the standard model in treating adolescent molesters has been that I feel it is a supportive type of therapy designed to control behavior rather than implement real change. This is a central thesis of this book and will be explored in detail elsewhere. A second reason for not embracing the standard model in my practice is that I have never felt that the local courts, attorneys, probation officers, or child protection workers would be the least bit supportive of this type of treatment. I have dealt with the problem by recommending placement where I felt the standard model was the treatment of choice.

The current climate in sex abuse treatment and the treatment of adolescent molesters suggests that an alternative to the standard model is necessary to treat the lighter weight outpatient and at least some of the more truly treatable adolescents in residential facilities. Much of the rest of this work will provide the theoretical and practical tools that will allow a clinician to do that.

Since 1987, my own interests have broadened. I have spent a significant part of my professional time treating boys who are only victims and not perpetrators of sexual abuse. This led to the 1992 publication of *The Diagnosis and Treatment of the Young Male Victim of Sexual Abuse.* I found much in common between male victims and adolescent perpetrators. There are also some significant differences. One of the commonalities is that molesters and male victims seem to share different varieties of what can be conceptualized as disorders of masculinity.

This moved my interest toward male development in the most general sense. What are the elements of successful maleness in American culture and subcultures? What is the interaction between male development and culture? Is maleness wholly shaped by culture? Are there cross-cultural regularities that suggest some inherent biological or biosocial determinants? These issues were dealt with at some length in *The Diagnosis and Treatment of the Young Male Victim of Sexual Abuse.* That work forced me to scour the psychodynamic literature for paradigms of male development. I found one which had only emerged in the 1980s and adapted it for use in understanding the dynamics of male victims. I proposed using the new model as the theoretical foundation for the treatment of male victims.

In returning here to adolescent perpetrators, I hoped to bring to bear what I have learned about male development to the study and healing of boys who molest others. This is one reason so much of this text has changed since 1987. I do not know where I will go from here, but I suspect it will be into further exploration of the disorders of masculinity. This concept seems to have value in explaining a great many of the sexually-related problems to which males are prone. The concept, I believe, can throw light on the problems of rapists, men who batter women, the perversions to which men are so much more prone than women, and even the male's greater propensity to crime and violence. But all that is for another book. Now this book must move on to an exploration of the literature.

Chapter Two

A REVIEW OF THE LITERATURE

A good review of the literature will allow the reader to develop an awareness of what is known empirically about adolescent molesters and to use that information to develop a more generalized understanding of the nature of this population. Careful reading of the literature may even shed some light on the dynamics which drive the behavior of those who molest. Such information is necessary, both to understanding whom and what we are dealing with, and to devising treatment plans that may offer meaningful help to the molester and enduring protection to society.

The literature on adolescent molesters, per se, is relatively limited. The literature touching on questions relevant to the understanding of adolescent molesters is much larger. An immediate problem is that much of the literature does not even distinguish between teenage boys who molest younger children and adolescent males who rape victims their own age or older. It is one of the central theses of this work that future research needs to distinguish between these two populations in order to develop a more meaningful database. Anyone wishing to become familiar with the literature on adolescent molesters must wade through a great deal of information about the much larger, undifferentiated group called "adolescent sex offenders," a group which includes both rapists and molesters.

The literature indicates that between 93 and 95 percent of adolescents who molest are male (Browne et al., 1984) (Davis and Leitenberg, 1987). My limited experience with female adolescent molesters suggests that it would be unwise to lump them with males. Because the problem of molesting or at least detected molesting is male, and because my experience is concentrated with males, literature regarding female adolescent offenders will not be reviewed, and the pronoun "he" will be used wherever adolescent sex offenders are referred to throughout this work.

Although the focus here is on adolescents, in certain cases the adult literature sheds very important light on what is going on with adolescents.

In those cases the relevant literature on adult sex offenders will be reviewed here. The focus of this review will be on the descriptive and empirical literature. Clinical literature will be touched on lightly in this chapter. The clinical literature will be integrated more extensively into later chapters where treatment, assessment, and related issues are under discussion.

DEFINING SEX OFFENSES

In addition to lumping rapists and molesters into a unitary category for research study, the literature suffers another problem. That is a problem of definition. Just what is an adolescent sex offense? Different studies use different criteria. Frequently, an age difference of five-years is required to define sexual contact between a younger and older child as a molestation. Nonetheless, any clinician working in the field is aware that many teenage boys are undergoing involuntary treatment in facilities for sexual contact with children two or three years younger than they are, contact which did not involve force. This is not necessarily indicative that such an activity is not molestation, but, technically, the literature is not meeting its own definitions when it includes such offenders in research studies. To deal with this problem, some researchers shorten the age interval necessary to define one party as a molester.

Another issue: what specific behaviors constitute a sex offense? Some researchers and clinicians define a sex offense as any act involving touching or penetration with an erotic intent on the part of the aggressor. Others include offenses that do not involve actual physical contacts in the roster of adolescent sex offenses. Ageton (1983), for example, obtained a phenomenally high incidence of adolescent males sexually assaulting others (5,000 to 16,000 perpetrators per 100,000 adolescents). The problem with this figure is that it was obtained by using a survey containing questions defining a sex offense as any kind of situation in which an adolescent male coerced another person into sexual acts. Verbal coercion was included in this definition. This definition would include some offenders who talked a partner into sex during a date. A common problem is that researchers often do not tell the reader what criteria they used to define adolescent sex offenses.

The reader will note other problems in the literature. Most of the studies of adults involve prison populations. Many of the studies of adolescents involve those in residential facilities. These populations are presumably more disturbed than those involved in outpatient programs. Many studies lack control groups. Many of the samples are small. Questionnaire studies are essentially self-reports, problematic in a population not known for its veracity. Although the literature is far from perfect, it has become richer and more informative since the original edition of this book.

WHY THE CONCERN?

Concern with adolescent sex offenders is relatively recent. It appears to have begun in earnest in the early 1980s and to have grown dramatically since that time. The reasons for this explosion of concern and the resulting proliferation of studies are multiple. Perhaps most basic is an increasing awareness that the adolescent molester is a vital link in a chain of molestation wherein younger children are damaged by older children and adolescents who have themselves been molested. The literature indicates that adolescents are responsible for 20 percent of the rapes in America and between 30 and 50 percent of all child sexual abuse occurring in this country (Davis and Leitenberg, 1987).

Twenty thousand sexual offenses committed by adolescents were reported by the FBI in 1981. The numbers have been growing since that time. They appear also to be the tip of an iceberg. Finkelhor found that only 35 percent of child victims ever report their victimization (1979). There is a growing consensus that adolescence is the time to intervene in these cases, both because adolescents appear to be more treatable than adult sex offenders, and because certain researchers have made some significant findings relevant to beginning treatment in adolescence. Abel and his coauthors (1984) believe that the average adolescent sex offender will go on to commit 380 sex crimes in the course of his life. Davis and Leitenberg (1987) published data indicating that 50 percent of adult sex offenders began their offending careers during their adolescence. Assuming treatment is effective, the sooner the treatment begins, the fewer children will be victimized.

ARE ADOLESCENT SEX OFFENDERS DELINQUENTS?

There has been much interest in the research literature in comparing adolescent sex offenders with other groups of incarcerated delinquents to see how the two populations compare. The essential question seems to be, is the adolescent sex offender simply a subspecies of juvenile delinquent? Rubenstein et al. (1983) found adolescent sex offenders and a control group of other delinquents similarly violent. The sex offenders differed, however, in that they were more likely to commit sex offenses as adults. Several studies have found that adolescent sex offenders have criminal records involving nonsexual offenses (Amir, 1971) (Van Ness, 1984) (Fehrenbach, 1986) (Schorr et al., 1966). These studies indicate incidences of other criminality in the history of adolescent sex offenders from 41 to 86 percent of the sample under study. Another study looked at a group of adolescent sex offenders compared with a control group who were known to be characterized by conduct disorders, but had not committed sex offenses. The adolescent sex offenders did not differ in their psychiatric symptoms or their degree of psychopathology from the other young delinquents. These writers concluded that sex offending is an aspect of a pattern of antisocial behavior, but they did note that the adolescent sex offenders differed from the controls in that 65 percent of them were victims of sexual abuse (Shaw et al., 1992). Truscott compared a sample of adolescent sex offenders with two other groups of incarcerated offenders, one violent and the other nonviolent juvenile delinquents. All groups were alike on the MMPI. Once again the adolescent sex offender group differed in having a history of sexual abuse.

Adolescent sex offenders have been studied in terms of their proclivity to substance abuse, most specifically whether they are more prone to commit sex offenses during a state of intoxication, or tend to be sober when the offenses occur. These studies generally indicate that drug and alcohol abuse is not a significant contributor to the sex offenses committed by adolescents (Groth, 1977) (Fehrenbach et al., 1986) (Van Ness, 1984).

ADOLESCENT SEX OFFENDERS AS VICTIMS

Somewhat surprisingly, this is an area of controversy. The existing literature publishes rates of victimization among adolescent sex offenders as ranging from 19 to 65 percent. The politics of the discipline become involved. Some researchers feel that perpetrators will fabricate a victimization in order to gain sympathy and attenuate responsibility for their crimes (Barbaree et al., 1993). These writers urge great caution in documenting victimization and even suggest that the perpetrator not be believed unless his victimization can be independently corroborated.

These writers seem to be unaware of the literature in the field of male victims, which suggests that males, as a group, tend to underreport their sexual victimization due to shame. Determining the victim status of a sex offender makes an interesting comment on the issue of self-reports. One dynamic, self-serving, skews the data toward higher instances of victimization. Another, shame in male victims, pulls the data back in the other direction. Who knows where reality lies in such a circumstance?

With these cautions in mind, the following table is offered.

Table 1.
Adolescent Molesters as Victims.

Author(s)	Date	% Victims
Shaw et al.	1992	65%
Becker et al.	1988	19%
Fehrenback et al.	1986	11%
Gomez & Schwartz	1982	38%
Longo	1982	47%

It is in this area of the prior victimization of perpetrators that the failure to separate rapists and molesters results in a significant defect in the literature. The studies that do separate the rapists from the molesters suggest that there are markedly different rates of victimization for these two populations. When they are combined, it seriously skews the overall numbers. It is necessary to go to the adult literature to illustrate this. Seghorn, Prentky, and Boucher (1987) studied a large sample of adult prisoners incarcerated for sex offenses. They did break them down into rapists and molesters. They found an incidence of victimization among the rapists of 23 percent, and 57 percent for the offenders who had molested younger children. Another adult study (Robertson, 1990) indicated that a population of homosexual pedophiles had a victimization rate of 73 percent.

Widon and Ames conducted a 1994 study of victims of sexual abuse. They looked specifically for criminal outcomes in general rather than specifically sexual crimes. They found sexual abuse in males to be associated with a higher risk of violent sex crimes, such as rape or sodomy. Adults followed in later life with histories of childhood sexual abuse, showed a higher risk than controls for sex crimes as adults.

The adult literature suggests that a high percentage of sex offenders in general are victims of sexual assault themselves. The greatest concentration of victims seems to be among molesters as opposed to rapists. More studies focusing on adolescents would probably substantiate the hypothesis suggested by the adult literature that prior sexual victimization is an important causal variable among adolescent sex offenders and that, as with adults, teenagers who molest are more frequently victims than are rapists.

A history of physical abuse in the sex offender population is a datum that is often left unstudied. Fehrenbach and his colleagues found an incidence of 16 percent in their adolescent offender population. Van Ness (1984) found 41 percent. Several students have turned their attention to the incidence of prior, age-appropriate sexual experience in the adolescent sex offender population. Groth (1977) found that 86 percent of his population had age-appropriate sexual experience prior to offending. Longo (1982) found 76 percent. Becker and colleagues (1987) found 59 percent.

RACE

Race is frequently omitted from descriptions of adolescent sex offender populations under study. Davis and Leitenberg, in their 1987 survey of the literature, conclude that black males are overrepresented among adolescent sex offenders, especially where forcible rape is involved. For all adolescent sex offenders, they find 64 percent to be white, and 30 percent black. When forcible rape is measured, 42 percent of the offenders are white, and 58 percent are black. No clarification is made as to why whites and blacks constitute 100 percent of those committing forcible rape. Presumably, this is occasionally done by Hispanics, Native Americans, etc. Shaw and his colleagues do provide racial data on their population, which was 50 percent white, 4 percent Hispanic, and 46 percent African-American. Theirs is a statewide program in Florida. Presumably, these figures reflect an overrepresentation of African-Americans and an underrepresentation of Hispanics.

Only Davis and Leitenberg (1987) attempt to explain the overrepresentation of African-Americans. They cite a 1947 article by Talcott Parsons describing greater anxiety about masculinity among black males as a result of oppression and slavery. This, in turn, is compensated for by "overriding stereotypic male characteristics, which in turn could lead to aggressive antisocial conduct, including assaultive sexual behavior."

THE CLINICAL LITERATURE

The clinical literature on adolescent sex offenders is reviewed by Davis and Leitenberg (1987). They conclude that reporting clinicians find the adolescent sex offender population to be characterized by low self-esteem, a sense of masculine inadequacy, fear of intimacy, gender identity confusion, sex role stereotypes, hostility to females, feelings of powerlessness and anger, poor impulse control, lack of moral development, belief in rape myths and, for pedophiles, cognitive distortions.

RAPISTS VS. MOLESTERS

The difference between sex offenders who rape and those who molest has been somewhat explored in the literature. Most researchers seem to accept whatever population is available to them under the name "sex offenders" without making further subdivisions. The classification of "sex offender" is a legal, not a clinical, or even behavioral entity. Prisons, residential treatment facilities, and outpatient clinic populations studied by researchers are in fact accidental samples of miscellaneous "sex offenders" lumped together due to court referral or community and/or family pressure. The sample usually includes rapists and molesters. It may also include exhibitionists, frotteurs, voyeurs, fetishists, cross-dressers, and makers of obscene phone calls. The majority of researchers simply proceed to study the population without further classifying. The results are then published as a description "sex offenders." Knight and Prentky (1993) express discomfort with this:

> ... juvenile sex offender samples typically comprise both rapists and child molester subgroups. Among adults, particular victim age preference subgroups have been shown to differ on a number of critical characteristics. It is plausible to speculate that these differences generalize to adolescent sex offenders.

To examine this issue in more detail it is necessary to turn to the adult offender literature, since this distinction between rapists and molesters has been the focus of little attention among those studying adolescent sex offenders. Seghorn's already cited study (1987) noted a number of crucial differences between rapists and molesters in a large prison population. Already noted was their finding that the men incarcerated for molestation had two-and-a-half times the incidence of victimization in their own past as those incarcerated for rape. Additionally, this study found that when rapists were molested, it was usually done by someone in their own family. Rapists were also found to come from more chaotic and disturbed homes.

Barbaree, Hudson, and Seto (1993) also profile the differences between a molester and a rapist population. They describe rapists as tending to be in their teens and their twenties. Incarcerated molesters are usually older. Molesters do not show the same diversity of nonsexual crimes as rapists. Psychiatrically, Barbaree and his colleagues found 30 percent of rapists to be antisocial personalities, whereas only 12 percent of molesters were so categorized (c.f. Abel and Becker, 1985). Nicholas Groth turned his attention to this issue in 1977. He concluded that molesters were less violent. None of his molester sample had used a weapon, whereas 30 percent of the rapists had knives, and 12 percent a blunt instrument.

THE BEHAVIORAL-COGNITIVE MODEL

Behavioral-cognitive theorists and researchers have had a major impact on the entire development of the discipline involved in understanding and treating adolescent molesters. This model was dominant in academic psychology at the time this discipline was created. It had instant appeal to those who were beginning to grope their way into the understanding and treatment of this population. The roots of this model go back into the early part of this century and lie in such areas as classical conditioning and operant conditioning theories.

The most recent and effective advocates of this theory were McGuire and his colleagues who published a seminal paper in 1965. This paper set forth a model which still has considerable power in shaping the thinking and treatment strategies of those working in this field. McGuire and his colleagues argue that deviant fantasies are transformed into deviant behavior when they are reinforced by masturbation. They see deviant fantasies as arising out of perhaps an initial seduction or other direct experience with a deviant act. The subject recalls the experience, masturbates with fantasies about it, and thereby reinforces, via conditioning, a proclivity to be involved in this kind of sexual behavior in the future. Rockman (1966) and Rockman and Hodgeson (1968) also published influential papers in which they claimed to have trained a male subject to become sexually aroused by boots by first showing him pictures of nude females, followed by pictures of boots. Similar studies were performed by McConaghy (1970) and Beech, Watts, and Poole (1971).

Subsequent studies have somewhat weakened these findings. Marshall and Eccles reviewed this research in their 1993 anthology, and concluded:

> The evidence, then, in support of the possibility that sexual preferences can be changed by pairing an externally presented CS and UCS seems, at best, to be weak and inconsistent. It seems unlikely, then, that such contingencies play an important role in the acquisition of deviant behavior. In terms of using such a procedure as a treatment intervention, the data suggests that would result in few subjects showing positive changes.

In spite of the weakening impact of subsequent research, the early research of McGuire et al. and the related studies which followed, the impact of these theories on the kind of treatment offered to adolescent sex offenders has been tremendous. Most of the currently recommended treatment interventions, as well as diagnostic understanding of adolescent sex offenders, has its roots in this early research in the field. It explains the emphasis on the reason there is so much focus on desensitization, masturbatory satiation, and the injunctions to adolescent molesters in treatment that they not masturbate to deviant fantasies. In fairness to the behavioral-cognitive school, it does need to be emphasized that these early studies put the emphasis on the behavioral side of the issue. Those who strongly advocate behavioral-cognitive theories as a foundation for treatment and understanding of adolescent sex offenders are now stressing the cognitive, as opposed to the behavioral elements. Specifically, much significance is now attributed to changing cognitive distortions which permit or facilitate the molesting of children.

THE PSYCHIATRIC MODEL

There has been a very recent counter-trend to the dominance of the behavioral-cognitive school. This has emanated from traditional psychiatry. Its principal focus has been to look for underlying psychiatric disorders in the adolescent sex offender population which contribute to or partially explain the behavior, or which need to be addressed in order to successfully treat the adolescent sex offender population.

Judith Becker has led the way in this area, although she appears to remain behavioral-cognitive in her essential orientation. In a 1988 paper, she notes that, in her judgment, the spectrum of adolescent offenders includes boys who have true paraphilias, but also those whose impulse control is damaged by conduct disorders and other psychiatric diagnoses.

She also sees impairment in social and interpersonal skills as contributing to their offending.

Kavoussi, with Becker and Kaplan (1988) examine the psychiatric issue in more detail. They approach a population of 58 adolescent sex offenders with standard, structured psychiatric interviews. They found 81 percent to be diagnosable. Forty-eight percent of these were conduct disorders, 18.9 percent substance abuse disorders, 8.6 percent adjustment disorders with depressed mood, 6.9 percent attention deficit disorder, and 5.2 percent school phobia.

Becker returns to this issue with other colleagues (1991) to study a population of 246 mostly black sex offenders. This study focused on depression, and found evidence of significant depression in 42 percent of the population. The article advocates that, in the future, sex offender populations be screened for depression as part of the diagnostic process.

Psychiatric issues have also been raised by John Shaw and his colleagues who operate the Elaine Gordon Center for the treatment of young perpetrators, in Florida. The program operates from a psychiatric model. Boys placed in that facility are placed under intense interdisciplinary scrutiny for both research purposes and treatment. In 1992 Shaw and his group published an article describing the Elaine Gordon Center population. Among their conclusions were that early adolescent sex offenders have a central antisocial core, but that there is also a great deal of psychiatric comorbidity connected with sex offending behaviors. In an unpublished presentation at Lake Tahoe, California in 1992, Shaw and his group indicated that they felt that there was a significant incidence of borderline personality disorder among their population. They also felt that the population was characterized by a generalized problem with impulsivity. Dr. Shaw was using serotonin reuptake inhibitors to control this impulsiveness. The group felt that 85 percent of the population at the center met the criteria for at least borderline traits, not the full syndrome of borderline personality.

The group also reported making careful measurements of testosterone levels as well as testing relating to levels of serotonin, dopamine, and norepinepherine in the blood of this population. The group also indicated they suspected a correlation of internalization of anxiety in some of the population with the compulsive behaviors.

Shaw and his group propose looking at the adolescent sex offender population from a psychiatric and multidisciplinary perspective, a perspective from which it has been very poorly studied in the past. I would anticipate this may be a growing movement in the field.

TYPOLOGIES

The issue of separating adolescent sex offenders into rapists and molesters begs the larger question of typology and classification. It seems to be widely known that adolescent sex offenders are a heterogeneous group (Barbaree, Hudson, Seto, 1993). These writers go on to argue that there is a need for research to develop meaningful subgroups "within which common factors and psychological processes contribute to the sexual aggression we observed." Knight and Prentky (1993) begin their discussion of typology with the statement, "Categorization is a necessary prerequisite and sustainer of all scientific inquiry."

It would seem impossible to work with adolescent sex offenders for any period of time without developing at least an informal working classification. Barbaree, Hudson, and Seto (1993) offer such a typology suggesting that the adolescent sex offender population can be meaningfully subdivided first into rapists and molesters, and then the molesters further subdivided into incest perpetrators, nonfamily perpetrators, homosexual perpetrators, and heterosexual perpetrators. Knight and Prentky are not satisfied to stop here. They developed a very complex multifactor system of classification, which they published in 1990, and again in 1993. This typology uses the degree of fixation and the amount of contact with the victim as primary variables. Offenders are also separated into rapists and molesters. Combining these variables creates 16 subcategories into which rapists and molesters can be placed.

Knight and Prentky were preceded in their efforts at taxonomy by O'Brien and Bera (1986). They divided the adolescent sex offender population into seven categories. These include naive experimenters, group-influenced, disturbed and impulsive offenders, offenders with low social competence, offenders driven by early childhood abuse, offenders driven by an impulsive lifestyle, and offenders driven and motivated by sexual preoccupation and compulsivity. Strangely, they do not seem to divide offenders into rapists and molesters.

Although these writers have begun to block out subcategories of molesters, the idea does not seem to have widely caught on in the literature. I could find no research which uses these categories as a basis for further study or attempts to verify their empirical validity.

SIBLING INCEST

Incest is a large and obvious subcategory of sex offenses. Adolescents who molest within their family are generally sibling offenders. This is the one subcategory to which some researchers have paid specific attention. Michael O'Brien (1986) studies a sample of 170 adolescent sex offenders, of whom 50 are sibling offenders. He compares these perpetrators with a group which molested nonfamily members. This sample is overwhelmingly white, with a very small admixture of Native Americans and African-Americans constituting only 6 percent of the sample.

O'Brien characterizes the sibling offenders as coming from more dysfunctional families than the other offenders. He also finds some evidence for multigenerational transmission of incest dynamics. These sibling offenders are more likely than the others to have been sexually victimized themselves. Both groups had little age-appropriate sexual experience with peers.

Becker and colleagues have explored the same population, publishing their work in 1986. In this case, the study group was 22 adolescent sex offenders who had molested siblings. Becker's population was comprised of 86 percent minority and inner-city youth. This study was unable to develop any unified profile for sibling offenders. Ninety-five percent had prior, nondeviant, nongenital sexual experience before having sex with their siblings. Becker's results are very different from those of O'Brien. O'Brien was able to separate sibling offenders from those who offended outside the family. He also found his whole sample, both sibling and nonsibling offenders, to be lacking in prior sexual experience. Perhaps the inner-city, minority nature of Becker's population contrasted with O'Brien's largely white population explains the differences. Culture is a largely unexplored parameter in the adolescent sex offender literature. No one seems to go beyond collecting descriptive statistics on the percentages of various racial and ethnic groups in the particular sample under study.

PROGRESSION

The issue of progression is a vital one. If adolescent sex offenders tend to start with more minor offenses and move into more serious and violent offenses, that is a vitally important piece of data to have available. Knight and Prentky (1993) suspect that there is a relatively large number of juvenile offenders whose deviant sexual behavior does not persist into adulthood. Marshall and Eccles (1993) note that experience with offending tends to increase the sexual and aggressive nature of the offenses. Abel, Osborne, and Twigg (1993) found evidence of progression in adolescent offenders, especially among the rapists. Turning to retrospective adult studies, Longo and McFadin (1981) found that many of the offenders in their study had been involved in such things as exhibitionism and voyeurism while adolescents. Longo and Groth, in a larger study (1983), found that a large part of their sample had engaged in compulsive masturbation as adolescents and prior to their sex offending. Another significant part of their sample had been involved in exhibitionism and voyeurism during their juvenile years. Their overall conclusion was that at least one in three offenders shows some evidence of progression from nonviolent to violent offenses as adults.

Hunter et al., in 1994, studied two samples of adolescents in a residential program. They found true deviant arousal strongest among adolescent sex offenders with only male victims, which is consistent with literature on adult offenders. They additionally found juveniles to be more fluid in their offense patterns, and with less correspondence between measured arousal and their offense histories. This is in marked contrast to adult offenders. Hunter's data might be interpreted to mean that there are two kinds of adolescent sex offenders. One is a group which has strong deviant arousal and male victims. This group is likely to progress into adult pedophilia. There may also be another group little commented on by researchers and clinicians. This group may offend only a few times and then not repeat the behavior.

All studies show that there is a group of adolescent sex offenders who do progress to more serious offenses and/or pedophilia. They also clearly indicate that many, and perhaps most, do not. Groth's (1983) progression rate of 33 percent is the only quantified figure in the literature. Whatever the exact figure, it would appear that there is a bimodal distribution of adolescent molesters in regards to progression. One group shows no sign of it and may drop out of a pattern of sex offending after one or more episodes during adolescence. A second group does go on to become serious sexual offenders.

VICTIMS INTO PERPETRATORS

Somewhat related to the issue of progression is the question of whether males who are sexually abused progress into perpetrators and, if so, with what frequency. This is obviously a vital question. Its major implications have to do with providing necessary treatment to male victims to prevent them from becoming perpetrators. It is clear that nowhere near all of the males who are victimized in American culture become perpetrators. There is no formal study addressing this topic.

Martha Erikson (1991) does deal with a similar issue in a population that has experienced physical abuse. She finds a crossover rate of about 30 percent from those victimized physically as children, who in turn batter others during their adult lives. She also took note of the factors which prevent victims of physical abuse from becoming perpetrators. They included the availability of a confidant, the absence of denial as a way of coping with the abuse, the absence of a tendency to idealize parents, an absence of preoccupation with the abuse, or rage and shame regarding the incident and the perpetrator. Also significant was the ability to acknowledge the pain and trauma involved in the incident.

Although incidence studies appear to be nonexistent on the victim to perpetrator question with adolescent sex offenders, several writers have devoted their attention to the factors that prevent victims from becoming perpetrators. Gilgun addresses this issue in a 1990 study of 34 men in treatment for sexual or physical abuse. Among the sexually abused men, nine of the 23 had no criminal history. Seven had become child molesters, and five were rapists. One had been involved in a nonsexual crime. Although the sample is very small, Gilgun has found a similar figure to Erickson. Thirty-five percent of her sample of sexually victimized males have become sex offenders.

Gilgun paid close attention to the factors which had kept some of the victims from becoming perpetrators. Her conclusion was that the presence of a confidant with whom the young male victim could discuss candidly what had happened to him was a key factor in preventing the victim from turning into a perpetrator of violent, and often sexual, crimes. Also significant in this transformation were being raised in a sexualized environment and an early onset of sexualized behavior. Being raised in a harsh, negative environment with troubled interpersonal relationships also seemed to predispose the child to victimize others.

She believes that conditioning factors also facilitate the process in which male victims grow up to become perpetrators. She notes that sexual behavior can be a tension reducing mechanism. As such, it may play a role in the victim to perpetrator transformation. Here the victim may begin to use masturbation, rape, and molestation as a coping mechanism to deal with high anxiety states. Finally, Gilgun notes that such early background factors as secure attachments and high quality early relationships also seemed to protect the victimized child from becoming a perpetrator.

Gerber deals with the same issue in a less rigorous way (1990). He stresses the need for positive, loving, well-balanced role models. He also feels that it is important that the child have some form of satisfying sexual outlet. He notes that longer duration or greater severity of the abuse situation and molest by a family member seem to facilitate the transition from victim into perpetrator. Like Gilgun, he feels that conditioning factors are important in this process.

In a 1986 study, Freeman-Longo also addressed this issue. Multiple perpetrators, a longer term of abuse, and male perpetrators were found in this study to be important factors predisposing the victim to act out sexually against others.

The psychodynamic literature is replete with studies of a clinical nature suggesting that the process of identification with the aggressor plays an important role in transforming victims of any kind of trauma into perpetrators of abuse as they grow older. The literature of social learning theory would stress the importance of negative examples who model sexual violence or exploitation for young male victims.

This literature has a remarkable coherence. It seems to stress that the strengths which the child had prior to his victimization play a major role in how effectively he copes with the trauma. Additionally, it is vitally important that the young victim have available to him family and social supports to help him overcome the traumatic damage. Chaotic and dysfunctional families seem to be highly connected with the victims who develop into perpetrators in later life.

PSYCHOMETRISTS

The adolescent molester population appears, until recently, to have been of relatively little interest to psychologists specializing in psychological testing. Hall et al. note in 1986 study that adult sex offenders in general are characterized by marked elevations on all clinical scales of the MMPI. Sixty-five percent of their sample were very significantly elevated on the scale for delinquency. Half of the sample was significantly elevated on scales for schizophrenia and depression. This is an incarcerated population. McCraw and Pegg McNabb (1989) have explored this population with the Rorschach test. They assessed for differences on this instrument between adolescent sex offenders and a more general juvenile delinquent population. The only differentiation found was a higher percentage of anatomical responses among the sex offenders.

Truscott (1993) compared adolescent sex offenders with violent offenders on the MMPI. The populations were essentially alike. Clinical interview, however, showed that the sex offenders were twice as likely to have a history of sexual abuse. The data from psychometry confirms the findings of other research comparing adolescent molesters with more generalized delinquents, again suggesting that adolescent sex offenders, as a group, are a specialized kind of juvenile delinquent, and that the main factor differentiating them from other young delinquents is a history of sexual abuse. It would seem that sexual abuse or other forms of sexualizing experiences have caused these juveniles to direct their aggression in a much more sexualized direction than other youth who come into severe conflict with the law without sexually troubled histories.

TREATMENT

Since the first edition of this book, there has been an effort to develop and standardize recommendations for the treatment of adolescent sex offenders. A large task force, under the auspices of the National Adolescent Perpetrator Network, worked on a project of this nature from 1986 through the publication of its preliminary report in 1988. The National Task Force released its most recent consensus report in 1993. This approach is probably most adequately and extensively summarized by Ryan and Lane in their 1991 work. More recently, it has been outlined by Becker (1993). It most recently appeared in a somewhat modified incarnation in late 1994 by Semarbeikian and Martinez. From here forward in this work, this approach will be referred to as the standard model for the treatment of adolescent sex offenders. It will be reviewed in more detail in Chapter Six.

The standard model has become the overwhelmingly dominant model, at least as reflected in the literature, for the treatment of adolescent sex offenders. Recently, there has emerged a tendency to suggest that this model be modified or amplified to include input from less behavioral-cognitive sources. Shaw and his group (1992) advocate a psychiatric-based approach, including a return to a greater role for individual and family therapy in the overall treatment process. They also advocate a judicious and appropriate use of psychopharmacology with this population (unpublished presentation, Lake Tahoe, California, November 1992).

Muster, in a 1992 study, describes the dominant model as confrontational and nonempathic. She surveys professionals in both corrections and mental health and finds greater support for the "confrontational and punitive therapy methods" among those working in corrections, while mental health workers surveyed preferred a more flexible and diverse approach.

It would seem that the discipline of treating adolescent sex offenders has gone through a recent phase in which there has been a battle of more or less one-dimensional schools of clinical thought to become the dominant modality. This probably reflects a developmental stage in a very young discipline. The result of continuing research and practice is likely to be a more eclectic approach, putting together data from diverse approaches for the understanding and treating of adolescent sex offenders. This point will be elaborated in the chapter on theory and theoretical approaches.

TREATMENT EFFECTIVENESS AND RECIDIVISM

At present, there are few published studies regarding the effectiveness of treatment with adolescent molesters. There are a number of adult studies on this issue. In general, the adult studies focus on inmates treated with behavioral-cognitive techniques. These studies include Becker and Hunter (1992), Marshall and Barbaree (1990), Dwyer and Myers (1990), and Marshall et al. (1991). These studies all report a relatively high level of success. There is some indication that rapists are less responsive than molesters to these kinds of treatment.

A study which does not share the enthusiasm of the others is by Furby, Weinrott, and Blackshaw (1989). This is a literature review covering 42 studies. The authors find these studies full of methodological flaws and conclude, "There is yet no evidence that clinical treatment reduces the rates of sex offenses in general, and no appropriate data for assessing whether it may be differentially effective for different types of offenders."

The authors of this study question all recidivism studies due to the "extremely low rates for reporting these crimes."

The objections of Furby et al. may apply to studies which measure their success by the recidivism of the population in treatment without a control group. It would not seem to apply to studies which compare recidivism rates of populations in treatment vs. those not in treatment. McGrath, for example, in a 1991 review of the literature on the treatment of adult sex offenders, cites data indicating that untreated sex offenders repeat at a rate of 60 percent, whereas those who receive treatment are only apprehended in reoffense in 15 to 20 percent of cases. This kind of data seems to render moot the issue of unreported offenses. Here the untreated offenders constitute a sort of control group giving some authority to the claim that treatment is effective.

Turning more specifically to adolescent offenders, there seems to be a general consensus that their rate of recidivism is lower than that of adult offenders (Knight and Prentky, 1993). Becker and Kaplan (1988) have done research in the area of treatment effectiveness with the adolescent offender population. They studied 300 offenders, of whom 68 percent entered treatment and 27.3 percent remained to complete the treatment process. Of this selective group who completed treatment, 9 percent had reoffended by the end of one year. It is also likely that the dropouts represent the highest risk group for reoffense. Becker's group does not look particularly good in terms of the effectiveness of treatment, although it is difficult to evaluate true recidivism with so many dropouts. As with many Becker studies, this is an inner-city, predominantly minority population.

Schram and Malloy report different data in another study (1992). Their population consists of 197 adolescent sex offenders treated in a residential facility in the state of Washington. This appears to be a group of boys who have been involved in some serious sexual offenses. Many of them had been treated in outpatient programs in the community prior to their placement in the residential program.

Schram and Malloy were able to follow the boys for up to five years after discharge, and found that only 12 percent were found to have committed posttreatment sex offenses. The bad news was that 63 percent of these adolescents were arrested for a nonsexual crime during the five-year follow-up period. This offers another confirmation of the essentially delinquent nature of the adolescent sex offender population. It also suggests that treatment for sex offenses is most specifically effective in the area of sexuality and of less value in containing other criminality.

Schram and Malloy paid particular attention to the 37 percent of the population who were not rearrested after five years. Their interest was in what factors predicted such a favorable outcome. This group was found to have no criminal record other than the sexual offenses for which they were treated. They had fewer school problems and were less likely to be victims of molestation themselves. They were less likely to have abused a sibling than someone outside the home. They had better social skills, were less likely to blame their victims, and were less likely to have been assessed as having deviant arousal. In general, it would appear that this successful group came into the residential program with greater social and psychological intactness. Bringing a higher level of functioning into the program, they were able to make better use of their treatment and avoid further involvement with the law upon discharge.

The differences between Becker's results and the results of the Schram and Malloy study probably have to do with both the nature of the populations and the nature of the studies. Becker's population was involved in an outpatient program from which the majority dropped out prior to completion. Becker's one-year recidivism is almost as high as the five-year rate for the Schram and Malloy study. Presumably there would be fewer dropouts from a court-ordered residential program which may make their results even more favorable in comparison to Becker's. Schram and Malloy's population was involved in a long-term residential program which was presumably more intense than can be offered in an outpatient setting. This may be an argument for the greater efficacy of residential treatment, or the differences may lie in the ethnic and/or socioeconomic differences between the two populations.

On a more theoretical plane, researchers within the behavioral-cognitive school have begun to criticize treatment emanating from earlier research in that area. Quincy and Earles (1990) review the literature on various techniques for treating deviant arousal in adult sex offenders. Their first caution is that phallometric measurements of sexual preferences can be faked by sex offenders. This brings into question one of the most reliable instruments for measuring the effectiveness of treatment. Regarding the issue of reconditioning sexual arousal, they contend that the better controlled studies employing phallometric measures indicate only mixed results. Looking specifically at masturbatory satiation, they say, "This method has been found to reduce deviant sexual interest, as measured phallometrically, in a small number of patients."

Clearly, we are seeing at least the beginning of a more careful assessment of the effectiveness of behavioral-cognitive techniques. There is much evidence indicating that these techniques are, to some degree, effective. It is likely that further research will confirm that behavioral-cognitive techniques need to be augmented by additional measures in order to increase the overall effectiveness of treatment with a very difficult population.

Chapter Three

THEORETICAL FRAMEWORKS FOR UNDERSTANDING ADOLESCENT MOLESTERS

The mention of the word theory will send many readers thumbing ahead to find something more interesting. It is hoped that the reader will tarry here for at least a while because some grasp of the theories underlying the thought and practice in any field is essential to anyone wishing to work successfully with this population. Theory provides a framework for both organizing thought and for enhancing understanding of what is an overwhelming amount of individual data about adolescent sex offenders. Without theory, we are looking at literally thousands of individual adolescent molesters in America, each of whom presents with a complex personality system which will generate megabytes of data. With theory we can gather together the most essential parts of this data and place it within a structure that makes it comprehensible.

Theories are also reservoirs of understanding from which we can draw hypotheses about how to intervene in the lives of adolescent molesters and how to promote change in their lives. Indeed, one of the basic questions asked of any theory in the social sciences is: how do human personalities develop and change?

Some clinicians are not very aware of theories that underlie their practice. These clinicians tend to call themselves eclectic and say that they do whatever works. I suspect that such practitioners tend to be influenced more than they realize by one or more of the theoretical systems that have been devised to explain the behavior and guide the treatment of adolescent sex offenders. Sometimes they direct us like reflexes, determining our behavior, shaping our reactions, and generally serving, for better or worse, as a kind of compass in our travels through the complex waters of the discipline of adolescent sex offenders.

A simple example of how theory shapes our reactions is: if we believe that sex offending is caused by the excess of a certain chemical in the brain, then that already has answered several questions about diagnosis and treatment. Viewed from this perspective, the adolescent will bear no responsibility for what he has done because he is responding to a bio-chemical imperative. This theoretical understanding will not suggest treatment involving cognition, interpretation, therapeutic relationship, or conditioning. Instead, the clinician will look for a way to decrease the problematic chemical, most likely a pharmaceutical.

PROMINENT THEORIES

Over the years, a variety of theories has sprung up to explain the phenomenology of adolescent sex offenders. Controversies have arisen about the weight to be placed upon various theories for understanding adolescent sex offenders. The range of theories that has been applied to understanding this relatively small population is incredibly wide.

Special concern with treating adolescent sex offenders probably has its beginnings in the 1970s. This concern exploded in terms of numbers of patients, therapists, and researchers in the 1980s. In the earlier part of this timeline, unitary theories appeared to dominate clinical and research thinking. Marshall and Barbaree (1990) feel that most researchers in the discipline still take a narrow perspective concerning factors that play a role in causing sex offending.

BEHAVIORAL-COGNITIVE THEORIES AND RESEARCHES

As noted in the last chapter, McGuire and his colleagues (1965) offered a comprehensive behavioral model of why males molest and how this can be changed. This model was still dominant when another article affirming and advocating it was published by Abel and Blanchard in 1974.

Briefly summarized, this model proclaims that deviant sexual arousal is the key causal factor. It is the engine that drives males to commit sex offenses. These researchers believe that deviant arousal emerges out of aberrant sexual experiences, either in very early life or in early adoles-cence, depending on the precise theoretical orientation of the scholar. Once a deviant experience has taken place, it becomes generalized and stamped in through a conditioning process involving either masturba-tion or further deviant sexual contact as a reinforcer. This model requires treatment by a series of reconditioning exercises. In the early days, these were predominantly aversive stimuli designed to eliminate the deviant arousal and encourage the substitution of more suitable sexual aims and objects.

The behavioral-cognitive theorists are generally academics. They like hard data, and they have access to elegant laboratories and large groups of sex offenders. The sex offenders studied are incarcerated and easily available for research. The earlier emphasis was on adult sex offenders for a variety of reasons. However, adolescent sex offenders have become the focus of increasing research and clinical experimentation through the 1980s and into the early 1990s.

Perhaps the high point of behavioral reconditioning came in the late 1960s and early 1970s when there was great interest in helping homosexuals to reorient their sexual interest toward the opposite sex. In the course of this research practice, it was discovered that the easiest cases to transform were those where there was a preexisting heterosexual arousal (Barbaree and Eccles, 1990). This suggests that, even in this age of enthusiasm, there was a growing awareness that sexual orientations cannot be created. If a weak sexual interest is present, it appears that conditioning techniques can strengthen it.

Researchers have found that pedophiles most closely fit the model outlined by McGuire, Abel, and Blanchard in their works of the 1960s and 1970s. They seem to generalize a sexual arousal that began with one child and extend it over a variety of children via either repeated sexual contact with children or masturbating to fantasies about children.

These researchers found problems when they tried to extend the conditioning models to the population of incest perpetrators. They did not seem to follow the model so closely. They tended to stay with either one child or a small group of children within a family. Their deviant arousal did not seem to generalize, a datum again not consistent with the theoretical model.

Gender issues also raised a problem. If one's sexual interests were determined by what first sexual experiences one had, in combination with further pleasurable experiences, in fantasy or reality, stamping in that kind of sexual activity until it became overwhelmingly preferred, it becomes very difficult to understand why the overwhelming number of sex offenders are male. If conditioning is the principal cause of sexual interest, then males and females ought to be roughly equal in representation among the sex offenders. Extensive research indicates that this is not the case.

By 1990, there was a good deal of dissatisfaction with the conditioning model. Marshall and Eccles (1990) reviewed the literature on conditioning as a cause of sex offending. They came to the following conclusions:

1. Most adolescent sex offenders do not have deviant arousal. Indeed, many express and manifest preferences which are clearly nondeviant.

2. A majority of those who commenced sex offending as teenagers, as well as those who had an adult onset of such behavior, say that they began to masturbate to fantasies about children only after repeated offending. In other words, fantasy and masturbation are not causal, but follow behavior rather than create it.

3. Support for a conditioning theory model of the acquisition of sexual preference is not strong.

4. Conditioning processes may play some role in nonfamilial child molestation, but as one small component in the overall complex factors.

5. Conditioning models may need to be modified in order to understand adolescent sex offenders.

Marshall and Eccles feel that cognitive learning, associative learning, covert conditioning, and observations of models all need to be incorporated to bring classical conditioning theory into conformity with the existing data. They are calling for something which has already begun to happen. It was becoming obvious that cognitive variables, i.e., the thought and reasoning patterns and intellectual conclusions of perpetrators need to be considered to understand why they behave as they do. Some researchers and clinicians working with adolescent sex offenders now cling to a more or less unitary theory usually styled behavioral-cognitive. This approach fuses the conditioning approach of the early literature with various cognitive approaches to create a hybrid discipline that still has a great deal of internal unity and consistency. It focuses on a series of relatively limited and very specific processes by which human beings acquire patterns of sexual behavior and by which these patterns can be changed.

In 1993, Marshall and Eccles seemed aware of the limits of behavioral-cognitive theory as a comprehensive model to explain adolescent sex offending. They argued for a multifaceted theory. They stated pointedly that the weight of their experience is that offenders have a developmental history that makes them vulnerable to a variety of influences and events that would be ignored by males who are not so vulnerable.

This vulnerability, we believe, arises most particularly by the failure during their infancy and childhood of the parents of sex offenders to insure that secure attachment bonds are formed between them and their children. Secure attachments provide the growing child with a view of others that is affectionate and empathic and that instills a desire for and the skills and confidence necessary to achieve intimacy with peers.

This is so fundamentally important, according to Marshall and Eccles, because where it is not present, a young male will have trouble relating to females in his age group. In the absence of a capacity for affection, intimacy, and empathy, the adolescent male will be likely to find appealing messages in the media that express attitudes toward women and children that objectify and demean them. The bonds of affection that bind human beings together and keep us from hurting and exploiting each other are not operative here. Add testosterone and the stage is set for sex offending.

This emphasis on attachment provides a potential link between behavioral-cognitive theory and many of the other theories already existing and prominent among those who work with adolescent sex offenders. Attachment difficulties play a key role in the psychogenesis of juvenile delinquency. One of the better established conclusions of the literature is that adolescent sex offenders are a specialized kind of delinquent. They share many diagnostic and behavioral traits with delinquents but are most prone to get into sex-related crimes. Marshall and Eccles' suggestions provide an opportunity to make a theoretical link between behavioral-cognitive thinking and psychodynamic theory. Marshall and Eccles work substantially within the framework of the behavioral-cognitive group, yet they insist that its insights are incomplete without input from attachment and developmental theories. Issues of attachment and the importance of early life events in shaping adult personality are foundational in psychodynamic theories of personality.

BIOLOGICAL THEORIES

Biological theories claiming that virtually every human behavior has biological determinants have been around for a long time. Such theories cycle in and out of fashion. Our culture appears to be approaching a peak in the prominence of biological explanations for all kinds of human behavior. Biologically-determined theories are currently conspicuous in the sex offender field. They fall into two rough categories. One stresses basic male aggressiveness as the cause of adolescent sex offending. The other has to do with biological theories about the origins of sexual orientation and behavior.

The male aggressiveness theory postulates that males are inherently more aggressive than females. This is not hard to prove. Reference to any statistics which measure violence or crime show an overrepresentation of males, particularly young males. As we have seen in the review of the literature, the adolescent sex offender population is a case in point. It is a group of delinquents involved in acts that involve violence or a ruthless disregard for the feelings and needs of others. This is an overwhelmingly male population which lends a gross statistical support to the hypothesis that there is some connection between maleness and a proclivity to become involved in sex offenses.

There can be many explanations for this. Male socialization in western cultures is preferred by some. Those who place great emphasis on biological determinism feel that adolescent sex offending is a sex-linked genetic trait. The human male is seen as inherently hypersexual and hyperaggressive due to his genetic and hormonal makeup. Marshall and Barbaree (1990) summarize this view rather concisely: "As we see it, the task for human males is to acquire inhibitory controls over a biologically endowed propensity for self-interest associated with a tendency to fuse sex and aggression." The central task of being male is thus to acquire "inhibitory controls over biologically-endowed aggressive tendencies."

Puberty looms very large in this model. Testosterone and other male sex hormones are usually seen as the major driving force of the male's hypersexuality and hyperaggressiveness. At the time of puberty, boys experience an increase in testosterone levels which brings the level to four times its prepubertal range (Sizonenko, 1978). Obviously, the recently pubescent boy must now cope with biologically-driven feelings of a very intense nature. Controlling the impulses generated by these hormones is an extremely difficult task for boys at puberty, particularly since they have had no prior opportunity to practice such control and restraint at such high levels of testosterone.

I have noticed in my practice that I get a significant percentage of referrals of boys who are in the midst of puberty and have just been involved in a sex offense. I have also seen a number of boys who committed their offense at the time of puberty, but were detected and referred for treatment at some later date. I believe that this can be interpreted, at least in part, as related to a difficulty in handling the surge of hormonally-driven sexual interest at puberty. Clearly, not all boys offend at puberty. Other issues, such as a tendency toward delin-quency, poor impulse controls, family dynamics, and many other factors seem to interplay with the hormonal factor to cause sex offending in some boys but not in others who are dealing with the same hormones.

It would seem that the male's struggle never stops. Barbaree and Marshall also cite research on men who are not sex offenders. Thirty-five percent of the men surveyed indicated that they might rape a woman if they were certain it would never be detected. This figure, of course, implies that far more mature males are potential sex offenders than ever act out in this way.

Among the most unitary of theorists in the biological camp is John Money. His writings (1990) reflect a view that the paraphilias are a brain disease best treated by chemotherapy. Dr. Money's other writings suggest that various hormonal agents can be used as the treatment of choice for sex offenders (1968, 1970, 1972).

Another group of biological theories centers around possible biological origins for sexual orientation, identity, and preference. The research of Le Vay (1991) and others regarding the genetic roots of homosexuality are well-known and are becoming the dominant popular view. To my knowledge, there has been no research on the genetics of the rarer paraphilias. Theoretically, if one sexual orientation is hereditary, it is but a small step to so interpret others. The evidence regarding homosexuality is still the focus of controversy, but that controversy will not be reviewed here.

Another area of some interest to biological determinists is the idea that there are critical periods in human development during which certain developmental tasks must be accomplished. They postulate a kind of biological timetable which unfolds according to a genetically-determined timetable. At each stage of this unfolding biological process, the individual human being establishes deeply ingrained patterns of behavior which are encoded in the neurological structure of the brain. Such structures are very difficult to modify once the window of opportunity is closed.

John Money has looked at such crucial stages in sexual development (1965). He presents rather convincing evidence that sexual orientation is established in the first two years of life and is extremely difficult to change after that. His research involved hermorphaditic children born with the traits of both sexes. In a research and treatment program, he and his colleagues found that if they were able to make a gender assignment of the child in the neonatal period, or at least before 18 months, the child could successfully accept the assigned sex. There were invariably

problems if the clinicians attempted to change the sex assignment after
18 months.

There is a great deal of information on these kinds of critical periods
done by biological researchers in the animal realm. The only carefully
researched critical period in human development is the one for the
acquisition of language. Language development seems to have an open
window from about age 2 through 12. Once that window is closed, it is
extremely difficult for a human being to learn a totally new language.
He or she will probably never speak it without an accent. Johnathan
Winson, who reviews much of this data in his book *Brain and Psyche*
(1985), feels that the development of language is neurologically pro-
grammed during its critical stage. If a new language is to be acquired
outside of the critical period for language development, it must be
acquired by other, less efficient, processes. He considers this a paradigm
for many critical learning processes in *homo sapiens;* processes which are
poorly studied due to the difficulty in doing research of this nature with
human beings.

The biological purpose of this kind of learning is to allow mammals to
adapt to the very specific environments into which they are born. Any
behavior that is purely genetically-determined cannot be modified to
adapt to unique or quickly changing conditions in which the mammal
may find itself. Critical-period learning allows the developing mammal
to make post birth but permanent adjustments that fine tune it to its
environments. Since the human being must cope with a complex social
as well as biological environment, I suspect that processes of learning in
critical periods are more common than most social scientists think.

Such processes would allow children to make adaptations to early
environmental challenges that they are not genetically prepared for and
are too young to cope with by rational problem solving. For example, if a
child is born into a physically abusive environment, he or she will
develop ways of behaving that allow survival in a pathological and
aberrant human environment. I believe similar adjustments may be
made via critical-period learning when children are sexually abused at a
very young age. If patterns of coping with dysfunctional environments
are stamped in neurologically at a very early age, they allow the child to
survive but cripple him/her with ingrained patterns of behavior that are
problematic in later life. This would explain why it is so difficult to
repair the damage done by physical and sexual abuse which occurs in
very early life. If the tenets of this theory are right, by the time most

victims come to treatment, they manifest a neurologically-imprinted pattern of adaptation. What was once an adaption may now disrupt the patient's functioning. Yet it is so deeply ingrained, it is very difficult to modify. Treatment is analogous to learning a foreign language after age twelve. It can be expected to be long and slow. Given the assumptions of critical period theory, learning new patterns in therapy will never be as efficient as the original, neurologically-based learning process.

While Winson has focused on critical periods in the earliest stages of life, Bateson (1978) suggests that the critical period for human sexual development may be early puberty. His argument is based on animal analogies. Apparently, there are a number of animal species that develop their lifelong patterns of sexual behavior at the time of puberty. Bateson interprets puberty as a time of the opening of a critical period in these species. What is imprinted at this time cannot be changed.

There is a fairly extensive body of research data suggesting that something like this may take place in human sexual development. Studies showing the onset of molesting behaviors between 13 and 15 years of age have been conducted by Awad, Saunders, and Levine (1979); Becker, Cunningham, Raffner, and Kaplan (1986); and Smets and Cebula (1987). These researchers more or less correspond to those by Feldman and MacCulloch (1971) and Storms (1981) who have examined the origins of sexual orientation. They consider it to be a phenomenon occurring at the time of puberty. They do not specifically formulate puberty as a critical period preferring to see the process as guided by the principles of learning theory. These researches are paralleled by those by Feldman and MacCulloch (1971) and Storms (1981). These latter investigators are looking at the origins of sexual orientation. They consider it to be a process occurring at the time of puberty guided by principles of learning theory. In this view, the developing child's first intense erotic experience, reinforced by orgasm, plays a role in fixing permanent sexual orientation. If this first experience is homosexual and is followed by unpleasant heterosexual experiences, the likelihood of an adult homosexual orientation is great. While they do not mention the term critical period, the notion that this process occurs most significantly and intensely at the time of puberty and then is fixed for the lifespan suggests a process closely related to, if not identical with, critical-period learning. When these ideas are applied to homosexuality the results are controversial. Applying them in this arena may generate more conflict than clarity, but these studies make the point that respected researchers believe in an imprinting process taking place in something like a critical period in human sexual development. The empirical researches on adolescent sex offenders are not as specific. They simply assign the onset of the problem to puberty. Nonetheless, they are consistent with a role for critical-period learning as part of a complex process by which sexual activity with children, like many sexual behaviors, is developed.

Only the most zealous would advocate that biological theories totally explain sex offending, and that no additional theories are necessary. These theories do strongly suggest that males have a great deal to cope with in terms of keeping their sexual impulses under control. To the extent that the problem is biologically-driven, these theories would suggest that some of the treatment should be pharmaceutical. Alternatively, from a psychodynamic standpoint, the patient should be helped to develop a very strong ego to continuously contain these strong impulses. It is, of course, possible that the biological argument is overstated, and that male sexuality is driven by cultural, family, and other variables.

Biological theories compliment well several other theories. They are not, in general, contradictive of conditioning or behavioral-cognitive theories. In fact, these perspectives articulate nicely in the area of early adolescent onset of lifelong patterns of sexual behavior. Some feminist theorists probably would agree with the portrayal of males as hypersexual and hyperaggressive and in great need of keeping their impulses under control. The school of feminism which prefers to see males and females as substantially equal in all physical and biological aspects would probably not regard these theories with favor.

SOCIAL LEARNING THEORY

This theory is immensely influential. It is related in spirit to behavioral-cognitive theory. It is, as it says, a variation of learning theory. It does not have the existential or metapsychological elements which make many practitioners and researchers uncomfortable with psychodynamic or trauma-based theories. It sees the human psyche as infinitely plastic and changeable by various reinforcement techniques. It also appeals to the behaviorally-oriented in the field because it adds an important element to the preferred behavioral-cognitive framework. This hitherto missing element is interpersonal relationship and its undeniable influence on child development.

One of social learning theory's key postulates is that children are shaped by their interactions with the people who are emotionally important in their lives. The reactions of those figures to the behaviors and communications of the developing child are powerful reinforcers which, in turn, shape the child's behavior and development.

Bandura is the best known and most frequently cited of the social learning theorists. Writing with Walters (1963), he gives a straightforward example of how social learning theory might explain the origin of sexual deviations. The case in point is transvestism. The authors offer a vignette to illuminate the workings of social learning theory in the development of a young male transvestite. A young boy is dressed by his mother in girls' clothing and jewelry. She also indicates that she had a girl's name in mind for him before his birth. The message to be reinforced is both implicit and obvious here. The boy takes on increasingly feminine roles as he grows older. His mother rewards these behaviors with demonstrations of affection and verbal approval. A beloved grandmother and enthusiastic neighbors join in to furnish a supply of women's clothing. Voila! A transvestite.

Bandura and Walter's vignette suggests shaping by reinforcement in the form of praise, love, support, and implicit expectations. Identification is another key social learning theory concept. A boy may have a father who is affectionate with him while modeling violence with his mother and neighbors. The father's affection for the boy, combined with their shared maleness, creates a situation where the boy identifies with and imitates the most important male figure in his life. He grows up to be much like his mentor.

Social learning theory has recently been offered as a comprehensive model for understanding and treating adolescent sex offenders (Sermabeikian and Martinez, 1994). The implications of social learning theory for treatment are that the same kind of reinforcement from and identification with emotionally important people in the patient's life can be facilitators of change in their treatment. Unlike psychodynamic theories, social learning theory postulates no obstacles to changing behavior by creating a proper learning environment furnished with emotionally charged individuals who will help the patient reshape his behavior through rewards and punishments or via identification or other processes outlined by the theory.

THE TRAUMA MODEL

This model is in widespread use throughout contemporary psycho-therapy. It is underrepresented as a theoretical framework within the sex offender field. It is probably the preferred theory in the closely related, but noncommunicating, field of treatment of victims of sexual abuse. This theory rarely makes it into even the clinical literature on sex offenders. It appeals mostly to those who focus on treating the victim issues of offenders when such issues are present. As noted earlier, the issue of sex offenders as victims is highly controversial. An articulate school of practitioners feels that the offender's victim status should be ignored lest he hide behind it as an excuse for his behavior.

The major hypotheses of the trauma theory are that trauma in early life shapes and, indeed, may warp all the rest of the individual's life. These traumata are often walled off from consciousness. Here they dominate behavior and feeling from their unconscious haunts (Summit, 1988). A specialized variant of this model is widely used by those treating adolescent sex offenders. Where the trauma is sexual victimization, the individual may become focused on issues of power and control. Males react with shame and rage to being under the sexual domination of others. The humiliation becomes a traumatic focus. The male victim seeks others to victimize so he can recreate his own traumatic victimization, but this time with himself in control. Since this technique provides only temporary relief, the behavior of molesting can become compulsive as the perpetrator needs to recreate the "healing" situation over and over again. Most clinicians or researchers asked about dynamic factors in the genesis of sex offenses will cite a need for power and domination as significant factors. This line of thinking is the main contribution of the trauma model to the understanding of adolescent molesters.

There are other, less widely employed, variations of the trauma model among those who treat adolescent molesters. Therapists who use post-traumatic stress disorder or dissociative reactions for the diagnostic understanding of sex offenders are adhering to a variant of the trauma model.

Clinicians treating adolescent molesters who are not victims of documented sexual abuse may feel this is not relevant in such cases. It should be kept in mind, however, that physical abuse and severe neglect can also set in motion factors leading to posttraumatic stress disorder and disassociative reactions. Physical abuse and neglect are part of the background of many adolescent molesters. Posttraumatic stress disorder and some of the milder dissociative conditions are probably more common among adolescent sex offenders than is generally realized.

The rate of sexual victimization during childhood among homosexual pedophiles, as well as among adolescent molesters who have male victims, are high and suggest that the trauma model has merit in understanding the roots of these particular problems.

The fringes of the trauma model, including repressed memory phenomena and multiple personality, have recently become controversial, with a number of lawsuits arising out of what often seems to be a misuse of these models. Any clinician proceeding into this terrain at the present time should proceed with great caution.

THE PSYCHIATRIC MODEL

This model views molesting as a manifestation of some kind of underlying psychopathology. Research emanating from this school examines sex offender populations for DSM–IV disorders. It also looks for underlying biochemical contributors to the problem, such as elevated or depleted levels of various neurotransmitters.

This school also advocates something close to standard mental health treatment for adolescent sex offenders. It gives a more central role to individual and family treatment than does the predominant behavioral-cognitive approach. Although it is not inherent in the model, those whose practice is rooted in the psychiatric model usually try to make use of the therapeutic alliance and transference and countertransference relationships as an important part of the treatment process.

The psychiatric model is probably most fully represented in the literature by Shaw and his colleagues. Judith Becker has recently made some forays into this area. As with other models, it is doubtful that the major adherents of this school would offer it as a complete and comprehensive explanation of sex offending. The psychiatric model appears to be another model which supplements understandings derived from other theoretical frameworks without claiming that it alone is the truth.

FEMINIST SOCIOLOGY

Feminists have a long-standing interest in the field of sex abuse. Indeed, they deserve credit for bringing American society's attention to the sexual abuse of women and children. White and Koss (1993) and Struve (1990) have written about adolescent sex offenders from a feminist perspective. This perspective sees sex offending as a manifestation of patriarchy. Adolescent sex offenders are simply expressing this culture's implicit teaching about male dominance and the right of males to treat women and children as chattel and to do with them as they please. This view sees rape as a mechanism for the subordination of women.

Marshall and Barbaree (1990) feel that cultural beliefs of this nature, expressed in patriarchy, facilitate and permit rape. They have more of a problem when considering them as an adequate explanation for the phenomenology of molestation. Feminist sociology is not inconsistent with the other models. Its theories relate to phenomena at the macro societal level rather than at the more individual levels at which most of the other theories operate.

PSYCHODYNAMIC THEORY

Historically, psychodynamic theory has had very little influence in the sex offender field. Psychodynamic clinicians generally are not interested in sex offenders. Much of the older psychoanalytic literature regards sex offenders as manifesting a perversion which is not treatable by psychoanalytic techniques. Some of Nicholas Groth's work suggests that he has been influenced by this model. His are the only commonly published writings which, to some degree, factor in psychodynamic considerations.

Psychodynamic theory is complex and has numerous variations. Some major tenets are shared by all of the psychodynamic theories. All are founded in the belief that people act as they do in large part because of early developmental experiences. The way they process these experiences during childhood leads to the emergence of enduring styles for coping with reality and relating to other human beings. The importance assigned to the early stages of life, and the powerful influence of these early stages over the rest of the individual's life are beliefs that psychodynamic theories share with the biological theory of critical periods.

Psychodynamic theory would also regard much of the force which drives adolescent sex offenders as emanating from unconscious factors, of which they may be only dimly aware. These theorists regard molesting as a symptom that plays a significant role in the psychic balance of the adolescent sex offender. Psychodynamic thinking portrays symptoms as adaptations. Symptoms are remnants of ways of coping with a less than perfect reality in early life. Molesting is a symptom of an early conflict. As a symptom, it is a way to try to accomplish some psychic goal of importance to the molester. The symptom was formed early in life at a time when the child's immature ego either had a distorted view of the world or when the immature ego was attempting to adapt to a grossly pathological reality such as physical or sexual abuse.

The molester's adaptation is to a distorted or pathological reality. The symptom, in this case molesting, becomes maladaptive when applied to a problem or employed in a reality context for which it was not designed. By way of example, a boy of three may be sexually assaulted by his mother's boyfriend. He feels little, weak, and helpless. He experiences the assault as a frightening loss of control to a more powerful adult whom he cannot trust. There are several ways his immature ego may cope with this. One would be to identify with the aggressor. He would then seek out others on whom to force sex. Now he no longer feels little weak, helpless, and out of control. He has, of course, acquired another problem. So has society. When this child formulated his symptom as a solution to his trauma, it relieved his anxiety. Carried into his adolescence and adulthood, the pattern becomes thoroughly maladaptive. Analysts and critical-period theorists would add that since the problem has its origin in developments in the earliest and most formative periods of life, it will be difficult to excise.

Psychodynamic theories are generally derided as "insight therapies" by those working in the adolescent molester field. There is a joke, often heard at conferences: If you treat a sex offender with insight, what do you get? Answer: A sex offender with insight. This derision seems to be based on the idea that insight is the main mechanism by which psychodynamic therapists attempt to change behavior and feeling.

Most of the contemporary schools of psychodynamic treatment attribute little significance to insight as a mechanism of personality transformation. Freud made a big fuss about making the unconscious conscious. That was many years ago. Most contemporary psychodynamic schools attribute the principal curative factor to the patient-therapist relationship and the examination of the nature of that relationship.

The psychodynamic theories fit well with the psychiatric model, with which they have enjoyed a long symbiotic interaction. To some degree, they are consistent with the trauma model, at least in its more moderate forms. In my judgment, psychodynamic thinking may have a great deal to offer in terms of explaining the behavior of the adolescent sex offender. Psychoanalysts have generally felt that their treatment techniques work best with the bright and verbal who are not crippled by severe psychopathology. They have always expressed reservations about treating the delinquencies and the perversions. This would suggest that techniques emanating from the psychodynamic school will be of limited use with adolescent sex offenders.

FAMILY SYSTEM THEORIES

Those who work extensively with families have developed a number of related theories to explain how family systems operate. There are many variations of family systems theory, and there is great variation in detail among these theories. It is beyond the scope of this work to discuss them all here. Only the more salient features shared by most family theorists will be examined. Here also will be integrated some observations on the role of family dynamics in generating some of the pathology in boys I have treated in over a decade of specialized practice with adolescent molesters.

Family system dynamics seem to be particularly prominent among boys who molest within their family. They are less important in the dynamics of boys who molest outside the home. Family systems theory sees human behavior as shaped by the family environment in which children are raised. Both positive behaviors and psychopathology are seen as a response to family systems pressure, and as an attempt to meet the needs of a family functioning as a system. In general, family systems theory postulates that each member of a family plays a significant role within the family unit. The roles balance and complement each other. The goal of the entire system of roles is to maintain an equilibrium. Dysfunctional behavior, such as incest and child molesting, are believed to result from pathological roles and an attempt to maintain a pathological equilibrium. Treating troubled families involves helping to establish a new and less destructive equilibrium.

This approach is probably dominant among those who treat incest. One of their frequent vignettes is a pathological family system in which the mother, due to her issues, has abandoned the role of mother and given it to a daughter. The daughter cleans, cooks, and looks after father's needs. After a while, this comes to encompass the father's sexual needs. The father has stepped out of his role as a father. He has now become a lover to his daughter. The entire system is in disequilibrium, producing grossly dysfunctional behavior.

The basic goal of treatment in this kind of model would be to return the parents to their proper role as parents, get them engaged in the proper sex roles with each other, and free the child to resume the role of a child in a normal family. Scapegoats play a vital role in preserving the equilibrium of dysfunctional families. The teenage perpetrator often occupies the role of a scapegoat in the family. If either parent in the family is emotionally disturbed or under serious pressure, they may attempt to improve their functioning by assigning the role of scapegoat to another member of the family. If the parents are having major issues with each other, one or the other of them may retarget their issues and their rage on a child in the family.

If the child is a boy and the family issues are sexual, this child may become an adolescent molester. One logical result of such a role system is that all of the sexual pathology is attributed to an adolescent perpetrator in the family. He is then detected and ejected from the family into placement. This follows the classic role of the Biblical scapegoat in which the sins of the community are heaped on a goat who is then driven from the community to die in the desert. Just as the Hebrews hoped their sins could be so removed from the community, so the dysfunctional family hopes that the whole family's sexual pathology will accompany the molester into whatever "desert" he is cast.

Another family system dynamic involves the parents. Parents who are victims of molestation seem to create family scenarios in which they can return to their own victimization issues. I believe that this is another attempt at self-healing. It is closely related to the trauma victims who keep plunging themselves into situations resembling the original trauma in order to attempt to work out the problem more successfully. Unfortunately, this often results in parents unconsciously creating family dramas in which children are molested.

SIBLING ISSUES

Sometimes a sex offense against a younger sibling is a way to get even with a parent who has made it clear that they overwhelmingly prefer the victim to the boy who becomes the perpetrator. Many different kinds of acting out can result from this family situation. In the case of boys who are otherwise predisposed to molest, the acting out takes the form of a sexual assault on the child who is favored. This is, in essence, using sex to express hostility and vengefulness toward the parent. Like rape, the crime is one of anger rather than sex.

Another permutation is a sexual act with a sibling in response to seductiveness by the mother. This seductiveness factor occurs frequently in the history of adolescent molesters. Carefully taken histories, particularly of boys in placement, yield evidence of a variety of sexualizing contacts with the mother. These include a history of sleeping in the mother's bed until somewhere between the ages of 8 and 12, taking showers with their mother until close to puberty, and even overt sexual contact with the mother, usually not going as far as intercourse.

These behaviors can create ambivalence in a young man. On one hand, his sexual feelings may be stirred by the sexual contact or near sexual contact with the mother. On the other hand, the thought of sex with the mother is frightening. Younger boys may see it as an engulfing act and therefore life-threatening. Others may be aware that this is probably the ultimate sexual taboo in their culture. Boys in this situation may develop an intense sexual frustration. They may also develop a rage with the mother for simultaneously stimulating and frustrating their sexual drive. Rage also probably serves a defensive role in their fear of incest and engulfment by the mother. If boys in this dilemma act out against victims, it is often with great anger. Eileen Yates describes a case with this kind of dynamic which culminates in the sadistic murder of a young girl (1978). A case from my own practice is also illustrative of the same principles:

Ricky U.

Ricky's mother had a history of extremely provocative behavior with him over a long period of time. He showered and slept with her until about age nine. She made a point of appearing around him in the nude. Ricky drilled a hole in the bathroom door and used it to observe his mother in the shower for two years. On one occasion, his mother told him that if he were not her son she would have sex with him. She did the next best thing and introduced him to some female friends who became involved with him sexually. Ricky was placed in residential treatment after he battered and sexually abused a two-year-old child for a period of hours. At one point the victim stopped breathing. As a result of this trauma, the victim spent thirteen days in intensive care. Like Eileen Yates's cases, it appears to be an example of near homicide resulting from conflicts centering around maternal seductions.

This case suggests the degree of rage which is generated by provocative and seductive behaviors. A closely related dynamic is revenge. Many adolescent molesters say openly that they molested a sibling who was favored in the family in order to express their rage with the parent who was favoring that child. In these cases, the parent is far too powerful to take on directly. A back door to hurting and getting even with the parent is to hurt someone who is valuable to them. In cases of this nature, the sexual assault upon a sibling is usually a forceful and sadistic act which is much more closely related to a physical assault than a sexual act. Where the relationship with a female parent is highly sexualized but not characterized by extreme hostility, we may see the emergence of a seductive and consenting incestuous relationship between male and female siblings. In this case, the role for the male is probably defensive against incestuous yearnings for a female parent figure.

A more subtle dynamic leading to molestation by boys involves a male child who is essentially unwanted by his family. This child may spend a lot of time wandering in the neighborhood on his own. If the father is absent, he may have an intense yearning for a father figure. He also has a strong and justified feeling that his own needs for affection are not being met at home. This kind of child is easy prey for a pedophile. Sophisticated molesters often operate by identifying such needy children and gratifying their emotional needs in exchange for sex. As noted earlier, once a boy has been molested by an adult or adolescent male, he himself becomes a candidate to become an offender. This is another instance in which family systems dynamics can contribute to the emergence of molesting pathology in male children.

THE PROBLEMS OF UNITARY THEORIES

It has been implied throughout this chapter that there is a deficiency in unitary theories. They are by definition one-dimensional and, therefore, almost inherently inadequate to explain the complex and convoluted behavior, history, and motivations of adolescent sex offenders. Virtually everyone practicing as a clinician in this field puts together some combination of these unitary theories to make something that is satisfying to them as a more or less complete explanation of the phenomena at hand and what can be done in the way of treatment to ameliorate the problem.

THEORETICAL SYNTHESES

There seems to be an increasing awareness among those working with sex offenders that the unitary theories are inadequate and that we need to struggle for something more comprehensive. Marshall and Barbaree have already been quoted as advocating a more eclectic approach, including sociocultural factors and biological processes. Marshall and Eccles (1993), however, do not believe that a comprehensive theory of sex offending is possible. They advocate a specific theory to explain each type of offense. Marshall and Eccles aside, there is certainly within the field a move in the direction of eclecticism. Both Becker and Shaw have shown a willingness to foray into previously little-explored psychiatric aspects of the behavior of adolescent sex offenders.

By far the most elaborate attempt to synthesize theories relating to adolescent sex offenders is that of Finkelhor and Araji (1986). The authors review a wide range of theories that have been offered to explain the phenomenology of adolescent sex offenders. They suggest that there are four basic factors which explain why young males turn into perpetrators. These are: (1) emotional congruence, (2) disinhibition, (3) sexual arousal, and (4) blockage of more normal sexual expressions. The authors are able to use these four principles to subsume under this rubric virtually all of the other theories that have been offered to explain the behavior and motivation of adolescent sex offenders.

This kind of grand unified theory of sex offending is significant. It may, however, lack the specific detail to make it meaningful and useful when applied to specific offenders. In addition to a grand and unified theory, I agree with Marshall and Eccles that there is a need for theoretical frameworks to explain what is going on with various subgroups of adolescent sex offenders. Perhaps the ultimate resolution will be that a global and eclectic theory such as that offered by Finkelhor and Araji will become widely accepted. Specific and detailed theories will need to be developed to explain the phenomenology of the probably multiple subcategories of molesters. It is likely that identifiable subgroups such as pedophilic adolescents with only male victims, frotteurs, or makers of obscene phone calls have unique and specific dynamics to explain their behavior. Ultimately, the behavior of each individual may have to be explained individually, using insights drawn from various theoretical orientations.

Chapter Four

A PSYCHODYNAMIC MODEL
OF MALE DEVELOPMENT

It is unfortunate that psychoanalytic theory has so little appeal to most of those who work with adolescent sex offenders. In my judgment, it has much to offer to the understanding of why some boys molest others and something to offer in the area of treatment. One of its salient advantages is that psychoanalysts are the only group of theorists who listen carefully to patients' words, fantasies, and dreams and try to make sense out of this material. In general, psychoanalysis has seemed to attract the best and brightest minds in psychotherapy. Those on the cutting edge among contemporary analysts have begun to integrate a number of diverse, nonanalytic data bases into their general theory. These endeavors include: (1) a new wave of direct observations of infants and children interacting with their mothers; (2) a formal science of psychoanalysis based on data, quantifiable measures, and sophisticated mathematical treatments; (3) integration of psychoanalysis and the evolutionary viewpoint of modern biology; (4) an active search for neurological and brain correlates for mental phenomena; (5) incorporation of data from anthropology, archaeology, and paleontology into psychoanalytic thinking (Langs, 1995).

It seems like folly to ignore this treasure trove of thought by some of the world's best minds. The reason this school of thought is so ignored throughout the sex abuse field is, in my judgment, the fact that the name "psychoanalysis" evokes in most modern therapists the ghost of Freud and classical psychoanalysis. Before I can ask anyone to consider the value of contemporary psychoanalysis, it is necessary to explore why classical analysis has caused the well from which seekers of understanding might drink to appear to so many to be poisoned.

CLASSICAL PSYCHOANALYSIS

Psychoanalytic theory, as developed by Freud and his disciples, consisted of a number of propositions which have not withstood the test of time. The major problem seems to lie in Freudian propositions about women and female development. It does not seem unfair to call them sexist. Freud's most celebrated and infamous idea is that women are traumatized by the mere fact of not having a penis. This renders the female a sort of second rate male, condemned to work out an identity without the presence of the magical penis, doomed, in a sense, to spend her entire life compensating for its absence.

Central to Freud's thinking about sexual development was the Oedipus complex. Freud considered the period of life between 3 and 6 years of age to be the most basic for formation of all later personality. He also felt that the Oedipus complex existed in unmodified form in all cultures. A number of psychoanalytically-oriented anthropologists dispersed across the world to gather data and, at times, manipulated it to arrive at the preordained conclusion.

Freud's hydraulic model of personality also troubled many. The idea of dammed-up energies flowing here and there, creating neuroses and other psychopathologies does not ring true. It is at best a metaphor and has no empirical support. It seems to have been discarded or ignored. The classical formulation of id, ego, and superego is also associated with the early Freudian school. While it may have some merit, its current cliché status makes it seem far from profound. The classical Freudians are still around. They are probably the best known psychoanalysts to those outside the discipline of psychoanalysis and those who follow it closely. When "psychoanalysis" is summarized in college courses, the usual focus is on the classical school and its dogmatic, and sometimes absurd, assertions. No wonder it is difficult to get college educated therapists to look at what is going on in modern psychoanalysis.

What is rarely, if ever, taught in these courses is that since at least the 1930s, psychoanalysis has been fragmenting and exploring areas only lightly touched upon by Freud. There has been an emphasis on exploring what happens in the pre-Oedipal period, i.e., the first three years of life, which most developmental theorists feel are the most important in the formation of personality. Outside of the orthodox analytic institutes, it is my suspicion that most analysts now would say that the events of the pre-Oedipal period are more important to personality development than what takes place in the Oedipal stage itself.

Penis envy has been at least de-emphasized or relegated to the status of a pathological aberration in most modern schools of psychoanalysis. Kernberg does not refer to it in the index of his influential book, *Borderline Conditions and Pathological Narcissism* (1985). Some analysts still adhere to the notion that penis envy is a key dynamic in female development. Phyllis Tyson still attributes great significance to it in a 1966 article reviewing female development. She cites as her source the influential Margaret Mahler (1966, 1975). Tyson (1989), however, has toned down the classic position:

> Where the mother/child relationship has been poor, penis envy as a developmental metaphor comes to represent a general sense of worthlessness, narcissistic vulnerability, inadequacy, deprivation, and damage.

Tyson feels that it is the discovery of anatomical differences rather than penis envy, per se, that function as a psychic organizer for the developing female. Peter Blos (1985) takes this a step further and states clearly his belief that the developmental lines of the male and female child are each *sui generis,* that is, independent and distinctly different sequences of development with separate milestones leading to separate ends in male and female identity development. Another important addition to the classical repertoire has been the discovery that at least some males have considerable envy of females, their anatomy, and their sexuality (Bettelheim 1955), (Stoller 1985), (Litz and Litz 1989), (Herdt 1981).

Another addition to Freud's pioneering work has been the concept of developmental lines. This idea was first elaborated by Anna Freud (1965), arising out of her extensive work with children. Gertrude and Reuben Blanck picked up the idea and elaborated upon it in a 1974 work. The Blanks point out that Freud focused on only one developmental line which they call psychosexual maturation. These are the classic stages known to every undergraduate: oral, anal, phallic, and genital. This line places male and female sexual development on a single line, creating much of the controversy that has surrounded psychoanalysis in the sex abuse field. Blanck and Blanck argue that development proceeds not along one line, but along a whole series of parallel lines. They list eleven. Anna Freud gives a different list in her 1965 work. Historically, it is the concept of multiple developmental lines which set the stage for idea that males and females follow separate developmental paths to the development of sexual identity. This, in turn, has immense implications for further understanding in the sexual abuse field.

THE MALE LINE OF SEXUAL IDENTITY DEVELOPMENT

A separate male developmental line has been implicit in recent psychoanalytic thinking. Blos (1985), who writes extensively about adolescence and spends much time on adolescent males, touches upon the idea but does not fully develop it. In spite of the fact that psychoanalytic thinking about developmental lines goes back to Freud himself, detailed and definitive papers on the topic of specific lines of sexual development in males and females were first published by Phyllis Tyson in 1982 and 1986.

This is an idea of major significance. It greatly enriches theory about why young males get into so many sexual problems. Their path to psychosexual maturity is convoluted and complicated. Because of the nature of male development itself, men are subject to a variety of disorders of masculinity which represent fixations and derailments in complex male sexual development. Molestation of children, the focus of attention here, is a result of such a developmental problem. Treating boys who molest is made easier and better informed when the main paths and byways of male development are understood. What is offered here is a synthesis of the thinking about male development drawn from several sources within the broad psychodynamic movement. For the milestones, I have relied heavily on Tyson (1982, 1986) and Blos (1985).

It is known that the male infant emerges from the womb with a strong propensity to be male (Money, 1965). A headstart on masculine development takes place in the womb. Numerous studies indicate that the testes secrete hormones *in utero,* and that these hormones act on the fetal brain to switch on certain circuits that promote male behavior (Money 1965), (Diamond 1965), (Young, Goy, and Phoenix 1964). The next milestone is the assignment of gender at birth. In most situations, parents are able to readily recognize the sex of their child, correctly identify it, and begin a socialization process that gives the child a shove in the direction of maleness. Of course, biological abnormalities exist which can complicate this process.

Tyson cites the discovery of the penis, with its genital sensations, and masturbation as a milestone in the development in the sense of maleness.

She also notes the importance of urinating in a standing position in the process of differentiating sexually from the mother and providing an early and visible gender link to the father.

A powerful and pervasive theme throughout the early years of male development is growing out of symbiotic fusion with the mother. If this does not happen, core identity will remain female. The logical outcome would be transexualism. A strong impetus is given to the development of maleness when the child recognizes his father or key male figure in his environment and he begins to identify with him. If he loves and admires his father, this both strengthens his gender identity and lures him away from symbiotic attachment to the mother.

The mother has important roles to play here. She must permit and encourage the boy's growth out of symbiosis with her. Otherwise, the boy will be placed in a horrible dilemma. He will have to choose to give up his mother's love, approval, and support in order to become male or to give up his quest to become fully male in order to please his mother by remaining in symbiotic fusion with her (Tyson, 1982). If he remains in such a state of fusion, he will be, by definition, feminine in his sexual identity. The logical formula is: Mother is a female; I am an extension of her; I am therefore female. If the mother communicates her liking and approval of masculinity, she facilitates the growth of her son's masculinity by providing narcissistic supplies for its development.

Finally, the mother must avoid devaluing the father lest the boy read this a general devaluation of masculinity and a denial of permission by the mother to form a gender bond with the father. The father also has responsibilities to communicate enthusiasm for his son's developing masculinity and to provide an admirable example of masculinity. If he devalues himself or is in chronic conflict with the mother, the father will make it very difficult for the mother to provide her necessary input for the boy's developing masculinity.

When parents work successfully in these ways to promote their son's developing maleness, they allow the boy to take the next developmental step. He cannot enter into a dyadic relationship with the father. Blos (1965) cautions here that what he calls "male isogender object relationships" are very poorly known. He speculates that for successful male development, the boy must form an intense relationship with a fathering figure.

This stage is postulated by Blos to be pre-Oedipal, meaning it arises around age three. This is a phase of idealization and identification with the father. The developing male shares what he perceives as the father's power by imitation of the father and submission to the father. This stage contains an implicit passivity which, for some males, can pose a threat of feminization. If a male becomes stuck in this developmental phase, he will spend his life in an unceasing search for father figures. This will, in turn, ensure an emotional infantilism just as significant as that created by an overdependency upon maternal figures (Blos, 1985).

Next on the young male's developmental odyssey is the Oedipal phase. Blos describes the boy as beginning to move away from the father, to "play big boy," and develop what he calls an "overbearing turn to noisy motions of self-affirmation" (1985). It is in this stage that the boy tests himself against the father. The classical situation of competing with the father for the mother comes into play. Ideally, it is resolved with a rapprochement between father and son in which the son gives up desires for the mother and moves toward other love objects. In ideal situations, this involves a friendly identification with the father. This, in turn, provides a foundation for peer and mentor relationships with other males throughout the rest of life.

The next milestone comes with puberty. Blos feels that, at or near puberty, there is a resurgence of the old idealization and identification with father. As with the pre-Oedipal situation, submission and passivity in relationship to the father characterize this phase. This often leads to some limited homosexual acting out, and to homosexually-tinged yearnings for the father's love.

This stage is followed by a reactivization of the Oedipal themes of competition. Ideally, these issues are again resolved through a relationship of cooperation, friendship, and identification between father and son. This process is not easy for father or son. Even if the process is proceeding well, Blos warns of "the usual, obligatory conflicts."

The vignette of male development offered here is far from complete. Failure at any point can lead into byways of sexual development some of which have been discussed, others which have not been. Throughout the process, the developing male must also strive to attain an integration of sexual and aggressive impulses that is balanced and nondestructive to self and others. If this balance is tipped in favor of the aggressive aspects of male behavior, a number of unfortunate outcomes, among them rape, may be expected.

The developmental theory presented here has several implications for the understanding of issues important in the developmental life of adolescent molesters. When something goes wrong at any of the critical

Table 2.
Development of Male Identity.

Age/Stage	Event	Developmental Goal	Pitfalls
Adolescence 14–18	Gradual separation/ individuation from older male models. Increased competition with other males. Dating, bonding to females.	Establishment of life long pattern of hetero-sexual relationships. Ability to love females, be a better father, etc.	Isolation from peers of both sexes. Too competitive. Fear of sexual relationships.
Puberty 11–13 ± one year	Hormonal upsurge. Resurgence of hunger for father figures. Transient homoerotic impulses. Same sex sexual experimentation.	Strengthen sense of male identity through renewed identification with father figures. Resolve or suppress homoerotic impulses.	Extreme vulnerability to molestation. Derail-ment of male identity. Life long gender, identity confusion.
"Latency" 5–10	Expansion of inter-action with older and peer males.	Learns competition, friendship, and team work with other males.	Becomes too competi-tive, can't relate to males. Male identity weakness.
"Oedipal" 3–5	Discovery of father. Hunger for connection with father figures.	Strengthening of male identity through iden-tification with and imitation of positive male figures.	Vulnerability to mol-estation. Identification with negative male figures.
"Pre-oedipal" 0–3	Beginnings of sociali-zation as a male. Dis-covery of penis, mas-turbation. Notation that girls are "different".	Early, irreversible sense of gender iden-tity develops (see John Money, 1965).	Gender identity con-fusion. Cross gender identification.
Birth	Assignment of sex.	Sociocultural defini-tion of child as male.	Misidentification due to anatomical abnormalities.
In utero	Hormonal masculini-zation of fetus.	Sets biological sub-strate for maleness, etc.	Biogenetic deviations from masculine, hermaphroditism.

stages in the development of masculinity, it is likely to result in a weakened sense of masculinity. Some of the problem areas leave the young boy more vulnerable to become a victim of sexual abuse.

If either parent fails to do their job in promoting the boy's sense of masculinity, the optimal development will not occur. Where the optimal development is not present, there will be a proclivity in some cases to attempt to repair or strengthen one's masculinity through one of the perversions. It is a contention of this work that pedophilia is one of the perversions. More will be said of this later.

SELF PSYCHOLOGY

Self psychology is explored here in part because it is rich in explanatory value regarding adolescent molesters because it is, in my judgment, the most comprehensive and plausible theory to explain the development of human personality in both sexes. When its insights are added to those of developmental psychology, a powerful theoretical and practical tool for understanding and treating adolescent molesters becomes available.

This discipline seems to be little known in the sex abuse field. It is an offshoot of psychoanalysis developed by Heinz Kohut and subsequently embraced by numerous followers. It represents the cutting edge of current psychoanalytic thinking and is the theoretical underpinning for much current psychoanalytically-oriented publication. Kohut's writings are exceedingly difficult to wade through. This has probably impeded his acceptance outside narrow psychoanalytic circles. For those willing to brave the jungle of jargon, there are treasures here for the clinician working with young males who molest others.

THE NUCLEAR SELF AND NUCLEAR GOALS

The nuclear or core self is the central concept of self psychology. Pathology and acting out are ways of shoring up gaps in the nuclear self or preventing its collapse. The structure of the nuclear self can be strong and intact or weak and buried beneath defensive structures. The nuclear self develops very early in life. Most of it is in place within the first two or three years of life. Self psychology sees the psyche as organized around two central concepts: ambitions and ideals. The life process is viewed as a struggle to attain the nuclear goals implied in the ambitions and ideals of the self. The person uses his or her congenital abilities as well as the skills they develop in life to push toward a nuclear program implicit in these ideals and ambitions. Anyone familiar with classical analysis will be struck by the existential nature of these concepts as opposed to purely hedonistic and sexual nature of the innermost self in Freud's thinking.

The concept of the nuclear self and nuclear goals are important in understanding all human beings and have important implications for the understanding of adolescent molesters. By appraising the strength of the core self we can understand the strengths and weaknesses with which we have to deal in treatment. Treatment goals will be better accomplished if they are tied to the person's own ideals and ambitions. More importantly for those working with adolescent molesters, I believe that goals relating to maleness are a part of the nuclear self of all males and that pushing for one's optimal maleness is, for most men, an essential part of their nuclear hopes and aspirations for their lives.

Where the nuclear self is weak, there is a constant danger of fragmentation. Fragmentation is a concept from ego psychology. It refers to the breaking up of the structure of the self resulting in such syndromes as psychosis, profound depression, delinquency, drug addiction, and/or other severe pathologies. Much of the sexual acting out by perpetrators can be interpreted as a mechanism to avoid fragmentation or repair the damage to sexual identity caused by various types of traumatic assaults on their masculinity in early life. Traumas affecting maleness include such things as molestation by males, parents who make it plain they would have preferred a female child, or a father who provides an extremely negative model of what it is to be a man.

Anything which makes a developing boy doubt his essential maleness or devalues that maleness can assault the self and particularly its ambitions and ideals in the area of masculinity. A coherent and well-developed sense of self allows for optimal social functioning. Individuals with this kind of self structure develop healthy relationships, get themselves through life well, and experience minimal danger of fragmentation.

The development of such a self provides a goal for the treatment of all patients who have the inner resources to work at this level including some of the higher functioning adolescent molesters. It is an ideal to be sought whenever possible. Sadly, according to the tenets of ego psychology, those who cannot work at this level can only be helped to develop various compensatory structures to cover over structural defects in the self.

SELFOBJECTS

Selfobjects are a key concept in Kohut's psychology. The term is clumsy but, if properly understood, is useful in the sex abuse field. I suspect that many of the transactions between victims and perpetrators have a selfobject quality for at least one of the parties. These relationships are one of the major vehicles males use to strengthen their sense of masculinity since sexual identity is part of the nuclear self. When masculine identity is damaged by trauma, the victim will seek out selfobjects to help in the repair process. This opens the door for the therapist to become a selfobject to the patient, and help him work out key developmental issues in the course of a selfobject transference to the therapist.

The term selfobject is obscure and technical. In simple terms, it means that people from birth to death are presented with and/or seek out other human beings with whom they can interact and, in the course of this interaction, either enhance the growth of the nuclear self or stave off its collapse. Selfobjects will be used to both ends in the course of a lifetime. Selfobjects would include parents, relatives, friends, mentors, and so forth. Selfobjects can also be inanimate objects such as paintings (pornography?) or famous individuals with whom the person has no contact, or figures drawn from entertainment, history or religion (Kohut, 1984).

Self psychologists who have focused on the perversions contend that here the selfobject has become sexualized. This perspective has the potential to explain some of the more bizarre paraphilias. It also suggests that the treatment relationship is likely to be sexualized by patients with sexual problems. This is a well-known phenomenon in psychodynamic theory. It seems to be subliminally known in the sex offender field but rarely talked about or published upon. These erotized therapeutic relationships can be difficult to handle if the therapist is averse to dealing with the kind of strong sexual transference from the patient that this situation implies. If the therapist is able to tolerate this kind of material, it constitutes a kind of treatment opportunity. This will be elaborated upon later.

The precise and technical meaning of the word selfobject reflects the fact that, because of the early developmental stage at which this mechanism forms, the ego does not distinguish fully between itself and the selfobject. The selfobject, although a separate entity, functions structurally as a part of the self. The other person is selected as a selfobject because of some desirable group of attributes they possess. In selecting a selfobject, we seek to borrow or to incorporate into ourselves something we lack, and desire or need to bring into our developing self. For a male who has doubts about his own masculinity, a male whom he sees as having masculine traits which he desires may become a victim of sexual assault. Or the victim may be envied for nonsexual attributes which the perpetrator sees in him or projects onto him. In either case, the molester tries to obtain something he does not have by literally fusing, in a sexual sense, with the victim. The fact that in molestation the victim must be younger should not be a significant objection to this hypothesis. Perpetrators lacking self-confidence can easily idealize a younger boy and project onto him traits they desire but do not have.

This hypothesis needs modification to explain why boys molest females. In such cases, the very act of engaging in sex with a female may serve the function of strengthening the sense of masculinity in a boy who lacks self-assurance in that area. Such a boy may lack the social skills and self-confidence to seek out a female peer with whom to validate his masculinity in some form of consenting sex. Instead, he may seek out a much younger female who will admire him uncritically and thereby validate his fragile masculinity.

I believe that there is a drive toward psychological maleness in men which is thwarted at their psychic peril. This drive seems to have its roots in both biology and the kind of nuclear goals of the male self proposed by self psychology. When this drive is frustrated or blocked, individuals dangerous to themselves and to society often emerge. The male's propensity for aggression in the sexual area is well-known. This aggressiveness seems to be heightened when a male cannot proceed along his developmental line toward mature gender identity. In the language of self psychology, rape and child molesting can be interpreted as compensatory structures worked out by males who have strayed from the main path of this line. For victims of assault and molest, this is devastating. For the perpetrator these behaviors are an attempt at self repair.

Where molest has been brutal and humiliating, males may attempt to repair the damage to their masculinity by assuming control, humiliating, and destroying symbols of the man who molested them. This would be an attempt to repair the damage along the traditional lines of the trauma model: recreate the trauma, but in a situation where you are now in control.

NARCISSISTIC BEHAVIOR DISORDERS

Self psychological thinking on the perversions is also relevant to understanding adolescent molesters who already manifest entrenched paraphilias. Goldberg regards the perversions along with delinquencies and addictions as narcissistic behavior disorders (unpublished paper presented in San Diego, CA., April 1994). Individuals manifesting this disorder are severely damaged. They are characterized by acting out as a defense against underlying depression and emptiness. Such individuals make little use of repression. They are aware of their disorder, their destructive wishes, and the fantasies that accompany them. Many want to preserve the acting out. The key defense mechanism is in the narcissistic behavior disorders is the use of primitive, archaic fantasies to defend against disintegration or depletion of the self. Indulging in intense, primitive fantasies stimulated by intoxication, criminal behavior, or sexual acting out mobilize a fantasy state which Ullman and Paul call narcissistic bliss. This state serves to obliterate anxiety, depression and other states of intense psychic distress (1981). Although the above discussion is in the formal language of self psychology, what is described fits very well with what professionals working with sex offenders say about them in other language.

Treatment of the narcissistic behavior disorder is more limited in scope than the treatment normally offered by self psychologists. The extent of damage makes full repair unlikely. Goldberg advocates forming an alliance with the small but weak intact part of the self which is still able to perceive and evaluate reality. Therapy needs to focus on strengthening this part of the self via reality-oriented interpretation and outright teaching.

Interpretation needs to be behaviorally-oriented. The patient should be made fully aware of the impulsive, misbehaving part of the self. Interpretations like, "You got upset and you acted out," followed by careful examination of why the acting out was undertaken, and the results of the acting out are an essential part of the treatment process.

Goldberg recommends that the patient be repeatedly confronted with the reality of his situation. Goldberg cautions that, for many patients, this kind of "instructional therapy" must be ongoing. It is essentially a supportive therapy which inhibits the acting out proclivity of the narcissistic behavior disorder. When the supportive therapy is withdrawn, there is a high risk that the problem will re-emerge. Goldberg feels that the therapy he prescribes for narcissistic behavior disorders is closely related to the techniques by which long-term self-help groups keep members out of trouble. Such groups are particularly common among those with narcissistic behavior disorders such as the various addictions. In the sex offender field, Ryan and Lane (1991) focus on identifying stressors which trigger acting out, identifying the acting out as part of one's abuse cycle, and focusing on the negative consequences of the acting out. This seems similar in content and spirit to Goldberg's recommendations for the narcissistic behavior disorders.

It would seem that self psychology, those involved in the treatment of sex offenders, and twelve-step programs have come up with some remarkably similar conclusions about how to treat a population they share but call by different names. The concept of the narcissistic behavior disorder seems to me to be a unifying one for these populations. It also seems to be a nosological entity that adequately describes the segment of the adolescent molester population that is at the most serious risk for becoming adult pedophiles. The elements uniting pedophiles and others with narcissistic behavior disorders seem to be multiple. They include the use of acting out as a way of coping with stress and a weak ego structure in which compulsive and impulsive behaviors are poorly controlled. A most basic feature seems to be the use of fantasy and acting out in order to cope with anxiety by using it to obtain a brief and narcissistic state of bliss in which panic, emptiness and fear of descent into profound depression or psychosis are temporarily blotted out.

NARCISSISTIC BEHAVIOR DISORDER, BORDERLINE PERSONALITY, AND NARCISSISTIC PERSONALITY

This would be a good title and subject for a book-length treatment of its own. Obviously, that is beyond the scope of this work but something must be said of it here to avoid hopeless diagnostic confusion. The term narcissistic behavior disorder is a new concept. It is not in DSM–III, nor does it appear in the recently issued DSM–IV. It is discussed here because of its great value in explaining the behavior of the most pedophilic of the adolescent molesters.

Many writers have noticed elements of "borderline personality" in some or much of the adolescent sex offender population. Jon Shaw and his colleagues seem to have the greatest current interest in this area. As a psychiatrist, Dr. Shaw seems to adhere to the concept as defined in

DSM–III. I use it more loosely to describe boys who show significant signs of severe pathology, but who are not formally diagnosable as psychotic. I believe it is a developmental issue determined by fixation in the separation/individuation stage of human development. I consider the term narcissistic personality to be a very specialized one more or less adequately described by DSM–III. It appears to be rare or absent in adolescent sex offenders. Where there is severe pathology in this population, I suspect it is either a narcissistic behavior disorder, borderline personality disorder, or the somewhat related antisocial personality disorder. I also suspect that many adolescent sex offenders combine traits of several of these diagnostic categories in one personality.

SELF PSYCHOLOGY AND TREATMENT

Within self psychology, Goldberg has outlined specific techniques that are suitable for narcissistic behavior disorders which I suggest include pedophilia and the perversions. Some adolescent molesters seem to be in the early stages of a pedophile career or to have other perversions involved in their sexual acting out with children. This subgroup of the population is best treated with the techniques outlined in the standard model of sex offender treatment. For those adolescents who are not entrenched in pedophilia or a perversion, self psychology also offers more general theories about how human beings can be helped in treatment. A basic premise of self psychology is that pathology arises out of efforts to maintain the viability and unity of the self. Self psychology outlines a treatment technique for strengthening the self and developing structures within the self which will allow the individual to function successfully in the world and to be free of feelings of overwhelming panic, anxiety, and fragmentation.

Transference is the key to this approach. It can be used with adolescents who have enough strength and motivation to establish a therapeutic alliance. Where this approach is successful, the patient will create a classic selfobject relationship with the therapist. The formation of this transference allows the patient to reactivate the process of sexual development at the point at which it was stopped. Patient and therapist should return to the point in psychic time at which the wounds creating the molesting behavior were inflicted. By a complex and technical interaction, including identification, interpretation, and a bond of empathy, the patient is helped to resume the growth process and to develop the structures of the self necessary to the creation of a healthy adult masculine identity. The transference takes one of its most difficult turns if the patient eroticizes the relationship. The meaning of the eroticization is a desire to merge with the therapist who is an idealized selfobject. Through this psychic maneuver the patient hopes to build better internal structures through incorporating those of a stronger self. In this kind of transference the specific technique is sexual. The wish to merge with an idealized object takes the form of yearning for sexual fusion with the proposed partner. This kind of therapeutic situation, with an offender who is strong enough to handle it, creates an opportunity to discuss all the feelings and fears that make the adolescent feel so inadequate. Through frank discussion with an empathic therapist, the adolescent may be able to repair some of the damage to the core of his sexual being.

In spite of the hoopla about "insight therapy," self psychology makes little use of insight and interpretation as curative mechanisms. Treatment and cure are the results of a complex interaction. Kohut (CF Goldberg, 1985) argues that the only interpretations that should be offered in the course of treatment involve the relationship between patient and analyst, specifically events which interrupt the selfobject bond between patient and analyst. By offering the patient empathy and understanding, the patient is able to identify with the therapist. Also unleashed in the patient are a series of transmuting internalizations which lead, in turn, to the development of an enlarged and strengthened self.

It is impossible to say what percentage of adolescent molesters can benefit from the approach outlined above, but some can. Clearly, the narcissistic behavior disorders will not be able to benefit from this kind of work. Another group that cannot use the most transforming kind of therapy are the psychotics and borderline personalities in the molester population.

Borderline personality seems common among adolescent molesters, particularly those in placement. Self psychology does not believe that borderline conditions and psychoses can be "cured." These pathologies are regarded as involving a gross structural deficit at the center of the self. Here, instead of a strong nuclear self with defined life goals, is a core of emptiness and/or chaos at the very center of the person's being. To ameliorate such a problem, self psychology offers the concept of the development of compensatory psychic structures. These structures provide ways of repairing the defects in the self to allow the individual to function and realize his nuclear goals. To be regarded as successful, treatment should also give the patient the ability to make efficient use of selfobjects throughout the rest of his life. Selfobject relationships allow individuals to draw on and use the strengths of others to enrich their day-to-day functioning. Compensatory structures and the ability to make use of selfobjects will allow even a person with damaged self to strive toward nuclear goals and, in many cases, to avoid fragmentation in the face of all but the most overwhelming stressors.

INDIVIDUATION

Moving outside of self psychology, other offshoots of modern psychoanalysis offer useful concepts for understanding and treating adolescent molesters. One such contribution is the concept of individuation. This word is often associated with Karl Jung, but it is not the Jungian idea that is discussed here. Individuation has been most recently elaborated by developmental theorists within psychoanalysis, particularly Margaret Mahler, Gertrude and Reuben Blanck, and Peter Blos. The basic idea is that to develop successfully, the individual needs to separate from the maternal matrix into which he or she is born. At the earliest stages in life, the individual exists in a mental state of complete fusion with the mother or mothering person, called a symbiosis. Anyone not developing out of this stage is *a priori* psychotic.

All subsequent development centers around separating and distinguishing oneself from the maternal matrix and developing a separate, discreet, and defended sense of identity. At the end of this process, the individual should be able to relate to others as independent and separate objects, rather than as parts of the self. Individuals who get bogged down at some point within the separating process, once the original symbiosis has been broken, are *a priori* borderline. Basic individuation is believed to be complete by 36 months of age. Problems arising after 36 months of age are of an Oedipal or neurotic nature.

Individuation has become a very important concept throughout modern psychoanalysis. The concept is particularly important for those who treat adolescent molesters. Males are born of women and pass through the earliest and most critical stages of development in a state of symbiotic fusion with the mother. Males must thus, in essence, reverse their basic identification from female to male in the course of successful development. The material drawn from cultures all over the world suggests that this is a universal task in male development (Lidz and Lidz 1989), (Herdt, 1981), (Breer 1992). A review of the anthropological literature suggests that males all over the world seem to feel a need to emphasize and exaggerate their separateness from the female. This issue looms large in the concerns of adolescent molesters about their masculinity, panic about possible homosexuality, and their proclivity to attempt to solve these problems by molesting others.

ROBERT STOLLER

Robert Stoller, a somewhat maverick psychoanalyst, has put great effort into the study of male sexual identity development. His vehicle for study has been the perversions, particularly transvestitism. Stoller (1985) views perversions in men as a failure in the individuation process as well as in male identity development. Both, of course, are closely related. The poorly individuated male who later develops a perversion has a tremendous fear of being re-engulfed by the mother. This fear is aggravated if the mother belittles, humiliates, or degrades the developing boy's sense of masculinity. Because of the boy's poor ego boundary and fear of reabsorption by the mother, he will have a great fear of intimacy. In Stoller's words:

> The non-perverse person does not powerfully fear intimacy because he or she is not afraid that it will lead to a merging that swallows up identity. (Stoller, 1985).

The most difficult cases seem to arise when a developing boy's sense of maleness is assaulted or humiliated by a female. This assault may take the form of some kind of feminizing behavior, treating the boy as if he were a girl, reinforcing feminine behaviors, or other such activities repulsive to the developing boy's ego. This is the classic situation that leads the developing male into the perversions. A central theme in transvestitism is to dress as a female. Dynamically, Stoller would say this symbolizes the assault by femaleness which the transvestite fears. When dressing as a female is a direct source of sexual arousal or is necessary for arousal in the process of having sex, the state of arousal, including the associated erection, is proof to the transvestite that although his maleness is under assault, he has retained his essential masculinity in the face of the assault. The preservation of male identity in the face of overwhelming attack is the goal. Stoller feels that men do not fear castration as is posited by classical analysis. Men's most basic fear is the loss of the sense of maleness.

Where male identity is poorly formed, the male must engage a number of defense mechanisms to prevent merging with females and thereby, feminization. True intimacy with a woman is threatening. Some perversions protect from the danger of being swallowed up by femaleness in situations of real intimacy by partializing females. For example, erotic interest may shift from the whole woman to an item of clothing as it does in fetishism.

I would add to Stoller's formulations that where issues of fear of merging with females and panic about feminization as a result are prominent, another defense mechanism is to seek an extreme degree of control over the female partner. Control itself is often seen by men as an aspect of masculinity. Hence control becomes a part of the dynamics of perversion, allowing sexual contact without danger to a fragile male identity.

This can easily be factored in to explain how the young male victim of sexual abuse becomes a perpetrator. The role of control as a dynamic in perpetration is well documented (see, for example, Salter, 1988). In many of the eclectic theoretical explanations, it becomes the prominent dynamic (see, for example, Ryan and Lane, 1991). If control of the sex object is understood as a mechanism for defending masculinity, then perpetration can be interpreted as a form of perversion which follows the dynamics outlined by Stoller.

RESISTANCE TO PSYCHOANALYSIS

This chapter began on the note that it is necessary to justify using even the name psychoanalysis among many who work with sex offenders. The sexism and rigidity of classical analysis have no doubt contributed to this and justifiably so. Also contributory is the fact that most of those who research and write in this field have their data bases in the most disturbed and damaged segment of the population. Most are working with incarcerated offenders. Becker seems to do some work among inner-city and minority youth and mixes rapists and molesters in her studies. Psychodynamic techniques are not likely to be effective with this part of the sex offender population. The fact that even contemporary psychoanalysis, as understood by most of those in the field, is irrelevant to the treatment of the population they know best probably makes psychodynamic insights into the nature of sex offenders seem highly suspect. To paraphrase an argument: "If psychodynamic therapy offers nothing to hard-core sex offender treatment, why should I pay any attention to what psychodynamic theorists think about how the problem arose?" I hope the preceding pages offer some perspective on this objection.

Chapter Five

CLINICAL OBSERVATIONS
ON BOYS WHO MOLEST

In earlier chapters, we took an extensive look at the research and existing theories about why adolescent molesters offend, and what can be done about it. This chapter will take a more personal turn. Here will be examined the things I have observed about adolescent molesters in the course of providing treatment to them. Since 1984, I have specialized in adolescent boys who molest others and young males who are the victims of sexual assault. During that time, I have seen approximately 300 adolescent perpetrators. Some of them passed through my practice in a few weeks, others stayed for years.

It has always been my intention, in working with this population, to create the freest possible climate for self-expression in group and individual therapy. In general, these young men have rewarded this effort on my part with a generous sharing of information about their psyches and their motivations. This data is of a more impressionistic nature than the research examined earlier. The conclusions and impressions are more like those of an anthropological field study than a carefully controlled statistical analysis. Nonetheless, this method has yielded a number of insights that seem to bear fruit if applied to the understanding and treatment of adolescent molesters.

HOMOSEXUAL CONFLICTS

A theme that has repeatedly recurred in my work with adolescent molesters is that a high percentage are wrestling with issues involving homosexuality. Clinicians working with adolescent molesters generally agree that most are not homosexual. Truly homosexual boys are a rarity in this population. Nonetheless, some kind of conflict about homosexual issues appears to be common among boys who molest. As my practice developed, I began to observe subtle and not-so-subtle conflicts about

66

homosexual issues in group discussion, dreams, and projective material. Whenever possible, I obtained MMPI test data at the time of intake.

The conflicts which emerge are not the issues of self-acceptance versus self-hate which are common in gay adolescents. With the molester population, the issue is more a gnawing fear that they may be homosexual, or may be thought by others to be homosexual. When groups have been at their best and most candid, some boys have been able to acknowledge sexual attractions to other members of the group.

In one case, this problem became so acute that I had to discontinue and separate the group in order to prevent acting out. This was a specialized group of males who had been molested by males and who had, in turn, molested other males. One boy in the group was freely admitting to being homosexual. Four others stated that they were afraid they might be gay. Two adamantly insisted they were not. Two boys reported that a third had made sexual advances toward them and expressed discomfort about this, including doubts about whether they could restrain themselves from accepting the proposition. The issue could not be resolved in group discussion.

This kind of experience has been rare. More typically, conflicts about sexual orientation are expressed in the form of homophobia. Some boys are so threatened when they perceive that other males are attracted to them that they will threaten physical assault. At times, the group process is dominated by a ritualistic and obsessive concern in which boys try to outdo each other in their hatred of homosexuals and homosexuality.

An adolescent in treatment with me for some time had forcibly sodomized a five-year-old boy when he was thirteen. He was never able to directly confront his conflicts about homosexuality. Towards the end of his treatment, he guardedly admitted that if he were incarcerated he might then become involved in sexual activity with other males through choice rather than force. This young man has a long history of antisocial behavior and poor judgment. His remarks about becoming involved in prison homosexuality led me to wonder if he was unconsciously maneuvering himself into a position where he would have no choice but to gratify his homosexual impulses. A long prison term for this young man is a definite possibility in the future. This may be superficially the result of his explosiveness, hatred of authority, and substance abuse. On a deeper level, it may be the price he is exacting from himself to gratify homosexual wishes in a way he can accept.

Another way of dealing with homosexual feeling and impulses is to attempt to repress them. Many adolescent molesters in group adamantly deny that they have any such feelings. They usually become angry when challenged on this issue. One boy maintained such denial for a prolonged period while in treatment. He came into group shamefacedly one day and admitted that he had been caught in his group home just about to perform an act of oral copulation on his roommate. Another boy with intense homophobia dreamed and fantasized about being sexually assaulted by larger, older boys who lived near his grandmother's home. Two other boys have shared fantasies in group in which they are attempting to masturbate with the stimulation of a picture of a nude female. Images of a nude male intrude into their mind and trouble them greatly.

A more malignant manifestation of a homosexual conflict is self-hatred in the boys who have molested younger males. Tim, age 16, molested a four-year-old stepbrother. He also molested a ten-year-old female. He was initially seen in an outpatient group, but his rigid and authoritarian father would not tolerate him in his home. Tim was transferred to a group home which continued to bring him for outpatient sessions. He was extremely agitated to find he had been assigned to share a room with an overtly homosexual adolescent. He was removed from the home after attempting to hang himself. It was subsequently revealed that the house parent at this facility had been molesting other boys. Apparently, the highly homosexual climate of this home was more than this young man could tolerate, and he preferred to die rather than give in to the temptations offered in that facility.

Over the years, I have given a number of MMPIs to adolescent molesters. Although my total sample is small, and statistically the sample is not a random one, the results were provocative. There is a consistent tendency for the patients I have seen to score high on scales four and five. I suspect that this profile showed up with far more frequency than it would in the general population. The literature does not support this as a common profile among sex offenders. To see if it is, I believe someone must try to replicate my findings with a larger random sample of adolescent molesters. To be meaningful, this sample must exclude rapists.

Assuming there is indeed a tendency for adolescent molesters to produce MMPI profiles with elevated scores on scales four and five, some interesting inferences can be made. Scale five was originally devised to measure masculinity and femininity in the person being tested. The MMPI was devised several decades ago. As such, scale five probably really measures what are traditionally feminine attitudes and values in a male. In contemporary society, no inherent masculine or feminine value would be ascribed to these qualities. Questions on this scale attempt to measure personal and emotional sensitivity, sexual identification, altruism and denial of traditional masculine occupations and interest (Lachar 1974). Educated males tend to score highest on scale five.

Adolescent sex offenders are generally not highly sophisticated or educated. Their age precludes any higher education. Most adolescent sex offenders are quite traditional in their sexual attitudes. They would regard the traits measured on scale five on the MMPI as indeed associated with femininity. When the scale is elevated, it probably points to the adolescent offender's perception of himself as feminine.

Scale four measures delinquency. The questions on this scale relate to impulsivity, low frustration tolerance, poor social adjustment, resentment of authority, and social alienation. This scale is elevated in many populations aside from adolescent molesters. Its elevation in conjunction with scale five seems significant in terms of psychodynamics. The elevated delinquency scale implies defects in conscience and lack of empathy for others. This may provide the engine which transforms intrapsychic conflicts into behavior. Specifically, if a boy has doubts about his masculinity or a strong deviant arousal to younger children, he could just ruminate about these feelings. If, however, he has a delinquent orientation, he is much more likely to act out these conflicts. The lack of regard for the feelings and needs of others implied in delinquency would be the vehicle permitting the adolescent sex offender to act out his conflicts on a child victim.

HOMOSEXUALITY AND THE ADOLESCENT MOLESTER: A HYPOTHESIS

The clinical data reviewed above led me to formulate a hypothesis that ego dystonic homosexuality is a major cause of sex offending behavior in teenage boys who molest. These homosexual conflicts can be conscious or unconscious. It is extremely rare that an adolescent molester has made a homosexual adjustment which he is able to accept. At the other end of the spectrum, it is also extremely rare to find an adolescent offender who has made a successful heterosexual adjustment. The adolescent molester seems to be in deep conflict about his own sexuality.

Much of this conflict centers around issues of sexual orientation, more specifically: "I might be gay and I don't like that." The act of molestation may be, in part, a defense against this conflict. The victim seems to play a symbolic role in helping the offender shore up his weak sense of masculinity. The defense of masculinity as a major issue for sex offenders follows the general outline in the chapter on male development.

Case Illustration
Clyde T.

Clyde is a black male who at age fifteen molested a five-year-old female cousin. He showed an elevation on scale five on the MMPI of 72, a significant elevation. This was his highest score on the MMPI. He spent considerable time in group identifying evidences of homosexuality and effeminacy in other group members. He adamantly denied any homosexual feelings of his own. Clyde was also aware of and obsessed with a highly effeminate homosexual male in his own ghetto community. He made several visits to a nightclub frequented by teenage and young adult homosexuals.

Clyde engaged in heroics to prove his masculinity. In the course of treatment, he claimed to be involved in episodes with prostitutes. He also described episodes in which he and a male friend would have sex with two females in the same room. A few times, with great embarrassment, he admitted that he had lost his erection while attempting these sexual adventures. This young man was never able to attribute these events to anything other than "horniness" and left treatment denying any homosexual conflicts.

This case seems to me to be an illustration of a young man with a strong latent homosexual conflict. It also suggests the degree to which many young offenders will resist confronting these conflicts. African-American culture seems to be intolerant of homosexuality in males. This, no doubt, played a role in the degree of denial and the intensity of Clyde's masculine protest. Unfortunately, these factors leave this young man with a guarded prognosis. He is obviously having trouble functioning heterosexually and may turn to younger females in the future if he cannot resolve these conflicts in a more socially acceptable way.

ADULT HOMOSEXUALITY AND PEDOPHILIA

The material that has been examined so far suggests some link between homosexual conflicts and molesting behavior in teenage boys. Neither Groth's 1978 research nor my own experience suggests that adult pedophiles have any recognized sexual interest in adult males. How can this discrepancy be explained?

The explanation may lie in the fact that adolescence is a period of congealing sexual orientation. Many adolescent males who do not commit sex offenses experience conflicts about homosexuality. Sometimes these conflicts are not resolved until the end of adolescence. There is a well-known period of homosexual experimentation characteristic of early adolescence. For the adolescent molester, the conflict is more sharply drawn. This young man is experiencing homosexual feelings and impulses which are unacceptable to him. He is attempting to deal with these conflicts in a way that assures him he is masculine. Dealing with the conflict takes the form of acting out. The acting out follows a standard pattern. Victims can be younger males, younger females, or children of both sexes. There may also be some experimentation with same-sex peers.

Toward the end of their teenage years, many molesters appear to come to a three-way fork in the pathway of life. Some go on to become adult heterosexuals. This is likely if their offending behavior against younger children has been minimal. Hopefully, this outcome can be made more likely with effective treatment. It would be interesting to know if these young men will retain a vulnerability to sex offending in the future. They may react to stresses in life by molesting during these periods of stress.

Another group of boys who offend as teenagers may go on to become homosexual or bisexual. This may be the least likely outcome without treatment. The degree of homophobia in this population is very high. This would probably form an effective block against the development of homosexual or bisexual orientation. A derived hypothesis of this interpretation would be that such men would be likely to turn to sex with younger children during periods in which their homosexual feelings and impulses are stimulated. This may be another route to the behavior described by Groth as regressed pedophilia.

A final group of teenage boys in the molester population no doubt grow up to be adult pedophiles. It would appear that in this population the homosexual conflicts become completely buried. It is possible that pedophilia may substitute for homosexuality and may represent a resolution of this conflict. This resolution is unfortunate for both the individual and society.

VICTIMIZATION

The role which a history of being molested by an older person plays in transforming young males into sex offenders is somewhat controversial. Most clinicians probably agree that it is an important factor. Some do not. Some caution that to believe molesters who say they are victims is to allow them to excuse their behavior.

Some boys do indeed seem to have a tendency to use their victimization as an excuse to reduce guilt and shame. On the other hand, a probably larger number withhold discussion of their victimization for some time because they are ashamed of it and, if it was at the hands of a male, because of its homosexual implications. On my own caseload, about 60 percent of the boys are victims. A colleague with a similar practice in San Diego reports about the same incidence. This figure has some support in the literature. Whatever the precise numbers, it appears that prior victimization is present in a significant percentage of the adolescent molester population. Estimates of the rate for sexual victimization of males in general in America run from three to 17 percent (Urquiza and Keating 1990). This overrepresentation of victims in the molester population suggests a causative role. Something about being a victim makes males more likely to become perpetrators.

Although I do not believe it has been addressed in the literature, my own caseload study suggests that molestation by a male is a more significant contributor to molesting in the future than molestation by a female. Other writers have noted this in passing (see literature review). Of the 17 boys in my 1987 caseload sample that I felt were prepedophiles, 15 had been molested by older males.

A link between a history of molestation by an older male and a later development of pedophilia makes theoretical sense. This kind of molestation is more likely to set in motion the homosexual conflicts discussed earlier. David Finklehor, in a 1979 study, found that female perpetrators evoke less fear in victims of both sexes. Victims have fewer negative feelings about being molested by females. It is also easier for a female to entice her victim into cooperation. Finally, Finklehor found that a higher percentage of victims of female perpetrators were actually interested in having the experience.

It is a clinical fact that the experience of being molested is often physiologically pleasurable for the male victim. The sexual organs of the human body are designed to respond pleasurably when manipulated regardless of the source of the manipulation. This phenomenon is the key to some of the intense conflicts experienced by the male victim. A very young male victim may find nothing but pleasure in the experience. Pedophiles prey on young boys who are starving for attention. These boys may be neglected at home. They may have no father in the home and crave an adult male figure as a father substitute. They are often easily tricked into compliance in sexual activity with the adult male perpetrator. In many cases, boys return over and over again voluntarily to repeat sexual acts with their victimizer.

As they grow older, this kind of history becomes a source of intense conflicts. In my experience with male victims, those roughly seven years of age and younger typically respond initially without severe conflicts and with pleasure elements predominating. These boys are easily sexualized. They then initiate a great deal of sexual activity with others in their environment, including other boys. Typically at this stage, the sexualization is indiscriminate. They will engage in a variety of seductive behavior with boys, girls, and adults.

As boys get older, most begin to perceive that it is not socially acceptable for a male to initiate sex with any other male or even to accept an offer of sexual activity with any other male regardless of age. This perception poses special problems for the boy who has been more or less consenting. He may begin to hear about "fags" at school. If he inquires of his peers what a "fag" is, he will most likely be told that it is a male who has sex with other males. This definition is most often accompanied by considerable repugnance on the part of the informant. This can set off a panic in the young victim when he realizes that he has either voluntarily engaged in such activity or has not been "macho enough" to avoid being forced into this kind of activity.

Adolescent subculture in America is generally intolerant of homosexuality. Teenage boys do not make much of a distinction between being molested by older males and being homosexuals. They can learn to make the distinction in the course of treatment. Without treatment, they are very likely to perceive themselves and others who have been molested by males as homosexuals. These boys become profoundly ashamed of what has happened to them.

This process has a feedback connection with the homosexual conflicts described earlier. The male victim suddenly finds that his peers will define him as a homosexual if he shares his victimization. He may actually have homosexual feelings triggered by that victimization. If this boy cannot accept these feelings, he may reach out and molest a younger female in order to prove to himself that he is not a "fag."

These kinds of dynamics are flagrant in the case material that follows:

The Case of Andy H.

Andy came into treatment at age 14. During the previous four years, he had been engaged in mutual sodomy and oral copulation with an adult uncle. He initially denied homosexual feelings. In the course of treatment, he was able to share that he was sharing homosexual attractions to other group members. He came to identify himself as bisexual toward the end of his treatment. In one session he described the day in which he committed the offense for which he was sent to a residential treatment program. On that day, Andy had been at the home of his grandmother. His uncle came to transport him to the home of some family friends where they planned to spend the day. In transit the uncle turned off the main highway and Andy and the uncle engaged in mutual oral copulation.

A few minutes later, Andy and his uncle arrived at the friend's home. Unfortunately, the friends had two children; a boy, ten, and a girl eight. Andy forced the ten year old boy to orally copulate him. Then, a few minutes later, he attempted vaginal penetration of the eight-year-old girl. Andy stated to the group that he molested the boy because he had homosexual feelings for him which had been stirred up by the incident with his uncle. He further stated that he had felt gay when he molested the boy. For that reason, he attempted to penetrate the eight-year-old girl to prove to himself that he was not a "fag."

This case indicates clearly how panic about being homosexual can drive a young male to molest a female. It also indicates that the sexual feelings can become so intense that they simply escape the perpetrator's control, causing him to molest his primary object of desire, a younger male. In this case, the uncle's molestation appears to have tilted Andy in the direction of profound homosexual feelings, which in turn made him feel very insecure about his basic masculinity. His attempt to resolve this dilemma was to have sex with a female to convince himself that he was not gay. His ultimate resolution of the conflict appears to have been to identify himself as bisexual. If he can accept that orientation, he may stay out of trouble with younger children. If he does not, he is most likely to molest younger females.

AMBIVALENCE

Another traumatic feature of victimization which feeds and fuels the conflict that turns some victims into perpetrators is profound ambivalence. In some cases, the perpetrator has first befriended a boy who is otherwise lonely and isolated or anxious for the attention of a father figure. This was probably how Andy's situation began to unfold. This kind of molesting is then done in a seductive way which accents the physical pleasure for the victim. In some cases, the sexual contact is demanded in exchange for emotional support, friendship, and parenting. In these cases, severe conflicts develop in victims. Darrell typifies the kind of ambivalence victims can feel for perpetrators.

The Case of Darrell Z.

Darrell is a 14-year-old white male committed to a treatment institution for juvenile delinquents who have been involved in a variety of criminal offenses. He was placed here after being involved in a series of burglaries. He has a history of substance abuse. Once in the program, Darrell admitted he had been molested over a period of at least a year by a neighborhood pedophile. Molestation took the form of mutual oral copulation and sodomy committed upon him by the adult.

These offenses came up in the context of group therapy and were reported to the authorities. Darrell was ambivalent about testifying against the man who molested him. He was reluctant even to give a statement to sheriff's deputies. He produced numerous dreams in which the offender was attempting to kill him by a variety of means. When questioned carefully, he indicated he had affection for the man. At other times, he indicated that he hoped the adult would get a long prison term and that he would testify in order to help this happen.

This young man has not molested another child. He has, however, acknowledged some homosexual attractions as well as strong fears that he may molest younger children in the future. He has made every effort to stay in the treatment institution as long as possible in order to avoid going home. The molester lives near his family. He is the only witness against the man, and the man will not be incarcerated if Darrell does not testify. He has openly expressed fears that if he is in the neighborhood, he will return to the man for more sexual activity. He hopes this problem will be solved by waiting in custody long enough for his family to move out of the area.

This case illustrates most of the issues about the molester experienced in young male victims. Almost always, victims have a profoundly ambivalent attitude toward the perpetrator. Typically, either one side of this ambivalence or the other is obvious at any given time. Very young victims typically verbalize little in the way of anger or hostility. As they grow older, the angry, hostile, and vengeful side tends to come more and more to the surface. By late adolescence, that may be all that is seen. The rage can become so intense that it mixes with homicidal preoccupations.

In Darrell's case, the profound ambivalence about the perpetrator flipped from affection to hatred on an almost daily basis. It is also obvious that he has no confidence in his ability to control his own impulses. If he is near this perpetrator, he will become involved with him again. He also feels guilty and ashamed about this. His inability to control his impulses, and their leading him into what he considers a homosexual act makes him very doubtful about his worth as a human being and about his basic masculinity. Sometimes he likes the perpetrator and wants to protect him. Other times he wants to testify and send him to prison. He is also terrified by nightmares about the perpetrator taking revenge on him. These assume a paranoid dimension at times.

From the standpoint of social learning theory, there is a danger that this man will become an adult model for Darrell and that he will imitate his behavior and become a perpetrator in the future. The fact that sexual contact with this man was pleasurable may also set up a series of conditioning factors leading him toward perpetration against young children. Finally, since Darrell is interpreting his acts with the perpetrator as homosexual on his part, all of the undesirable consequences of an unwanted homosexuality are likely to be in place. This may further push him toward molesting younger children as a defense against these unacceptable homosexual impulses.

BOYS MOLESTED BY FEMALES

The preceding remarks apply only to boys who have been molested by males. Currently, that is 77 percent of my practice. Six percent of the boys I presently treat have been molested by females. Hence, I have focused more extensively on victims of male perpetrators. The issue of boys molested by older females is also important and should not be ignored. It is likely that molestation by females is more common than statistics indicate. The attitude of this society is very casual about older females molesting male children, or at least has been so until very recently.

Male victims themselves do not seem to protest too much about molestation by a female. They typically interpret it as a desirable experience which did not cause them harm. Being molested by an older female carries no stigma with adolescent boys that I have been able to discern. This is in part due to the fact that it does not violate our cultural taboo on sex between males. The glaring exception is molestation by mother, which is devastating (see Breer 1992 for an elaboration). It is also likely that molestation by any closely related female will cause serious conflict because of the incestuous implications.

It may be that molestation by an older female is more traumatic when it appears at a very young age. Generally, below age five serious problems resulting from victimization by older females can be detected. The younger the child, the greater the problem. The trauma manifests itself in the form of fear of females and fear of sexual activity with females. Perhaps the very large size of the female compared with the child contributes to the development of this fear. Specific sexual acts may have an engulfing quality to the small child and frighten him for that reason. The thinking of very young children is known to follow rather different processes than that of adults. Very small children may have fears that are exaggerated by the primitive nature of their cognition. For example, if a perpetrator puts her mouth on his penis, she may wish to devour it. In treatment, males molested at a young age by females will express fears such as falling into the vagina or that their penis will become trapped in the vagina.

POWER AND CONTROL

Any discussion of the defense of maleness as a dynamic in adolescent molesting makes numerous references to issues of power, control, and dominance. Many clinicians and researchers consider this the primary cause of molesting behavior. These thinkers consider sexual crimes not really to be about sex but about power. That may be true in the most abstract form. It can be argued that power, control, and domination are culturally determined aspects of masculinity and not intrinsic to it. It can be argued with equal force that they may be rooted in the biology of masculinity. Whatever the etiology, maleness in America is often equated with it power, control, and dominance. Adolescent molesters are hypersensitive to issues of masculinity. It is not surprising that power issues loom large in their sexual pathology. The need to have power over and dominate the sexual partner are part of the molesters' definition of masculinity. Since he feels so inadequate, he is driven to select a much younger partner to be sure he stays in control and thereby reinforces his sense of being masculine.

Jonathan, a probably psychotic boy in a treatment group, addressed everything very bluntly. He had already told me he was bisexual. He had regular sex with boys his age. Yet he remained attracted to little boys. I asked him why. With his usual candor and brevity he said: "Guys want to butt-fuck you or they tell. Little boys keep quiet and you can butt-fuck them." I followed up with a question as to why he objected to being butt-fucked. His answer, "It makes me feel like a girl."

Octavio Paz, a major modern Mexican intellectual, addresses the issue of power and control in homoerotic relationships in Mexican culture in his well-known work *The Labyrinth of Solitude.*

> It is likewise significant that masculine homosexuality is regarded with a certain indulgence as far as the active agent is concerned. The passive agent is an abject, degraded being. Masculine homosexuality is tolerated then on the condition that it consists of violating a passive agent. As with heterosexual relationships, the important thing is not to open oneself up, at the same time to break open one's opponent.

Although the subject is homosexuality, the elements are similar to what I perceive when adolescent males molest. Passivity is the archetypal enemy of the masculine in their thinking. It is a greater threat to the molester's sense of male identity than having a male partner. Where the perpetrator has a deviant arousal to sadism, humiliation, and control, destruction of the self-esteem of the passive victim is part of the erotic pleasure. I suspect issues of sadistic control are also often involved when molesters molest young females. The only work of caution I would add is that I suspect these issues are already overworked by clinicians practicing in the field. Power dynamics are important. We need to be aware of them, but we also need to remain aware that molesting is a multiply-determined behavior which has different causes and mixtures of causes in different individuals.

FAMILY OF ORIGIN ISSUES

The family is the cradle in which personality is nurtured and developed. The dynamics which take place within a family system sometimes have a powerful shaping influence on the sexual pathology of boys who become molesters. Boys who molest, as a general rule, have some kind of serious problem in their relationships with their fathers. Those who have absent fathers are often furious with them for leaving. They can also be angry and disillusioned if the father is emotionally absent or presents a flawed example of maleness. In the most extreme cases, the fathers actually molest their sons. In these cases, they themselves sexualize the child in such a way that simultaneously loses one of the most important relationships in their life, the father-son bond.

We have already discussed molesting as a specialized form of juvenile delinquency. An emerging body of data on juvenile delinquents indicate that the role of the father is profound in controlling delinquency. Boys raised without fathers are many times more likely than boys raised with fathers to become delinquents. This finding seems confirmed with adolescent molesters. The role of the father in preventing delinquency is complex. One aspect of it is to provide a nondelinquent model with whom the boy can identify. Another aspect is to set limits on the boy's behaviors, sexual and otherwise, something which mothers often have considerable difficulty in doing. The boys I work with are much more willing and able to accept authority and limits from males than females.

SEXUALIZED SYMBIOSES

Many of the boys who molest have problems in their relationship with their mothers. A significant subset, which often includes those with the most severe offenses and those in residential treatment, seem to be involved in symbiotic relationships with their mothers which have become highly sexualized. The mother presents as overprotective of the child and overinvolved in his life. The child reciprocates with a similar entanglement with the mother. These symbiotic relationships are characterized by overprotection, seduction, and destructive hostility on both parts. It would seem that the symbiosis is carried out within the parameters of a sadomasochistic relationship. Such cases are a minority, but the psychopathology is so extreme that these offenders probably do a great deal more damage and are at greater risk of offending than those where this dynamic is not present. A particularly pathological case suggests the kind of risk involved. This case concentrates the most toxic elements of these disturbed relationships in one complex case.

John

John comes from a family in which both the males and females are victims of physical and sexual abuse. John has seen a series of men who are physically abusive to his mother. He has seen fights between his mother and her husbands and boyfriends which border on homicidal. The mother's involvement in this seems to be a need to pit males against each other. For a long time she lived in the same household with both her husband and a boyfriend with whom she was carrying on a sexual affair. Prior to that, she had a long history of cheating on her husband which she made abundantly known to her son by means of frequent, intimate conversations.

John became involved in these games at an early age. His relationship with his mother was always a stormy one, characterized by sadomasochistic maneuvering in which both came to participate. Episodes of sadistic acting out by the mother alternated with periods of seduction and overindulgence. The mother would urge the stepfather to discipline John for violations of household rules. The stepfather's discipline technique was a severe beating, often all over the body with a belt, leaving bruises. The mother watched these episodes. Afterwards, she would take John to the bathroom, insist he undress and take a cold shower. She would watch while he showered. This continued until he was twelve years of age. The purpose of the shower was to cause the bruises to become less obvious so school authorities would not suspect child abuse. A voyeuristic interest on the mother's part was also likely.

John came to my attention after he molested his sister by means of oral sex and attempted intercourse. The sister at that time was nine. John was fourteen. John was placed in a residential facility. When he ran from this facility, his mother hid him from law enforcement. During this period, she had him share a bedroom with the sister he had molested. John also reports that after frequent fights between his mother and stepfather, the stepfather would leave home. On these occasions, the mother invited John to sleep with her in her bed in order to comfort her. This and the shower incidents suggest that the mother is sexually attracted to her son. She may have offered the sister to him in lieu of herself as a sexual partner.

John's reaction to his mother's behavior is manifest in a dream disclosed in treatment. John is in a room, in bed. A female figure who is either his older sister or his mother comes in. The woman tells him to take off his clothes. He says, "No." The woman then takes his clothing off for him, and, in his words, "sits on his face." In relating this dream, John could not specify whether the figure was really his mother or older sister. As he related the dream, the figure seemed to oscillate between the two. This seems to be a defensive maneuver, an attempt to prevent himself from becoming aware of the incestuous nature of his bond to his mother.

Some clinicians might expect this young man would hate his mother and welcome the separation from her. This is not the case. He is obsessed with her.

After being returned to residential treatment from his AWOL attempt, he continued to maneuver to secure permission to live again with his mother. During the second treatment episode, the mother separated from the stepfather. At that point, his zeal to return home became almost unmanageable.

This is obviously an unusually pathological situation. It is presented here because it contains an example of almost everything that can go wrong in a sadistically erotized mother-son relationship. Rarely will the clinician encounter anything this dysfunctional, but many of the elements will be found in cases toward the more disturbed end of the molester spectrum.

John has an intense and apparently unbreakable symbiotic bond to his mother. They engage in mutual sadomasochistic behavior with each other, and the sister becomes the victim. It is likely that John's mother is herself a victim of sexual abuse and is acting out her ambivalent and often intensely destructive attitude toward males in her interactions with her son.

It is this swamp of enmeshment from which the presence of the father can often rescue the boy. If John had had a strong father figure consistently in the home, he might have been able to identify with the father and gradually extricate himself from a pathological symbiosis with the mother. Where these kind of dynamics operate, it is very important that treating clinicians be aware of them. Such intense symbiotic relationships almost inevitably result in reoffense if the boy is returned home. Yet in these kind of cases, both the boy and his parent are constantly agitating for his return home. Under current conditions, they are frequently able to convince the court that the boy ought to be back in the home, something which serves the best interest of no one involved, including potential victims.

Regarding mothers, I should stress that many mothers are raising difficult boys alone and doing the best possible job in that area. When their sons offend, it is not their shortcoming, but simply the fact that other dynamic factors operating in the boy's life overwhelm their best efforts and good intentions. This section is not an attempt to say that mothers are, in anything like a majority of the cases, major contributors to the boy's perpetrating behavior. When this kind of mother-son dynamic is, in fact, present, the cases are especially difficult and dangerous. These boys tend to be among the most disturbed I see. Typically, they are in residential treatment facilities.

MUTUAL HATRED

There is another variant of the pathological mother-son bond that needs to be discussed. Here the sexualized elements are absent or minimal. There is a deeply entrenched hatred between mother and son. Often it is rooted in the mother's identifying her son with a male who has previously molested or otherwise sexually mistreated her. Sometimes the boy stands *in lieu* of a hated former husband or boyfriend. In these cases, the explicitly sexual elements in the relationship are missing. The relationship is nonetheless full of hatred and destructiveness. Doug's case is an example of how pathological and molestogenic this kind of mother-son relationship can be.

Case Example:
Doug Y.

Doug is a 15-year-old male in residential treatment. He was placed after molesting his younger brother and sister. The mother is an intelligent but low-functioning woman. Prior to age 7, Doug was molested over a prolonged period by a neighbor couple. At that age, he was removed from the mother's home and placed in foster care. He remained there until he molested his siblings while on a home visit. Once in placement, Doug was anxious for reconciliation with his mother. To provide family therapy, it was necessary to go to the home since she would not keep an appointment at a professional office. During one family session, the therapist noted that the mother repeatedly insisted that the brother whom Doug had molested sit on his lap. When he pointed out to his mother what she was doing, she became angry and insulting.

Later in the treatment process, this young man was given a one-day home pass. On that pass, the mother prohibited him from contacting his girlfriend. She left him alone with the two children he had molested. Doug had enough ego strength to break with his mother. In a final family session, he told her he felt that further contact was not in his best interest. Following this call, the mother repeatedly used the younger children to attempt to lure Doug back home. She had the children place phone calls and beg him to come for a visit.

The mother was a victim of molestation as a child herself. Her preferred solution to this problem appeared to be to turn her own son into a molester and destroy him. Doug feared that his younger brother would be used for the same purpose. He was probably right. Doug resolved his issues with his mother by terminating the relationship. This, however, was done at great cost. For years afterward, he simmered with rage against her. It is one of his writings which is used in another chapter to show the intensity of the rage in the adolescent molester population. Nor did the case end happily. After several years in treatment, Doug left the residential program. A few months later, he was living with a former foster father from whose home he had been removed when the man attempted to molest him.

CLOSING THOUGHTS ABOUT BLAME

In reflecting upon the clinical material offered in this chapter and the more theoretical material in Chapter Two, it would be easy to infer from it that adolescent molesters are simply not responsible for the acts they commit. Their behavior is, in essence, determined by a whole series of biological, social, and psychological factors. The important distinction here is that to offer an explanation is not to offer an excuse. It is vitally important that this point be communicated to adolescent molesters in treatment. Regardless of why they committed their offenses, society will hold them responsible for what they did, and it is their responsibility to learn to control their tendency to act out sexually in spite of the origins of these tendencies. On the other hand, to deny the existence of powerful dynamic factors which shape the adolescent's behavior is to say that events in psychic life happen without any cause. Ultimately, this would take us into chaos theory wherein events happen unpredictably for unknown and unidentifiable reasons. If molesting is caused by factors that are random, unpredictable, or unknowable, there is no foundation on which to base treatment. Treatment of the adolescent offender is, in my judgment, better served if the issues causing this behavior are clearly identified and targeted for resolution.

Chapter Six

WRITINGS, DRAWINGS, AND DREAMS

Everyone who works with adolescent molesters is aware that this is often a difficult population with whom to communicate verbally. The offenses for which they must be in treatment are generally laden with shame. There seems to be something about teenage males as a group which makes them difficult patients in psychotherapy, whatever the reason for their coming.

Fortunately, many adolescent molesters enjoy drawing and are prolific and often expressive in their drawings. Some of them engage in expressive writing that says a great deal about their underlying feeling state. Through writing and drawing, many of these young males are able to present their feelings more poignantly than they ever do in words.

Dreams differ from drawings and writings in being spontaneous creations of the human brain. They do, however, share some features in common with writing and drawing. This commonality is that all three involve an access to the unconscious. When dreams are communicated frankly and honestly, they are probably more revealing than either drawings or writings. Most human beings seem to have some kind of intuitive awareness that dreams reveal as much about themselves and their lives as do drawings and creative writing. Resistant patients of any kind tend to resist sharing this kind of material with a therapist.

Many adolescents will only engage in any of these activities under great pressure in the course of therapy. Dreams seem to evoke the greatest resistance. Many adolescent molesters claim never to dream or never to remember their dreams. Others are prolific dreamers. A difficult group will make up elaborate stories and present them as dreams. These creations are generally easy to spot because they are much more organized than true dreams, and their message is much more compatible with the kind of message that the adolescent offender wishes to present when putting his best foot forward for a therapist or his treatment group.

These caveats aside, I find that most adolescent molesters are willing to draw with minimal encouragement. Indeed, there have been times when I have asked nonverbal boys to concentrate on drawing in group. Their contribution to the group process is to present the drawing they have done in group for discussion by the group. Obviously, this could be misused by a very devious offender attempting to avoid basic issues, but for a withdrawn, anxious, and schizoid young male, this is often some of the best communication that can be evoked for purposes of discussion.

Writings, drawings, and dreams are all media which allow for a form of nondirect, metaphoric communication. Patients do not have to "own" as the material presented as directly as they would if they presented it in words. Often they are unaware of its underlying meaning. If confronted with something they are unready to face, they can deny its meaning.

The intent of this chapter is to look at some of the writings, drawings, and dreams of adolescent molesters with a view to the light they can shed on underlying, intrapsychic, and emotional issues. This will help to put flesh on the rather bare theoretical bones that have been presented in previous chapters on theory and research. The fit is not perfect, but if we look at these productions of adolescent molesters, many of the interpretations and inferences drawn from the research literature and from theory present themselves here in graphic or written form.

The rest of this chapter will be a selected sampling of writings, drawings, and dreams. The overall quality of much of this material leaves me with the feeling that we are dealing in many cases with young males with severe psychopathology. Much of this material has a borderline or psychotic flavor to it which will be apparent on examination.

DRAWINGS

Sexualization

Sexualization is manifest in almost all of the drawings of adolescent molesters. Even where a drawing is presented here to illustrate another principle, its sexualized nature is often blatant. This sexualization seems to be a causative factor in the adolescent's offending behavior. Frequently, it has its roots in a time when the adolescent molester was himself a victim. Sexualization is one of the early and immediate impacts of being sexually molested at a young age. This is abundantly documented in the literature on victims of both sexes (Finkelhor and Browne, 1985) (Friedrich et al., 1988) (Hewitt, 1990).

Figure 1. This drawing reflects the intense sexualization and sexual chaos in a boy molested by a stepfather. The stepfather molested two other children in the home. He forced this boy to have sex with his sister while he watched.

Figure 1 is by a male, fourteen years of age. It is also illustrated in my 1992 work on male victims. This young man dropped out of treatment as a victim and has returned as a perpetrator. This drawing portrays such intense sexualization and such pansexual chaos and dysfunctionality that the fact that this teenager has become a perpetrator is not at all surprising. In this scene, an adult female is molesting two younger children. An adolescent or adult male seems to supervise from the edge. The entire scene is framed by two large erect penises.

This young man was from a large family in which the stepfather molested all of the children. The children were aware of what was going on with each of them and the stepfather. This child was molested by the stepfather and forced to have sex with his sister. The mother was unprotective and defensive of the stepfather. The kind of out-of-control sexuality represented in this drawing seems to have been accepted by this young perpetrator as acceptable, at least in the context of his family background. This points to the inner generational transference of this kind of incestuous behavior. Although the perpetrator here is female, there is no documentation that this boy, or any of the children, was actually molested by the mother in that home. The meaning of this is unclear, but could be that the father's behavior ignored by the mother caused this boy to consider his mother to be a comolester. It could also be that the general climate of intense sexuality in the family vicariously sexualized this boy's feelings about his mother causing him to yearn for her sexually. It is, of course, possible that she molested him and was never caught.

COMPENSATORY HYPERMASCULINITY

Figure 2 is a drawing by a young man I treated when he was nine. He was molested extensively by a foster father who apparently obtained a foster home license for the purpose of molesting children. In this drawing, this child has accentuated every conceivable masculine trait. Stomach muscles are prominent, as are the pectorals. He wears a military style helmet and puffs on a cigarette in a kind of tough-guy style. Sexualization is reflected in the dog sucking on the penis. I lost contact with this child when he was ten and hope he has been able to avoid becoming a perpetrator.

Figures 3 through 6 represent before and after drawings by two different boys. These were produced as a group assignment to draw pictures of

Figure 2. This drawing illustrates sexualization and masculinity strivings in a boy molested by a male foster parent.

themselves at the time they were molested and pictures of themselves now. Figure 3 is one boy's picture of himself at the time of his victimization. He appears to be trying, as much as possible, to distance himself from the experience. The drawing communicates fear. His position suggests that he is off balance and disoriented by what has happened to him. He was molested repeatedly by his mother's boyfriend. Figure 4 is the same child's presentation of himself in the present. When he left his parent's home, he was placed with an aunt. He molested one of her young children and had to be placed in residential care, hence the group home reference. In his presentation, he shows himself as far more assertive and aggressive than in the self-portrait at the time of his victimization.

The ill-fitting pants suggest that he does not feel that he has not yet completely grown into this new role. The figure seems to have a beard, suggesting additional masculinity strivings. This boy became affiliated while in residential care with a street gang and adopted a number of stereotyped gang attitudes. These seemed to me to be part of his compensatory exaggeration of his masculinity to defend against the feeling of being traumatized and victimized as a helpless child at the sexual mercy of an older male. This raises the interesting issue of gang involvement as a manifestation of a disorder of masculinity, a topic that would take us far beyond the scope of this book.

Figure 5 is Jose's portrait of himself at the time that he was molested. A very small, somewhat frightened figure is overwhelmed by the couch, which may represent the experience of being molested by an older relative. His presentation of himself in the present is more fanciful than real. He remains a slight and frightened child. In his presentation, however, he actually labels himself in gang graffiti as big and bad. Muscles are exaggerated as is an aggressive stance in this "myself as I wish I were" portrait. This young man is seriously flirting with gang activity and may still be drawn into it. As with the previous artist, gang involvement on his part would be an attempt to defend himself against feeling weak, helpless, and sexually victimized and instead to feel like a powerful criminal victimizer of others.

HOMOSEXUALITY

It has been noted elsewhere that boys in treatment for molesting younger children generally do not seem to be comfortably homosexual. Most of them, however, have great conflicts about this issue. The greatest conflicts are, not surprisingly, in the boys who have been molested by older males and then have molested other males. The first reaction to the experience of being molested is sexualization, which often leads to sexual approaches to other males.

The boy who drew Figure 7 was molested at a young age by a teenage male relative. He seems to have become totally preoccupied with sex between males. This drawing illustrates sexualization as well as the kind of homosexual issues that are often activated by molestation. This child

Figure 3. This perpetrator/victim drew this to illustrate how he felt at the time of his molestation. He was raped by a custodial grandfather who also physically abused him. Fear, helplessness, and withdrawal characterize his mental state at that time.

molested a young female. The only sense I can make of this was that it was an attempt to deal with the terrible conflicts about his attraction to other males and to assure himself that he was heterosexual.

Figure 8 needs no interpretation if you know the code. This child was attempting to write "I am a queer." He believed that the word queer was

Figure 4. This drawing is by the same young male who produced Figure 3. This drawing was produced after he was requested to draw how he feels now as opposed to how he felt at the time he was molested. Both drawings were produced in one session. He obviously feels better now. Gang identification has become the vehicle for his masculine protest.

Figure 5. This and Figure 6 are another pair illustrating how the boy felt at the time of his victimization and at the present time. Figure 5 shows a little boy overwhelmed by his environment. He is physically small. Dress features suggest infantilism. Weak presentation of the left hand suggests helplessness. The forceful right hand may indicate the aggressiveness that made him a perpetrator.

spelled cure. The drawing openly reflects his concern about strong sexual feelings for other males triggered by his own victimization at the hands of an older male. The very enlarged penis figure again is an indication of the intense sexualization experienced by many adolescent molesters.

FEAR OF FEMALES

Figure 9 also speaks for itself. This young adolescent had molested both his brother and sister. He had been molested by an uncle who resided with the family.

Figure 10 presents an even more intense fear of females. The story that goes with this is that the women in the picture kidnapped men, imprisoned them in the cage above the campfire, castrated them, roasted their penises, and then ate them. This young man had molested a younger sister. He himself had been molested by his mother.

Figure 6. Once again helplessness has been transformed into pseudohypermasculinity. The formerly helpless victim has become a gangster. Big muscles and an aggressive stance suggest the intensity of this boy's drive to be masculine.

EFFECTS OF VICTIMIZATION

Figures 11 and 12 are by the same young male. He was molested by his father and molested his younger brother. Figure 11 was actually drawn as his response to a request that he draw a picture of himself as he felt at the time of his victimization. This is, of course, an unlikely reflection of his feelings at that time. It is more likely how he wishes he felt.

Figure 12 points in the most oblique ways to one of the most difficult parts of the victimization with which child victims have to deal, the pleasure element. Unless done with brutality or with the severe accompanying pain, there is often a physiological pleasure response to molestation.

Figure 7. This boy was molested at age four by a teenage male. He has been thoroughly sexualized. In this case the focus is on sex with other males. The large penis suggests the degree to which sexual feeling dominates his life. This boy denies any sexual interest in other males.

Males who have been molested are profoundly ashamed of this. Here the patient very covertly communicates his anxiety about pleasure experienced in being molested. The dog with whom the human is having sex is being asked, "Good dog, enjoy it yet?" by the perpetrator. The dog says secretly to himself, "You don't know, but yes I do." It is probably this feeling of guilt and shame regarding pleasure that provides one of the key elements that cause a statistically elevated percentage of young molested males to feel or fear that they are homosexual. In a 1985 study, Johnson and Shrier found molested males self-identifying as homosexual at seven times the frequency of controls. These drawings give some clue as to how that phenomenon arises.

Figure 8. This drawing illustrates two key phenomena in victim/perpetrator dynamics. The very large penis is one more depiction of sexualization. The homosexual anxieties of boys who have been molested is illustrated here. This boy meant to spell out "I a queer." His poor spelling lead to the wording, "I a cure."

Figure 9. This drawing by a young adolescent victim and perpetrator illustrates anxiety about basic maleness which is here presented as castration. Fear and hatred of mother in particular and probably of females in general is also presented in this drawing.

PSYCHOTIC THEMES

Figures 13 and 14 were produced by Tom while he was in a residential treatment program for sex offenders. He had significant problems with substance abuse. He came from an extremely dysfunctional family that had abandoned him. Figure 13 suggests a profoundly depressed young man with marked feelings of worthlessness. This figure is horned, indicating it is demonic and very probably a self symbol indicating how terribly evil this adolescent feels. The staring eyes are often seen in

Figure 10. This young victim and perpetrator develops clearly in this drawing the theme of fear and hatred of females that is prominent in the psychodynamics of this population. The females in this drawing kidnap males, castrate them, then roast and eat their penises.

individuals with paranoid trends in their personality. These themes were well developed in writings Tom left in my office. They were not reproduced here because they were plagiarized from heavy metal music. Tom had memorized them and was offering them as his own writings. The theme of this material was extreme paranoid distrust of others. Figure 14 may express underlying suicidal impulses or perhaps fear of fragmentation of the self. Those working with adolescent sex offenders, particularly in residential programs, are going to encounter a high percentage of severely disturbed adolescents in those programs. Tom's graphic material suggests that he is one of them.

Figure 11. This boy was molested by his father. Usually this creates a complex love-hate relationship. By the time this boy drew this picture of how he would like to take revenge, any positive feelings had been drowned in a sea of wrath.

Figure 12. This drawing presents the best kept secret of many male victims, that, for some of them, there was a pleasure element in their victimization. This boy distances himself from those painful feelings by putting the words in the mouth of the dog. The perpetrator asks if he is enjoying it. The dog says that he is. Usually, this material becomes available for therapeutic discussion only after less threatening issues have been explored and a strong therapeutic alliance has been developed.

Figure 13. This adolescent presents a number of themes common among the more psychiatrically disturbed perpetrators. Depression and low self-esteem are implied. He sees himself as irremediably damned. This boy was into Satanism, also common among the most disturbed molesters. The demon is probably a self-symbol. As such, it implies an identification with evil that may foreshadow a psychotic depression and/or serious and violent offenses in the future.

WRITINGS

Sexualization

As in their drawings, adolescent molesters' writings reflect a high degree of sexualization. A high percentage of their spontaneous writings are simple sexual fantasies, typically of a wishful, heterosexual nature. Occasionally they will write about their attraction to younger children and their fear that they may act on it. One of the most intense and dramatic writings produced in group was done by a 12-year-old boy who was probably borderline or psychotic. In very large, elementary school letters, on an 8½ × 11 paper, filling the entire paper, he wrote, "Butt fuck you rub down, and suck your dick, and lick you down to your dick."

Figure 14. This drawing illustrates another theme limited to the most disturbed of sex offenders. This is fear of personality disintegration. In this case, I believe the boy feared psychotic decompensation. This issue could also be suicide. This is an almost literal presentation of what self-psychologists call the fragmentation of the self.

This appeared to be aimed at another boy in the group and was an undisguised proposition, indicating the extent to which this boy had lost all ability to control his sexual impulses. He was in residential care when seen. He had been repeatedly molested by older boys in residential care for years, and now was engaged in extensive sex with other children in the residential program.

Sexualization is similarly reflected in the writings of a 14-year-old boy who had also been molested in residential care. He wrote the following on a notepad and gave it to me at the end of group:

> You are reading a Playboy magazine and the next day you fuck a girl, and she finds the Playboy, and she says, "You fucking pervert." So you go and slap her in the face, and you grab her, and rape her. She tells the police and her parents and the police come and put you in jail. And you go to court and they say you're not guilty. And you go and rent triple X rated movies. You also rape another girl and you rape your mother, and they find you guilty, and you go to jail, and they rape you. What would you do?

In this brief writing, this boy embodies many of the themes we have talked about. There is a quality of out-of-control sexuality, which I call sexual chaos. There is a complete inability to control sexual impulses. At least in fantasy, this boy is seeking out sexual experiences of every conceivable kind without limits. It is no wonder this child molested a young girl while baby-sitting. The offense was far less extensive and violent than this writing would suggest. This boy's future behavior is of obvious concern.

Rage is a common theme in the writings of adolescent molesters. It comes through in the following passage written by a fifteen year old during a group session.

> I fucking hate this place. I think the staff are total assholes. Sam can go to hell and Frank can stick his rackets up his ass. Sandy used to be a bitch like my mom, but my mom still is. I wish I never got into this fucking shit. This fucking sucks, the whole fucking program. I hate that fat bitch who I have as my mother. I hate the shit she puts me through. I think she is a total fucking bitch asshole motherfucker and a pendenjo. I'd like to kill that fat slob. Fuck, fuck, fuck, fuck. I hate you, I hate you, I hate you, I hate you, I don't give a shit if you die. Bitch, bitch, bitch. This whole world is full of shit.

This material needs very little in the way of comment. Obviously, this young man is mad at the entire world. The sequence with which he develops his rage, however, is interesting. He starts with his hostility to the program in which he is placed, then to specific staff members. As he writes, his rage with his mother emerges. It becomes increasingly intense as the writing continues. This young man appears to have actually been decompensating while he was producing this material. In addition to illustrating a kind of generic rage that many adolescent molesters feel, it illustrates also the severe conflict which some of these boys have with one or both of their parents. This was written by Doug whose case was presented in more detail in the previous chapter.

DEPRESSION AND SUICIDE

Depression and suicide are somewhat common themes for adolescent molesters. They seem to show up more commonly in the writings of boys who are in residential programs, boys who are probably therefore more psychologically disturbed than those left by the courts in the community. One offender produced this poem dealing with his feelings of depression:

> As I see the rain my tear hits the bed. As for my soul, I feel pain. As for my heart, I feel loneliness. As for my mind, I feel confusion, as if our love has drifted away.

This was written by a young man who yearned desperately for human contact. He told me that he would often wake up crying, just wishing someone could hold him. My suspicion is that, at depth, what he was looking for was a mother. He was in placement and was totally rejected by his family. That is probably what he was talking about when he made references to love drifting away.

Suicide is an issue that shows up in both explicit and veiled form in the writings of teenage offenders. The following is an explicit reference to suicide as written by Travis on a styrofoam cup during a group session.

> I was a shadow. I was about to kill myself. Jim, Dad, Mom, Sally, and Judy were there. Jim was on one side, and all the others on the other. I was in the middle. Jim asked me what it would solve and I said, "nothing and everything."

Travis added two notes to clarify the above statement. Arrows were drawn to the words, "nothing" and "everything." The explanatory comment, "no emotion in statement" was added. Regarding the word shadow, he made the following comment: "PS, shadows have no feeling, that's why I was a shadow." Jim was a male staff member to whom Travis had become very attached. He seems to be turning to him for support. This is a good illustration of the use of transference for repair of the self. This boy seemed to be attempting to form a father or older brother bond with Jim. He could then use this to help him repair his damaged maleness.

Travis's family had abandoned him. They are the figures standing opposite him. If they are all he has, he will commit suicide. But he has Jim. Here he models how he would like to use Jim as a confidant and support. Unfortunately, he tried this same technique with another young adult male before his arrival in the treatment program. That man took advantage of Travis' need for male support and attention and established a long-term, sexual relationship with him. Instead of resolving his problem, this episode set the stage for homophobia and molesting of a younger female. This case had a happy ending. Travis' willingness and ability to form working alliances with other males served him well in the program. It was an obvious strength in his therapeutic work with male therapists. He graduated successfully after several years in the program.

Two poem-like writings produced by another offender deal with suicide in a more oblique manner.

> He loved her, he said, but she could not hold, she said. Until God said, go ahead. She went ahead, but he couldn't go ahead, and now look, he's dead.

On the surface, this is a charming and playful writing. Beneath the surface is this young man's desperate need for someone, hopefully female, to love him. Once again it points to affectional deprivation in early life and the yearning for a mother figure. There is no specific mention of suicide, but when the protagonist cannot go ahead toward his beloved, he ends up dead. The same young man produced a second poem.

> There is an island out there, small but beautiful. Why it's so beautiful I don't know. Why it's there, nobody knows. Everybody thinks because it's so small it's an ugly island, but this island lives off other islands. Why he's there, he does not know. All he knows is that it feels good. All the other islands did not give him a chance. Now look, the small and beautiful island has vanished. He wasn't big enough to live. Now he's believed to be dead.

This poem is autobiographical. The island is the patient. What seems to be dealt with is not so much suicide as a wish not to be alive. The first line deals with this young offender's narcissism. He sees himself initially as beautiful. Others, however, think of him otherwise. He conveys here a sense of utter isolation. He is an island. Other human beings are islands. There is no connection or communication. His terrible emotional dilemma is revealed in the next line. "This island lives off other islands." Even though he is isolated, he cannot live without others. But the relationship he establishes is parasitic and destructive of the other with whom he is involved. This was an offender who nearly killed his victim. His basic hedonism comes out in the line, "All he knows is it feels good." This hedonism may be a defense against his isolation, emptiness, and despair. He continues, "All the other islands did not give him a chance." This projects blame for his problems onto others. Clearly, he does not see himself as a viable human being: "He wasn't big enough to live." Profound depression and perhaps suicide are the remedies suggested by desperation of this young offender's situation.

HOMICIDE

The anger of many adolescent molesters is so intense that some contemplate homicide. References to an urge to kill have been reproduced elsewhere. There seems to be a special concentration of murderous impulses where homosexual feelings are involved. Sometimes this is interwoven with the molester's victimization. A murderous rage is often directed at the adult who molested the young man. In placement, fights often occur between boys who have a covert sexual attraction to each other.

Writings involving homicidal feelings are relatively rare. The clinician or case manager working with this population may encounter verbal statements involving homicide before running into anything the adolescent will put into writing. Here is a sample of references to homicide, again by Travis, from whom we heard earlier in this chapter.

> One time I was in bed with Tom (the young adult male who molested the writer over a period of many months), and he was sucking me off. I reached up and grabbed him by the groin hair and yanked them. He screamed, and I pushed him off, got up and walked away laughing. Another time I told him to close his eyes, and I quickly handcuffed him. I knocked him to his knees and told him to suck me. He started. I couldn't get hard so I told him to quit. I went behind him and tightened the cuffs. He asked me to stop and I laughed. I picked him up. I threw him down on the bed and left him there for awhile. Then undid it and said I was joking. I wasn't. I didn't care, and I wanted to kill.

This case is particularly sad. Tom was a major source of emotional support; unfortunately, he demanded sex in exchange. This seems to have triggered a mixture of love and homicidal rage.

DREAMS

It is relatively rare to get adolescent males to share their dreams in group or in individual therapy. When they do, however, these dreams are generally an invaluable source of insight. They point to the most basic issues with which the adolescent is wrestling. A 15 year old in a residential program for molesting his female cousin related the following dream:

> A little girl about eight wants to have sex with me. I keep saying no. I offer her to the other guys in the program. The other guys don't want sex from her. She comes back to me wanting sex with me. I say no, and I wake up frightened.

Current biological theories involving dreaming suggest they are a problem-solving mechanism, posing a central question and then attempting to answer that question with some kind of course of action (Hobson, 1988; Winson, 1985; Cartwright, 1978). In this dream, the young offender's question is how to deal with his impulses to molest female children. His initial solution is to send her away and offer her to other boys. The defense mechanism here looks like projection. "Those other boys are molesters. I am not."

But projection does not work. The problem returns to haunt him. Another problem is implied. The other boys have said no. This may be an implicit recognition that his problem is worse than that of the other boys. This young man is left with no real resolution of the dilemma. He says no, and then his anxiety causes him to wake out of the dream, probably before it becomes a dream of actual molestation. This dream presents a core treatment issue, whether or not the patient wishes to be a molester. It goes right to the point. It also flags the high level of anxiety this offender feels about his deviant arousal. This dream is a treatment tool that allows the therapist to go to the essential issue while at the same time suggesting a favorable prognosis. A good prognosis is suggested by fact that this molester was willing to share such a dream and that he has so much anxiety about its content.

The next dream was related by an adolescent who had been molested by his mother and who had molested a younger boy in foster care.

> I am a vampire with fangs. I am kissing and biting the neck of a woman. I suddenly become very aware of the fangs and that it will be very hard to eat with them.

This young man has been drawn into an intensely ambivalent relationship with his mother because of her molesting him. She has sexualized the relationship, leaving him profoundly ambivalent about how to relate to her. The kissing and biting metaphor indicate an intense fusion of hostility and affection. The very obliquely presented solutions to the problem are: (1) kill mother and get her out of my life, or (2) love mother physically and sexually and gratify my impulses. He then adds a reality note recognizing that the degree of hostility which he feels for his mother and which he transfers to other women is probably going to make it very difficult for him to meet his needs for nurturance and affection from females.

A 14 year old related this dream in group.

> I am in bed with some guy my own age. I am fondling him and he is fondling me.

Tony was troubled by this dream. He was very anxious after sharing it with the group. After a pause he blurted out, "I didn't even try to stop it." This dream led into a discussion of Tony's sexual attraction to another boy in the group. He was able to figure out that the attraction was based on the fact that this other boy looked tough and masculine. This other boy smoked cigarettes; Tony recognized that he had recently taken up smoking in order to imitate him.

The associations here allow for interpretation. This young man is attempting to use sexual contact with males he admires as a way of incorporating a masculinity that he does not feel he possesses. If he had directed this kind of feeling at younger males, they would become his victims. Tony's principal problem had been molesting younger boys, although most recently he had molested a young female, probably in an attempt to shore up his feelings that he could be heterosexual by having sexual contact with someone female. In discussing his male victims, Tony stated that he had selected them because he admired their masculinity. Even though they were younger than himself, Tony's victims appeared to represent a kind of idealized masculinity with which Tony is trying to merge through sexual contact.

Mark shared this dream with the group.

> I am watching television. All of a sudden the screen is filled with angels and devils. The devils come out of the television. They come up to me and tell me to molest someone. The angels come out next and they have a fight with the devils. The devils keep telling me to molest while they fight the angels.

Once again the problem is, "Am I going to molest again? Once again there is tremendous conflict. This dream wrestles with the problem via the primitive defense mechanism of splitting. This boy is dividing the world into entities that are all good and all evil. He sees himself in the same light, alternatingly incredibly evil or very good. The evil part of him wants to molest. He may well connect all sexuality with the devil. He is locked in a struggle, and the question is posed but not answered. A troubling aspect of this dream is that it has the same structure as a command hallucination. Mark was a very troubled young man. This dream and the sum of his behavior led me to wonder if he perhaps was not hearing voices. With a primitive personality structure characterized by an extensive use of splitting, Mark is likely to shift back and forth between good and evil behavior in an unpredictable way. Prognosis is poor as it often is for mentally ill offenders.

SUMMARY

In this section, a wide variety of projective material from the adolescent molester population has been examined. In many senses, this material reproduces and illustrates dramatically the inferences that have been drawn independently from examining the research and the theoretical and clinical data available on this population. As such, it enriches our understanding of why molesters do what they do. Skillful use of this kind of material in treatment provides a way for adolescent molesters to communicate their deepest issues and fears. Dreams, drawings, and writings provide a window to the psyche, a window which an adolescent molester who is willing to share them throws open to the therapist and others wishing to help him resolve his conflicts.

Chapter Seven

ASSESSMENT

C areful assessment is the beginning of all diagnosis and treatment of any emotional or behavioral problem. Assessment is like the foundation of a house. If this foundation is aligned incorrectly or inadequately, all subsequent treatment efforts built upon this foundation will compound the initial error. The final result in such a case will be something that is neither accurate diagnosis nor meaningful treatment.

Adolescent molesters are among the most difficult of all populations to clinically assess. They share evasiveness, manipulation, and secretiveness with other types of delinquents. In addition to this, the adolescent molester has a problem in the area of sexuality. This is an area in which most members of our society have deep conflicts. Since their problem deals with sex, it is covered under a mantle of shame and guilt which often makes it difficult to get accurate information.

Shame and guilt are not the only reasons it is difficult to find out what is really going on inside the mind of the adolescent offender. Frequently, they are not even the major reasons for secrecy and evasiveness. Nor is the problem limited to the youth with whom we deal. Their parents are often as anxious, sometimes more anxious than their progeny, to cover the boy's problems with a shroud of secrecy and deception. The motives for concealing can be either conscious or unconscious.

The reasons for concealing the thoughts, feelings and fantasies that clinicians need in order to help them are multiple. Sometimes the most important reason is legal. Molesting children is against the law. Adolescents who have done this are usually aware of the illegality of their behavior. Admitting new offenses or additional details of already discovered offenses may get the adolescent into further legal trouble.

Sometimes these young men and their families conceal on the advice of their attorneys. In other situations, the families do not know what they can share, and what they cannot share without getting into further difficulty with law enforcement. Such families often come into treatment with considerable fear and distrust of the clinician. Out of perceived self-protection, important, often vital, material is concealed.

Parents are often at the forefront of the withholding. They do this for a variety of reasons. Some are simply overprotective of their child. They wish to shield the young man from the legal and social consequences of his act. Some parents hold to an almost delusional belief that their child has not committed a sex offense. Their line of reasoning proceeds along the line, "He is such a nice boy, he could not possibly have done that." I recently interviewed a perpetrator and his mother. I saw the two of them separately. The mother told me that her son had fondled a five-year-old neighbor girl two years before our interview. She attributed the incident to teenage curiosity. The boy, when interviewed with his mother, told her clearly and frankly that the offense had been oral copulation and that he did not feel that it was normal.

Adolescents are usually part of a family system. When they come to the attention of law enforcement and therapists after an act of molestation, they must take into account the demands and pressures of the family system. The fathers of many of these offenders are homophobic. This poses a dilemma of severe conflict to a young man who has molested a male. In this kind of situation, the adolescent is likely to deny or minimize. In some cases the teenager and one parent may enter a conspiracy to conceal the full facts from the other parent.

Often, when a son is arrested for molesting, the parents feel profound shame. They feel that, if they had been adequate parents, the problem would not have arisen. Sometimes the parents are so full of shame, they must deny to themselves and others what their son has done in order to avoid profound depression or even suicide. Here the adolescent offender will instinctively conspire to protect the parent by maintaining vigorous denial. In working with this kind of case, it is vital to keep parental shame to a minimum in order even to make an adequate assessment, let alone undertake treatment. Such cases usually require individual or family therapy for the parents to deal with their issues in a way that does not immobilize the adolescent's treatment.

Another group of parents who cannot deal with their sons' molesting are those who idealize, overprotect, and/or infantilize their boys. Their need to deny the sexual offense at times approaches the delusional. If the parents and their child are cornered by a court conviction and ordered into treatment, such parents usually resist and undermine treatment. Scott's case illustrates this situation.

Scott L.

Scott was referred for treatment after he had been convicted of molesting a 7 year-old girl two years prior to the time of referral. The offense was an ugly one involving physically dragging the child into the bathroom, attempting penetration and consummating oral copulation. Charges were not pressed at the time. Neighborhood gossips, however, hounded Scott mercilessly. To get even with one of the principal sources of gossip, Scott and a girlfriend invaded the victim's home and did thousands of dollars worth of damage to the contents. Scott was placed on probation for this.

For some reason the sex offense charges were resurrected. Scott failed badly a polygraph test regarding the offense. He was subsequently convicted in the juvenile court. The mother's position shifted back and forth between, "He is innocent," and "too much is being made of a very small matter." She engaged an expensive attorney to either get Scott completely off from the charge or to minimize any consequences of his actions. Her principal questions of the therapist were, "How much is it going to cost?' and "How long will it take?' After Scott was convicted, the mother arranged her work schedule to be at home whenever he was. This was to protect him from possibly still resentful neighbors whom she feared might frame him with further charges.

This woman appears to be a borderline personality. She has a highly idealized vision of her son which is clashing with the reality of his offense. The boy truly has some strengths, but these are all the mother is willing to see. She is resorting to nearly delusional tactics in order to preserve her idealized version of her son. Obviously, she would be an obstacle to any clinician trying to figure what was really going on in her boy's psyche. I suspect that preserving this image of an ideal son is essential to the mother's preservation of her own sanity. Her teenager cannot help but respond to this pressure by sharing in her denial and evasion.

This case illustrates what is probably denial for the purpose of preserving the mother-son bond and the mother's emotional stability. Resistance can also come from attempting to preserve the offender's own intrapsychic equilibrium. In some cases, the sex offense can be regarded as a symptom. As a symptom, it is a defense against a deeper anxiety. Groth et al. (1978:53) discuss what they call the "internal crisis issue" in a young offender named Robert. They raise the possibility that this young man's sexual offenses may have been "a last defense against going insane." In cases where molesting is a symptom, serving as a defense against psychosis, strong resistance can be expected to any attempt to penetrate into the nature and roots of the offense. Symptomatic behavior in this kind of situation would be seen as literally life preserving by the offender.

NATIONAL TASK FORCE RECOMMENDATIONS ON ASSESSMENT OF SEX OFFENDERS

The formidable obstacles to getting good information with which to assess adolescent molesters has caused the specialized discipline which treats them to devise specialized protocols for assessment (see Revised Report from the National Task Force on Juvenile Sexual Offending, 1993). The focus here is on the special problems and responsibilities involved when one treats sex offenders. The Task Force's protocols stress the need to verify everything about the offense that is related to the clinician by the offender. This means getting access to the victim's statements, police and probation reports, psychological evaluations already on file, etc. It also involves contacting all significant people who have been involved with the offender in the past. The family must be interviewed and assessed for strengths and problems.

The Task Force rightly stresses the responsibility of those assessing sex offenders to consider issues of victim protection and community welfare. A high priority is placed on assessing the offenders' potential risk to the community, his capacity to retaliate against the victim, or to traumatize the victim if he remains in the community. Since community and victim protection are priorities, confidentiality is not. If the perpetrator is to remain in the community, the ability of the family to provide adequate supervision and control must be carefully assessed.

The National Task Force's recommendations also stress that assessment is an ongoing process that begins at the time of referral and continues into treatment aftercare. A therapist working in this area needs to shed the notion that an assessment can be completed in one session. This is a concept which seems to have become tolerated by some mental health practitioners because of the demands of hospital settings. Psychiatric hospitals usually have a few days or, at best, a few weeks in which to work with the patient. A quick assessment must be made in this kind of situation. These constraints rarely apply to the diagnosis and treatment of the adolescent molester.

Assessment is really a process rather than an event. Several interviews will be necessary in order to do a thorough job of even the intake. The assessment should continue as treatment proceeds. Once an adolescent is placed in treatment, new information will be elicited. New facts, feelings and fantasies continually emerge in the course of treatment. The therapist should obtain a copy of the police report and review it carefully in the course of diagnostic study. Police reports are often not available at the time of intake. Generally they are not released while a prosecution is ongoing. Nor are police reports infallible. They are, at times, based on faulty procedures or even bias. On the positive side, they often include verbatim interviews with victims and witnesses which can be helpful. They also contain the initial reaction and remarks of the young offender.

One young man in treatment only admitted his offense after being confronted in group with polygraph data suggesting that he was lying when he denied oral copulation with his victim. Another offender neglected to tell his therapist that his victim had spent 13 days in intensive care after the assault. He also did not mention that the two-year-old victim had stopped breathing. This information was contained in the police report. The offender acknowledged it only when confronted with the police reports. If the clinician had not obtained these reports, vital information would be lacking and the diagnosis woefully inadequate.

CULTURAL FACTORS IN ASSESSMENT

The National Task Force places major emphasis on cultural awareness. They point out that minority males are often socialized in ways that cause them to equate violence and masculinity or that force them into violence and criminality as an adaptation to the world with which they must cope. Cultural factors in both assessment and treatment are vitally important issues. The way cultures shape maleness and its expression varies considerably from culture to culture. America is emerging as a diverse, multicultural society, and it is now necessary to think beyond black, white, and Hispanic. The term Hispanic is itself misleading since it includes aristocrats from Madrid with Maya Indians from the outskirts of Guatemala City in the same category.

In my 1992 book on male victims, I devoted two chapters to the subject of culture. It is a suitable subject for an entire book on sex offenders. An exhaustive review is beyond the scope of this revised edition. It needs to be said, however, that those working with sex offenders need to familiarize themselves with cultural issues. This can be done by attending workshops, reading, and listening carefully to your patients who bear other cultures.

PSYCHOLOGICAL TESTS AND OTHER PROJECTIVE DATA

The National Task Force declares that there are no infallible tests of instruments for evaluating sex offenders. They do not mention specific tests or procedures in their written reports. I suspect there was a great deal of behind-the-scenes controversy in this area. In the mainstream of those treating sex offenders there is a distrust of the routine psychological tests used in mental health settings. Some in the field have devised specialized pencil and paper tests for sex offenders. These are generally card sorts inquiring about the adolescents' sexual interests and cognition scales to test for distorted perceptions such as, "Women enjoy being raped."

I believe these kind of instruments should be included in the battery of tests used at the time of intake. They have limitations. They are self-reports and, as such, can be distorted by those wishing to mislead. The card sorts with explicit sexual questions need to be used in intake with informed parental consent. Many of the clinicians in the field either use or would like to use the plethysmograph. This will be considered later.

I believe that many of the traditional psychological tests are also valuable with the molester population. These include the MMPI, projective drawings, sentence completion tests, the Rorschach, and the appropriate Weschler Intelligence Scale. These tests do not say much about the central sexual issues, but they do reveal a great deal about the individual who is having the sexual problem. Psychotherapy as a discipline has learned that some techniques either work or do not work with certain types of patients. For example, patients with low IQs are not likely to respond well to therapies requiring a lot of memorization and formal learning. In the presence of severe pathology, it is necessary to proceed with cautions that are not necessary with less disturbed patients. It is my clinical experience that the more disturbed and impulsive offenders are the most likely to reoffend or otherwise act out while in treatment. This kind of data is very important to any treatment planning.

Looking more specifically at the tests, the Draw-A–Person Test and the Kinetic Family Drawing are particularly helpful. Many of a patient's sexual concerns are reflected in drawings of the human figure. The Kinetic Family Drawing asks the patient to draw a picture of each person in his family engaged in some activity. The result sheds significant light on family relationships and family dynamics. Weschler Intelligence Scales and the Rorschach are valuable assets to diagnosis and treatment. The Weschler gives a detailed analysis of the adolescent's intellectual functioning. It can also give hints as to organicity and deprivation and neglect in early life. The Rorschach provides data on personality structure and ego functioning. It can help evaluate the quality of the offender's reality testing. It also yields data on personality style and characteristic defense mechanisms. It is particularly useful where severe psychopathology is suspected. Molesters may attempt to manipulate the results of psychological testing. Tests are not infallible. Some are easier to fake than others. With the brighter and more evasive offenders, projective drawings and the Rorschach seem to yield the most reliable information.

Where appropriate, the MMPI should be used. It has deficits. I believe it is easily faked by the bright, sophisticated offender. In my opinion even the validity scales do not always identify the malingerer. It is important to try to establish a climate in which the offender will take the test truthfully. Assuming a cooperative examinee, the test has several advantages. When interpreted using a system focusing on the interaction of the highest scales such as that described in Lachar (1974), my clinical experience has been that it has an uncanny accuracy about personality make-up and probable response to treatment. No one claims that it identifies sex offenders, that there is a "sex offender profile," or that it predicts recidivism. Rather it should be regarded as a source of hypotheses about treatment approach. In this sense, it is a valuable contribution to the data pool about the offender.

OTHER PROJECTIVE DATA

In addition to psychological testing, there is a variety of projective material which can be helpful to the clinician in making a complete assessment of the adolescent offender. Sexual fantasies accompanying masturbation are particularly important. They reveal basic diagnostic information about what motivates the offender. This material is difficult to get. It is probably the most carefully guarded secret of the teenage molester. Many of these young men do not admit that they masturbate, let alone admit that perverse fantasies accompany this activity. When an offender will share such information, it is usually late in the treatment process. Sometimes it can be elicited early on as a condition of acceptance into a treatment program.

Adolescent molesters are more willing to share dreams than masturbation fantasies. A percentage deny dreaming at all. In my experience, prognosis is poorer and treatment slower for this group. The majority of adolescent offenders seem to remember their dreams and are willing to share them in treatment. Where this is the case at intake, the data provided is of great diagnostic value. Therapists who work extensively with dreams often find that the initial dreams related often lay out in detail the patient's most basic conflicts.

Other easily obtainable projective material involves eliciting three wishes from the offender and asking what animal he would most and least like to be. Wishes tell a lot about personality style. Some adolescent molesters produce wishes which indicate how evasive they are. Examples of this kind of response might be: (1) to be out of this legal mess, (2) lots of money, (3) three more wishes. Other wishes can be revealing of basic conflicts. For example: (1) for my mom and stepdad to stop fighting, (2) to live with my real dad, (3) to have a new red Ferrari. Here the first wish points toward fighting in the home. The second is a wish to get out of the home and/or pursue an idealized parent represented by the father. The third suggests strong urges toward masculinity and success. Much time could be spent with this offender exploring the ramifications of these wishes.

The animal an individual would most like to be makes a statement about self-concept. Sometimes it deals with an idealized concept rather than their actual self image. For example, different personality inferences would be made about an individual who wanted to be a leopard as opposed to one who wished to be a tortoise. The animal least desired as a self symbol sometimes makes a comment about the offender's conscience. For example: "I would not want to be an alligator because they attack and hurt people. The response, "I would not want to be a mouse because they get stepped on," suggests that the molester feels small, inadequate, and possibly in fear of attack.

A word about eliciting projective material. It is often necessary to reject an initial refusal to provide this information. If a youth tells me that he never dreams, I usually follow with the statement that everyone dreams, the difference is in whether we remember them. I will also ask them to search their memory to see if they can come up with any dreams. Once the dream is presented, it is often necessary to ask further questions. This often gets the teenager to reveal dream content he would have otherwise withheld. Coaxing and encouraging is also sometimes necessary to get the three wishes and the animals. With the Draw-A–Person test, it is important to stress that stick figures are not acceptable, nor are happy faces. These will tell you that the young man is evasive but little else.

THE FAMILY INTERVIEW

A family interview yields important diagnostic information. There should be at least one session involving the entire family and a follow-up session with the adolescent and both parents. Minimally, the adolescent should be seen together with whomever is parenting him in his home. If his victim is a sibling living in the home, it is better to wait a while before including the victim in any family session with the perpetrator. A conjoint family session with the victim and perpetrator can yield valuable data, but it can be traumatic to the victim. This interview should be delayed until well into the treatment and planned in concert with the victim's therapist.

The family interview allows the clinician to see the system in which the offender lives. It also provides information about how his personality has been shaped by family dynamics. It is in the family interview that the therapist often learns that the father is homophobic or that the mother is overindulgent and overprotective. Issues involving the parents' own victimization or offending may also come up in this context. Eric's case indicates the importance of a family interview in making an assessment.

Eric F.

When Eric was referred to treatment, he was living with distant relatives. He had been placed there after molesting his two younger sisters. These caretakers refused to be involved in Eric's treatment. Subsequent investigation revealed that Eric's relatives had children in the same age range as those he had molested, and he was babysitting them. The probation officer returned him to his own home at that point. Things went well for a few months, but the parents began to call both the therapists and the probation officer to complain that Eric was disregarding their instructions. He was coming and going as he pleased, carrying on a passionate sexual affair with a girl his own age, and refusing to take any household responsibility. They wanted him placed in an institution.

The mother and stepfather came for a family interview. When the therapist arrived, mother and stepfather were engaged in passionate embrace on his doorstep. The interview indicated that the stepfather was using physically abusive discipline in his attempt to control Eric. The mother alternated between bursts of tears and guilt, and venomous rage toward her son. A brief period of family treatment resulted in no change. The parents refused to continue treatment, and Eric ran away. He was subsequently arrested for stealing a car while on the run. The probation officer recommended placement to the juvenile court.

This young man's parents were as impulsive, confused, and disturbed as he was. The parents themselves were too immature to parent. Their basic drive appeared to be to get Eric out of the home to avoid the responsibilities of parenting. As such, no treatment in the home was possible. Placement turned out to be necessary. Many mistakes could have been avoided in this case if a thorough family study had been made shortly after Eric's arrest.

THE PENILE PLETHYSMOGRAPH

The penile plethysmograph is widely used with adult sex offenders in both evaluation and treatment. Its use with adolescents seems to be growing and becoming less controversial. Its advocates favor using it for assessment because they believe it provides the most empirical way to measure male sexual arousal. Any clinician considering using it in the assessment of juvenile offenders should be aware of its strengths, its limitations, and the controversy that surrounds it.

What is the penile plethysmograph? Technically this device is a mercury and rubber strain gauge through which a very low level electrical current is run. This gauge is hooked up to a computer to record and process responses. To use the device the gauge is placed around the penis. By measuring the electrical resistance in the mercury column, the examiner can tell to what degree the penis is dilating, i.e., becoming erect in response to visual and/or auditory stimuli. The device measures not only the fact of erection itself, but the degree of tumescence of the penis. It can thereby measure nuances of the sexual response. It can tell not only that the offender is stimulated but to what degree he is stimulated by material being presented.

How is this instrument used? It is properly used in a laboratory setting by trained technician or researcher. The offender is asked to place the device around his penis. Typically the subject is then shown a series of still photographs, movie, or video material which is sexually explicit. A typical subject will be shown people of both sexes and many different ages. Nudity and a wide variety of sexual activity is portrayed. Some of the activity involves violence. Some does not. The goal of this technique is to show the clinician and/or researcher what kind of sexual response pattern is typical of the individual under investigation. It will show sexual responses to young children if this is the preference of the subject. Homosexual and heterosexual preferences can also be reflected in this technique. The examiner can also tell if the subject is sexually excited by violence or humiliation of the sexual partner.

A series of questions can be raised about the validity of the technique. The most recent literature has still not reached any consensus about its validity. Barker and Howell (1992) review the literature and conclude that it is the best available tool for discovering male arousal patterns and that it is useful in the treatment of sex offenders. They acknowledge, however, that there are no standards for its administration or for interpretation of the results. They note that the results can be faked. Their conclusion is that the plethysmograph is best used in conjunction with data collected from a variety of other sources. Simon and Schouten (1993) challenge even these conservative conclusions. They feel that Barker and Howell underestimate problems in faking and standardization and that their data suggests more guarded conclusions about the use of the plethysmograph.

Other recent researchers have found more specific and disturbing problems. Eccles, Marshal, and Barbaree (1994) found that the plethysmograph did not distinguish rapists from nonrapists in a controlled clinical trial. Proulx et al. (1994) come to similar conclusions regarding rapists and nonoffenders. Castonguay et al. explore the problem of men who have minimal responses to plethysmograph stimuli and are therefore very hard to assess. Adams et al. (1992) focus on voluntary control of erectile responses. They find that many subjects can suppress their responses in a way that would conceal deviant arousal. It was much more difficult for subjects to fake an arousal that did not exist.

The empirical implication of these recent studies is that the plethysmograph is likely to err in the direction of a false negative, i.e., it will say there is no deviant arousal when there is. Another problem is that, even where deviant arousal is found, clinicians should realize that the presence of deviant arousal does not predict deviant behavior. It will not predict who will molest in the future. The issue of the degree of erection is also important. Sometimes the test shows a 5 percent or 10 percent erectile response. What does this mean? How should it be interpreted?

Are such individuals concealing a stronger arousal or do they have a weak arousal which is not clinically significant?

The objections raised to the plethysmograph up to this point have been scientific ones involving validity. There are also issues involving both ethical and emotional considerations. The mere mention of the plethysmograph evokes a strong emotional response in many people. A program in Arizona became the focus of hostile publicity in the *Arizona Republic* in 1992. The paper found the clinicians were using the device on boys as young as 12. The program was featured in several articles including one in which the use of the plethysmograph was called "taxpayer funded child abuse" (*Arizona Republic* June 14, 1992). The ACLU became involved, and the state legislature was considering placing severe legal restrictions on its use.

The plethysmograph was used for a period of time in the California Youth Authority. After a vociferous public protest, it was banned from the institution by order of the Governor. I once raised the possibility of using this instrument in a residential facility where I do some work. My question was exploratory, not declarative. The probation officer assigned to the institution immediately reacted that she would have to consult her supervisor on this matter. She was uncomfortable with the concept. The program psychiatrist and administrator responded with associations to *Clockwork Orange* and *1984*.

The emotional issue here is related to the ethical one. The plethysmograph is an invasive instrument. It gives us information which is based on physiology and is in no way volunteered by the patient. As such, it is a relative of the polygraph and the urine test for substance abuse. Additionally, its indiscriminate use on minors may expose them to sexual stimuli more deviant than they have already experienced or fantasized about thereby suggesting behaviors not previously conceptualized. The National Task Force on Juvenile Sex Offending enjoins caution in this area in its 1993 report.

As an invasive device, use of the plethysmograph runs a risk of alienating the adolescent from those who treat him. It is generally better to get the patient's full and informed consent before using this device. I do not use it in my practice. The community in which I work would be totally unsupportive of its use. It is probably most useful with hardcore populations in institutional settings. Even in such settings, anyone using it should be prepared to deal with a storm of criticism.

THE HIGH FUNCTIONING OFFENDER

Another area for great caution is when dealing with the intelligent, sophisticated, high functioning offender. These young men are often good at covering their tracks and appearing to be either minimal offenders or victims of erroneous accusations. Scott, whose case was discussed earlier in this chapter, is such an offender. Few people in our society wish to believe that a hard-working, intelligent young man who is a successful athlete is also a sex offender. Needless to say, any offender will traffic on this social goodwill. Scott admitted part of his offense after being confronted with polygraph evidence. He went through a psychological evaluation which failed to turn up the fact that he was deeply dissatisfied with his adoptive parents and fantasizing about returning to his birth parents. The examination also failed to turn up his hatred and contempt for his adoptive mother as weak, stupid, and vacillating. This information emerged in treatment after Scott developed some trust for the therapist.

With the bright and manipulative offender, extra caution is indicated. Important statements should be scrutinized. Many of these offenders play a shell game with reality which is very difficult to disentangle. In the assessment of such cases, corroborating or elaborating documents and testimony should be especially pursued. One of the best techniques with the high-functioning offender is to take him into exploratory treatment. I have had cases where, at the time of intake, I literally could not tell what the offender did and what he did not do. A period of treatment of both the individual and family usually breaks down their ability to continue concealment. The true nature of the situation usually emerges in the course of this kind of exploratory treatment.

USING ASSESSMENT RESULTS

At the end of the assessment process, a wide range of data about the offender will have been gathered. At some point, this will need to be categorized and assembled into a report. The report should include all the elements of a regular mental health evaluation including an extensive social history, a developmental and medical history, an assessment of family function and dynamics, mental status, previous treatment episodes, educational background, and criminal-legal history. Projective and test data should be reviewed and integrated into the report.

Since the presenting problem is sexual, particular attention needs to be paid to sexual issues. A careful sexual history should be taken. This should include milestones in male development and an attempt to place the individual offender at the point wherein his male development was arrested if that appears to be identifiable from the data. Sexual and masturbatory fantasies should be examined and evaluated in terms of their meaning. An evaluation should be made as to whether there is deviant arousal and, if so, to what. Nondeviant sexual fantasies and experiences should also be included. To the extent possible, a sexual history of the parents should be taken.

Issues relating to the offense for which the adolescent is being evaluated should be examined in detail. Similar attention should be paid to previous sex offenses. There is another series of important questions: How did the perpetrator involve the victim? Was there force or threat of force? What was the extent of sexual arousal? How much planning was involved? Does this offender show signs of progression? Are there sadistic elements in the offense? Bizarre elements? Is there reason to suspect undetected offenses? The data should be used to make an assignment of the adolescent to one or more of the categories of sex offenders which clinicians and researchers have found useful in treatment planning and risk assessment. Is this offender a sibling offender? Is he a prepedophile? Is he low functioning or mentally ill? This list could go on. It is intended to be suggestive of what should be included rather than exhaustive.

This data is assembled not just from the perpetrator, but from all available sources. Once it is collected and reflected upon, it should result in a comprehensive picture of the offender as a human being and as a sex offender. It should be pulled together into a dynamic hypothesis about why the offender became involved in an assault upon a child. It is vital to assess the degree of risk the adolescent poses in the future and whether he can be safely left in the community. The dynamic formulation about the molester's sexual pathology will become the foundation for his treatment whether it is in the community or residential.

Perhaps of greatest interest to the community is the clinician's appraisal of the risk posed by the offender. Referral sources are interested in the likelihood of recidivism and the amount of physical danger an offender might pose to future victims. Certain situations imply a much greater risk of recidivism than others. Incest cases are particularly tricky. The victim is likely to be in the home. Even though there is often not as much psychopathology as in nonincest cases, there is a greater risk of recidivism if the offender remains in the home due to the constant availability of victims.

In any criminal justice situation, the best predictor of recidivism is history. Offenders who have many victims over a long period of time are very likely to repeat their acts. Repetitious offending implies a compulsive quality to the behavior. The adolescent molester may be so driven to offend that, psychologically, he cannot stop. Some offenders are psychotic or severely borderline in their personality structures. By definition, such adolescents do not perceive reality accurately or make good decisions based on their perceptions. This means that their behavior is inherently unpredictable. Impulse control is by definition poor in this population. Because of these personality factors, this kind of adolescent offender is a high recidivism risk. These offenders can often be identified on the basis of mental status alone. Their associations are loose, their ideas often bizarre. There is usually an undercurrent of paranoia that can be identified in their verbalizations and their careful scanning of the examiner. Instinctively, the clinician may "feel" the underlying craziness. Diagnosis should be further confirmed by psychological test data and the assessment techniques discussed earlier.

Like the psychotic or borderline molester, the intellectually low functioning offender is a high risk. Because of intellectual deficits, they have poor impulse control. Because of their limited intelligence, they may see themselves as peers of younger children. In a sense, this is true. Developmentally, they may be nowhere near their chronological age. From their perspective, offending is simply having sex with a peer. This, combined with poor impulse control, creates a significant potential for reoffense.

In my clinical experience, the most important predictor of recidivism is the unsupportive family. Unsupportive here refers to the family's stance toward treatment. These are the families who assist the offender in denying what he has done. They often place the adolescent in a position where he cannot admit his offense without alienating his entire family and perhaps be ejected from his home.

At the other extreme are parents who scapegoat their son. As soon as the offense is discovered, they turn on the young man with pathological viciousness. Typically, they demand his incarceration in juvenile hall and refuse to be involved in any kind of treatment program. These offenders usually end up in residential treatment for obvious reasons. Sometimes, however, the family has a "change of heart." This is often based on the pathological needs of the family system. The real need is to get the offender home, covertly encourage reoffense, and then repeat the scapegoat drama.

Another pathological family situation which predicts recidivism is the parent who is acting out his own pathology through the child. This is common in all kinds of delinquency. Antisocial parents act out their antisocial impulses through their children. They themselves may appear to be pillars of the community while their child steals, assaults, or deals in drugs. In the more specialized realm of the adolescent molester, this kind of dynamic sometimes operates where the father has been an offender himself. Clinicians often encounter families in which virtually everyone has been molested. Parents in such families should be watched closely for acting out their own needs to offend and/or to be victimized through their offspring.

A vital assessment question involves the potential to harm or even kill a victim. This is a difficult issue to address. It is well-known that a small minority of adult pedophiles are sadistic. Torture and homicide are often involved in their offenses. This picture seems to be rare among adolescent molesters. Some of its precursors may be present in offenses involving sadistic mistreatment of the victim. As in the case of recidivism, the most reliable assessment tool is history. If a young offender has a history of sadism and force connected with acts of molestation, such acts are likely in the future. Adolescent molesters are rarely candid about the use of force and the enjoyment of the victim's humiliation and pain. For that reason, it is important to review police and probation reports. If possible, direct contact with the victim is also desirable.

Less reliable than a history of force and sadism, but still significant, are fantasies and projective material revealing this kind of fantasy directed toward victims. Caution is indicated here. Most adolescent molesters produce fantasies involving more violence than their actual acts have ever entailed. What this means psychodynamically, I do not know. It does suggest that there is not a one-to-one relationship between fantasy and action in the teenager who molests. A history of violence outside of the sexual area is probably significant in predicting violence toward victims of sexual assault. If a young molester's background includes nonsexual offenses involving violence, it seems logical to infer that his past or future sex acts may also involve violence.

A history of physical abuse of the adolescent perpetrator may also point to the possibility of violent sexual offenses in the future. It is known that physical abuse of children predisposes them to abuse their own children in later life. It is also connected with delinquency in adolescence and criminal careers in adult life. The link here seems to be that physical abuse damages a child's ability to bond to other human beings. It also generates an underlying rage which seeks expression in interpersonal relationships. Many victims of physical abuse attempt to escape from the anxiety caused by this abuse by identifying with their attackers. When these traits are found in an adolescent offender, the stage is set for violence if their pathology has turned them in the direction of sexual assault.

As in the case of recidivism, the presence of psychosis or severe borderline pathology raises a greater possibility of violence directed toward victims if these individuals become molesters. The essence of the matter is that psychosis makes future behavior unpredictable and unconstrained by the boundaries of reality. Anyone working with psychotic adolescent molesters needs to proceed with great caution and be aware of the potential risks posed by this group.

A CONTINUUM OF SEVERITY

Once again in the study of the adolescent molester, we are confronted with a continuum. This one involves the risk which the adolescent poses to the community. At one pole, there is a kind of offender which most clinicians would agree poses little risk to the community if proper treatment measures are implemented in a timely manner. The classic case of the low-risk offender is one who has a single female victim. The offense involves neither penetration nor force. The family is supportive of treatment. The offender admits his offense and talks freely about it. This kind of young man responds well to outpatient treatment. The major risk here is that the offense will be regarded as teenage curiosity or experimentation and no treatment offered. Without treatment, prognosis is guarded, especially if the potential for reoffense in the distant future is considered.

At the other end of the continuum is the offender with multiple victims who are either all male or mixed male and female. Here the family is unsupportive. They are either unwilling to be involved or actively harmful and destructive. This offender has used force or threats of force in obtaining compliance from his victims. In the worst case scenario, he totally denies his offense. Slightly less serious are those who minimize and blame the victim.

COMMUNITY vs RESIDENTIAL TREATMENT

The goal of all clinical assessment is treatment planning. The basic decision any clinician must make is whether the offender can be treated in the community or will need treatment in a residential facility. Community treatment is appropriate where the dangers of recidivism and physical harm to victims are low. The young offender who denies his offense poses particular problems for treatment. I do not believe it is possible to offer meaningful treatment to an adolescent who denies having committed a sex offense. Some clinicians accept this kind of individual into treatment and continue treatment in spite of continuing denial. If the patient is denying that the offense ever occurred, for what problem is he being treated?

If a young offender denies his involvement in an offense, it is my policy to see him for up to six sessions. This applies only if the young man is otherwise suited to the outpatient or residential program where he has been placed. I would not continue the treatment beyond six sessions under any circumstances if the denial continued. In general, denial points to serious problems. It can imply many things. It may reflect poor reality testing. It is not good functioning to continue to deny an offense admitted or proven beyond reasonable doubt in court. Denial may reflect emotional rigidity. The perpetrator may have no other way of coping with problems beside denying their existence to himself and others and hoping they go away. It may also reflect a passive-aggressive style of relating to others. This kind of adolescent becomes involved in desperate power struggles. He may be resisting parents, law enforcement officials, and/or his therapist by refusing to admit. This list is not exhaustive. There are probably other reasons that teenage perpetrators deny. None of them imply the possibility of rapid and effective treatment. While in a state of denial, the molester is probably also at high risk for reoffense, particularly if he has easy access to victims.

If the denying offender is in outpatient treatment, he should be remanded to residential care if the denial persists. Denial in a residential treatment facility is more difficult to deal with. One strategy might be to remove the offender from all treatment and make it clear to him that he is just serving time until he discusses his offense. Another might be to leave him in the facility's treatment program but make it clear that no advancement through the program is possible until he deals candidly with his problems.

In making an assessment, the clinician's task is to ascertain how quickly denial can be broken through. A brief period of outpatient treatment might be recommended for molesters who otherwise seem safe in the community. It should be made clear that residential treatment will be recommended if no progress is made.

Two other criteria for successful community treatment have been discussed earlier. One is a supportive family. The second is the lack of available victims in the home. Another consideration about the family is that they must have the emotional resources for community treatment. Some families are well meaning. They would like their son to get the treatment that he needs. They are, however, disorganized and incapable of carrying out a regular treatment plan. Typically, these families do not get the child to his appointments. If they do get him there at all, attendance is erratic. Even if they get the child and themselves into the treatment situation, they have trouble making use of what they learn in the process.

Another consideration is that the community must have resources appropriate to treating adolescent molesters on an outpatient basis. There is almost universal agreement among specialists in this field that group therapy is the treatment of choice. If only one treatment modality is to be offered, it should be group. In some communities, there is no clinician with sufficient background to operate such a group. Even in some medium-sized communities, there may be only one or two such groups available. These groups may be filled and therefore unavailable.

Another factor which must be considered before deciding on community treatment is the sophistication and intensity of the available treatment. With unlimited resources and unlimited specialists, a high percentage of adolescent molesters could probably be treated in the community. Neither resources nor specialists are unlimited in the newly emerging discipline of treating the adolescent molester. A treatment plan involving group therapy two times per week complemented by family and individual therapy is not likely to be carried out in most communities. Enough trained therapists to offer this much treatment to a large number of adolescent offenders simply do not exist in most areas.

The bottom line here is that all clinicians and case managers operating in the field of the adolescent molester must adhere to the demands of the reality principle. We should not make treatment plans that are unlikely to happen. To do so is a disservice to both the patient and the community. Based on my clinical experience, I would "guestimate" that about one-half of the adolescent molesters can and should be treated in the community. This presumes that the community in question has enough qualified therapists and case managers to meet the demands of treating this many teenage perpetrators in the community.

About half of the adolescent molesters should ideally be treated in a quality residential setting. This is necessary both because of their more extensive treatment needs and because of the need to protect the community. It may also be necessary because of some of the unfortunate but realistic considerations discussed earlier. The groups who very clearly belong in residential treatment are the psychotic and severely borderline, the low-functioning, and those with unsupportive families. Returning to the concept of a continuum of severity in sex offenses, any molester close to the more severe pole of the continuum belongs in a residential setting.

What has been written here so far is quite idealistic. It is predicated on the assumption that there are abundant quality residential programs for adolescent offenders. This is clearly not the case. Many residential treatment facilities exclude adolescent molesters. Others maintain a routine program with no special provisions for the treatment needs of the molester. Their treatment may consist only of seeing a psychologist every other week and a social worker once a week. If their offense is talked about at all, they are fortunate. Some programs make an effort to transport molesters to special outpatient groups in the community for treatment.

Some residential facilities are not at all selective about whom they take. Anyone the placing agencies will pay for is welcome. These are basically warehouses. They are particularly bad because they run the risk of aggravating the sex offender's already serious problem. Residential facilities without intensive supervision have high incidences of consenting and nonconsenting sexual activity between residents. If the facility is all male, the activity is homosexual. In view of the role of homosexual anxieties in the etiology of molesting behavior, this type of "treatment" is most unfortunate.

If therapists and case managers are to err, it is better to err in the direction of placement than in the direction of community treatment. Even in attempting to live up to these standards, there will be mistakes. Some offenders who belong in residential treatment will be left at home.

Some who should be left at home will be put into residential facilities. We live in an imperfect world. The best clinicians and the best case managers can make errors in judgment. The most that can be asked of all of us is that we put forth our best efforts to secure necessary and appropriate treatment for adolescent perpetrators. In the course of doing this, we must never lose sight of our responsibility to protect victims and the community at large.

Chapter Eight

TREATMENT OBJECTIVES:
STRATEGIC vs TACTICAL

Among those who treat adolescent molesters there is considerable discussion about the tactics of treatment, specific types of intervention designed to obtain specific and measurable objectives. There is very little thinking about the overall strategic goals of treatment. By strategic goals, I mean: What is the grand design of the treatment plan? Where does the clinician intend to go with the client? There are two general strategic goals in any kind of psychotherapy. These two strategic goals lead to very different treatment strategies and very different outcomes. One kind of strategic goal leads to treatment planning which aims at the ultimate resolution of underlying problems. The hope is to treat so thoroughly that the dynamics which generated the molesting behavior no longer exist. The more limited strategic goal aims at the containment and management of symptoms so that the client and society are protected from the consequences of the patient's acting out.

Since psychotherapy draws much of its metaphor from medicine, let us look there for clarification. In the case of a simple disease caused by bacteria, a resolution-oriented approach would be antibiotic therapy. By eliminating the bacteria from the patient's body, the underlying cause of the disease is removed, and the patient is no longer at risk. The management model within medicine would apply to diabetes. In this case, no one expects to resolve the underlying condition. Things which aggravate the diabetic's weakened ability to manage sugar are carefully avoided. Medications are given to keep the insulin level in a range wherein the patient will not suffer the ravages of the underlying disease process. Foods high in sugar are avoided, and overweight is avoided as a stressor which will aggravate the underlying condition. Again, no effort is targeted to resolve the underlying condition because medicine has no cure for that at this time.

Taking the analogy back to psychotherapy, twelve-step programs are classic examples of a management approach to a problem. The twelve-step approach is widely used with the addictions as well as with a number of other intractable problems with which psychotherapy has considerable difficulty dealing. Within psychotherapy, it has been the psychodynamic approaches that have aimed at the resolution of underlying problems rather than symptom management. The track record of these approaches has been very mixed and depends a great deal on the kind of patient with whom the approach is used.

It is a major thesis of this work that some, perhaps many adolescents who molest younger children, are amenable and suitable subjects for a treatment approach which aims not at symptom management, but at the resolution of their underlying problem. This statement may be controversial since it is completely outside of the traditional approach to sex offenders in general. The traditional approach is what I call here the standard model. It has been largely borrowed from clinicians and researchers working with adult sex offenders. In its basic premises, it is based on the assumption that sex offending in adolescents represents an intractable and incurable problem that must be dealt with by a management model of treatment.

THE STANDARD MODEL

This model focuses on a reconditioning of physiological responses and an effort to change the cognitive distortions that allow or promote sex offending. This process is facilitated by a variety of techniques emerging out of behavioral-cognitive theory. Among these techniques is cognitive restructuring. This involves making explicit and modifying the erroneous ideas that underlie sexually assaultive behavior. For example, if the adolescent believes women enjoy being raped, he is cognitively restructured by being informed that women do not enjoy this. Cognitive restructuring belongs to a group of techniques that are aimed at making some degree of change in the underlying psychic structure of the molester.

The problem here is with the nature of the human psyche implied by the cognitive restructuring approach. The implication is that *Homo Sapiens* is engineered in such a way that behavior is determined by simplistic formulations about the nature of reality. If a person acquires an erroneous belief, it will determine his behavior until such time as he/she is re-educated by being informed of the correct belief. This flies in the face of everything that has been learned about the complexity of the human brain and psyche in the last century. Sex offenders may have erroneous beliefs, but they are likely to be part and parcel of larger psychiatric problems and not amenable to simple "restructuring" via the provision of information. The offender who believes that women like to be raped believes this for complex reasons. The belief is probably connected to all of his beliefs about women and sex. It is likely rooted in his relationships with key male and female figures in his past. It may simply be a rationalization that allows him to rape which is what he wants to do for other reasons having little to do with misinformation.

The standard model also includes a number of techniques to extinguish or suppress deviant interests. The most common of these is masturbatory satiation, in which the offender is urged to masturbate repeatedly. The initial masturbation is to be with a healthy and age-appropriate fantasy. Subsequent masturbation is to be with deviant fantasies. The material is to be recorded on audiotape and checked by the therapist to be sure that the adolescent is complying with the requirements of the treatment program. It is not clear to me whether this is simply intended to decrease deviant arousal or whether there is a presumption that this practice will result in an increasing attachment of the adolescent's sexual interest to the healthy and age-appropriate fantasy.

Becker acknowledges the difficulty of using this approach with adolescents in her 1993 publication. She states that the adolescents she treats resist this technique by claiming it is against their value system, or other resistances. To get around this difficulty, Becker substitutes verbal satiation (Becker and Kaplan, 1993). Here the adolescent is told to look at pictures of naked children and say, over and over, what they did to their victim. Verbal and masturbatory satiation are often done while the perpetrator is attached to a plethysmograph to measure erectile response. The exercise continues until the erotic response is extinguished. Aversive conditioning is sometimes part of the standard model. This is what most people think of when behavioral-cognitive treatment is mentioned. In aversive conditioning, the offender is encouraged to self-inflict some kind of aversive punishment when he begins to experience deviant arousal. For example, if he becomes sexually aroused at pictures or fantasies regarding young children, the offender will sniff ammonia as his penis begins to become erect. Sometimes this technique is done while the offender is hooked up to a plethysmograph. The aversive measure is administered at the directive of the plethysmograph technician. The literature generally describes this technique as obsolete, although I am aware of its continued use in one large outpatient program in California.

These conditioning techniques are strong medicine. They involve exposing adolescents to powerful sexual stimulation and carefully monitoring their sexual responses. As such they are bound to arouse community controversy. I could not possibly stay in practice in my community using masturbatory satiation and the plethysmograph. There would simply be too much concern from parents, attorneys, and social workers about the use of such techniques in a private, outpatient practice.

The standard treatment model emanating from the recommendations of the National Task Force (1988, 1993) also includes anger management and the development of social skills. Justification for the anger management component rests in the assumption that mismanaged anger is a causal factor in sex offending. Sex offenses are typically regarded by practitioners of this model as acts where anger plays a greater role than sexual gratification.

Teaching of social skills is another essential component of the standard model. It is intended to help the young offender establish age-appropriate sexual outlets. The theory behind this would appear to be that once the adolescent develops the necessary social skills, he will establish the age-appropriate sexual relationships which will in turn be reinforcing and literally seduce the adolescent away from deviant sexual interests.

In the standard model of treatment, group therapy has a central role. These are highly specialized groups in which peer and therapist pressure is directed intensely at adolescents who are in denial or are minimizing their problems. Some of the more aggressive residential programs require periodic monitoring by the penile plethysmograph in order to verify that the adolescent is not withholding information about deviant arousal from the group. This approach is sometimes also paired with a polygraph for added verification of the offender's statements.

The standard model of treatment does not at all emphasize the patient-therapist relationship. It places heavy emphasis on therapeutic work being carried out in a group setting, with individual treatment as a kind of ancillary approach. Ryan and Lane (1991) consider individual sessions largely a supplement to the group process. They cite such goals as drawing out painfully shy clients, addressing uniquely personal concerns, conducting physiological testing, or other similar secondary purposes, which include "confrontation of destructive group dynamics."

The standard model also places very little emphasis on dealing with the perpetrator's own victimization. Some practitioners seem to be aware that this is a relevant issue in the treatment of a perpetrator who is also a victim of sexual abuse. Others, however, fear that the issue of victimization will be used to avoid taking full responsibility for one's perpetration. There are additional injunctions that perpetrators not be allowed to fabricate victimizations in order to gain sympathy and other advantages in the treatment program.

Another way in which the standard model differs from other models of treatment is that the usual rules of mental health treatment do not apply. The central focus is not the patient, but protection of the community. Confidentiality is considered a negative factor which prevents professionals from working together to protect potential victims (Barbaree and Cortoni, 1993).

A central feature of the standard model is working with the offender on his abuse cycle. The abuse cycle is a regular pattern or cycle of events which start out with relatively innocent events, culminating in an act of molestation. Typically, the abuse cycle is urged along by stressors in daily life which in turn escalate the adolescent in the direction of further sex offending as a means of tension reduction. The abuse cycle approach stresses helping each individual adolescent identify his own cycle and then giving him a series of tools with which to cope with the events at each step of the cycle. Armed with this information, the offender can now, hopefully, break the cycle before it culminates in more molestation. Techniques for avoiding stressors, techniques for reducing the impact of stressors, and avoidance of masturbatory fantasies about children are important examples of ways in which adolescents can be taught to intervene in their own abuse cycle.

Understanding the abuse cycle is a key to another key element of the standard model: relapse prevention. The meaning of the term is obvious and the aim noble. The central element of relapse prevention seems to be maintaining awareness and vigilance about one's abuse cycle in a prolonged aftercare period. Aftercare includes continuing supportive treatment and a quick return to more intensive therapy if the offender appears to be losing control of his abuse cycle.

It hardly needs to be said that the standard model is practiced largely within institutional settings and in outpatient settings where the overwhelming majority of patients are court ordered. Most of these techniques would be very difficult to use with a voluntary population that could leave treatment at its own discretion. I see the standard model as something that has arisen out of the frustration of therapists at having to deal with a group of highly disturbed, institutionalized patients who are, in many cases, a menace to society. These techniques may represent the best that can be done with men who are deeply entrenched sex offenders and who are characterized by severe sexual pathology and strong recurrent deviant sexual interest in children. Research also indicates that they are reasonably effective techniques. I suspect that they work best where some kind of motivation from the molester is elicited to get him to be involved in his own treatment. The standard model of treatment for sex offenders is essentially a package of tactics which stress supportive techniques, albeit supportive techniques with a somewhat heavy-handed and correctional emphasis.

HETEROGENEITY AND THE STANDARD MODEL

The literature clearly indicates that the adolescent molester population is a heterogeneous one with many subtypes. This clearly implies that different patterns of personality and psychodynamics require specific and different treatment interventions. Little consideration appears to be given to this issue by those publishing and presenting within the discipline. Most of the techniques advocated by the standard model seem to be most appropriate with pedophilic and prepedophilic adolescent molesters. We have no good data on what percentage of adolescent molesters have a long-standing deviant arousal to children as opposed to a transitory episode of deviance occurring at the time of their offenses. Marshall and Eccles (1990) conclude from their literature review that the majority of adolescent sex offenders do not have deviant arousal. It seems likely that pedophilic offenders are concentrated in residential settings because of the courts' tendency to send the more serious offenders to placement. It seems logical that a significant segment of boys seen for sex offenses in outpatient practices are not pedophiles.

One of the particularly optimistic suggestions of the research literature is the idea that sexual preferences and patterns become fixed in adolescence rather than in much earlier life (Bateson, 1978) (Feldman and MacCulloch, 1971) (Storms, 1981). My own clinical experience is that boys seem to have a great deal of plasticity in their sexuality during adolescence, a plasticity which steadily decreases as they approach adulthood.

If this reading of the data is accurate, those treating adolescent molesters will encounter some young men whose deviant sexual acts with children were indeed an aberration in their general developmental struggle, an aberration which can be relatively easily treated and resolved. It is my hypothesis that a significant percentage of adolescent molesters are not wrestling with pedophilia, but can be regarded as manifesting some type of disorder of masculinity along the lines discussed earlier in this work.

Two ideas have exciting implications for those who treat adolescent molesters. One is that sexual orientation, including an orientation to young children, is not yet fixed in adolescence. The other is that most of the problems seen by those who treat adolescent molesters, including the problems of boys who are developing toward pedophilia, are essentially manifestations of some kind of disorder in the development of male identity. These ideas have significant implications for the way cases are managed and the way in which treatment is provided. The most exciting implication is that we can aim at a resolution of the underlying problem rather than simply containing the pathology.

TREATMENT IMPLICATIONS
OF THE DEVELOPMENTAL MODEL

The details of how problems in male development lead to molesting were discussed in some detail in Chapter Four. They will not be repeated here. An understanding of the developmental model leads to a number of inferences about what kind of treatment should be provided. Following the suggestion of ego psychology and psychodynamic thinking in general, the basic treatment need is to reactivate the adolescent's developmental struggle and help to resume and complete his aborted masculine development. This can probably only be done in the context of a therapeutic or treatment alliance between the therapist and the adolescent. It must be an alliance that involves both transference and empathy. Treatability by this model indeed must be defined by the ability of the adolescent to form and sustain such a relationship. An inability to form this kind of relationship is a diagnostic indicator that the standard model is probably a more appropriate way of dealing with the problem.

Both the literature and clinical experience suggest that the father-son relationship is vitally important in male development. This truism will probably elicit very little controversy. One of the implications of father problems in this population is that it is most desirable to have a male therapist and to work on male bonding issues as a key part of successful treatment. To my knowledge, this issue has not been raised in the treatment of adolescent molesters. It has, however, been raised by those treating male victims of sexual assault and homosexual males who are uncomfortable with their sexual orientation (Nicolosi, 1991) (Dimock, 1990). Both of these writers stress the need for an empathic relationship with a fatherly male therapist and a group therapy relationship with other males as keystones of the treatment approach. Since both of these writers are dealing with patients who have major issues in their masculine development, their inferences can logically be extended into the treatment of adolescent molesters who have similar issues.

This does not mean that there is no role for female therapists in treating adolescent molesters. It does mean that, in the majority of cases, much of the treatment should be provided by a male therapist. Some work with a female therapist is desirable as a part of the overall treatment process in order to work on issues of relating to females, reality testing in a male/female context, and mother issues. Female therapists can also handle much of the process of therapy itself, including the teaching and interpretive elements, but they will have serious problems in helping the patient work through the most basic and essential male issues. Males with problems in their masculine development need male models with whom they can identify. They need to work on issues of developing nonsexualized, but affectionate, relationships with other males. They need a place where they can safely work out issues of cooperation and competition with a father figure.

THE CENTRALITY OF GROUP

The developmental approach to resolving the psychic conflicts which result in molesting suggest that group therapy with other males is an important part of the treatment process with this population. It provides an all male context in which to explore male relationships. Males do not behave the same when females are present. There is a strong tendency to flirt with the females and compete with other males when males are seen in a mixed group. Confessing a sexual weakness or inadequacy in a mixed group is extremely difficult. Even the presence of a female coleader slows progress on male issues. Such a group also helps reactivate the basic male issues with which the adolescent molester has often ceased to struggle. Peer therapy groups should mimic the peer groups which are endemic among boys throughout latency and adolescence. The therapist, of course, brings to such a group a structure and purpose not present in the more loosely organized peer group. Such a group can unleash an almost tribal process of initiation, growth, and change.

SEXUAL ORIENTATION AND TREATMENT

Many who first listen to my ideas during formal presentations conclude that the course of choice would be to help many of these boys accept what appears to be an unrecognized or unwanted homosexuality. This is rarely what the patients themselves want. Overwhelmingly, adolescent males who molest younger children do not wish to be homosexual and will quite explicitly state that their goal is heterosexuality. Many will state that they consciously prefer pedophilia with younger females to homosexuality if that is their choice.

The first rule of psychotherapy is to start where the patient is at and to help him work toward his goals. On the few occasions when I have veered away from this and encouraged more acceptance of homosexuality by boys in treatment or by the treatment group, it has evoked a strong negative transference and has been labeled as attempting to transform the boy or the group into homosexuals. This creates an almost unresolvable treatment impasse.

Nonetheless, there are some boys who will need this kind of help. In some cases, it may be necessary to take them out of their group and see them only individually or to refer them to a group for boys with strong homosexual inclinations who are exploring the possibility that they may be homosexual.

It is important to distinguish the problem I am addressing. I am speaking about adolescent molesters, not gay adolescents who have not accepted their homosexuality. They are not the same thing. I only rarely encounter a boy who is comfortably bisexual or homosexual. Adolescent molesters are, as a general rule, not boys who are homosexual and not accepting it. They are young males but who have severe conflicts centering around fears that they may be gay. Where this dynamic prevails, much of their acting out can be interpreted as a desperate maneuver to assure themselves that they are heterosexual.

SUCCESS AND RECIDIVISM

A reviewer of the original edition of this work commented that he would like some indication as to how successful my approach was. That seemed like a reasonable request and/or criticism. I will share such statistics as I have. I have been in specialized practice with adolescent molesters and young male victims of sexual assault since 1984. I have seen a total of 336 young offenders (excluding those who came only once or twice). Of those, 144 were in residential settings and 192 residing in nonresidential settings in the community. Of that population, I am aware of 6 who have reoffended as of the end of 1994. That calculates out to a 2 percent rate of recidivism.

A source of added optimism is the fact that none of the reoffenses have occurred since 1989 when I started using the more specific male developmental orientation. When offenses have reoccurred, the most common situation involved siblings where the court or child protection authorities had decided to leave the perpetrator and victim in the home. One of the other reoffending boys was living in a group home with younger males, another high-risk situation.

Obviously, there are problems with this data. Everyone is aware of undetected offenses. We find out that our patients have reoffended if they are arrested or if they tell us they have reoffended. This leaves a great deal of room for offenses to occur about which we have no knowledge. Additionally, I screen out cases from the community that seem to be high-risk. I often have the opportunity to make a recommendation to the court regarding residential versus outpatient treatment and frequently divert the high-risk cases into residential facilities. The age of my clientele also gives them many years to reoffend. Some may do so long after I have retired from practice.

Even if my calculated reoffense rate is much higher than 2 percent, it is still in line with or below the recidivism rates for programs that have been studied. In addition to a formalized rate of recidivism, there are other ways of measuring success. In looking at my clientele, I consider their ability to form long-term, intimate, and ultimately sexual, relationships with peers to be one of the best prognostic indicators for a good outcome. When they begin to date and show a strong interest in individuals in their own age range, I am encouraged. Higher self-esteem and a strong sense of masculinity are also good prognostic indicators. The ability to form a treatment alliance with the therapist and with peers in group is also a good indicator of a positive outcome. When boys feel secure enough to discuss previously unknown things about themselves, such as their more intimate sexual feelings, deviant sexual impulses and fantasies, and even undetected previous offenses, I am encouraged about the outcome. At the present writing, about 70 percent of the boys I see respond at least by the end of their treatment in the ways outlined above.

CONCLUDING THOUGHTS

In this chapter I have outlined something very different from the standard model. My problem with the standard model is that it does not aim at deep and enduring change in the adolescent molester. Combining the insights of ego psychology and a psychodynamically-derived model of male development allows us to put together a program of real change for adolescents with enough ego strength to benefit. No one makes claims of this nature for behavioral-cognitive techniques.

These techniques, so widely lauded in the sex offender literature, have the implication that molesting is a problem like alcoholism or diabetes, a problem that can be managed, but never fully resolved. Boys who come to treatment as adolescents deserve an opportunity to work on their problems in a way that may offer an opportunity for resolution rather than symptom control. A boy with an entrenched paraphilia probably cannot abandon it. Those who come to treatment with a lesser degree of sexual pathology do have an opportunity to do more than just contain the problem. Adolescence is a window of opportunity, a time when sexual orientation for many boys is still in flux. For these reasons, teenage boys who molest need to be carefully assessed. Those who can be treated in a way that will resolve the problem should be offered such treatment.

My argument is not that all adolescent sex offenders should be treated with psychodynamic techniques. It is that, particularly in outpatient settings, boys who are amenable to this approach should be identified and the standard model of treatment modified to take advantage of the opportunity their greater psychic strength. If after careful diagnosis, a true paraphilia is found to be present and entrenched, the standard behavioral-cognitive techniques should be employed.

Even where the therapeutic alliance and other traditional mental health techniques are employed, behavioral-cognitive elements can be integrated into the overall treatment as important supplemental techniques.

There is no reason that boys cannot be exposed to the best of both psychodynamic treatment and behavioral-cognitive treatment in the course of a comprehensive and meaningful treatment program. The problem is not the presence of behavioral-cognitive techniques in the treatment of sex offenders, but with the routine absence of psychodynamic ones where they are indicated.

Chapter Nine

SPECIAL GROUPS FOR ADOLESCENT MOLESTERS

The majority of professionals specializing in the treatment of adolescent molesters feel that group therapy is the treatment of choice. If only one modality is going to be used, it should be group. The reasons for this are multiple. Adolescent molesters are inclined to deny and minimize their offenses. The use of group allows the mobilization of peer pressure to secure a candid discussion of the offense. Teenagers are good at picking up each other's evasions and manipulations. Once a suitable group culture has been established, adolescents who molest are not reluctant to challenge each other on these maneuvers.

Anyone who has worked with a group of adolescent molesters has seen a typical sequence. Boys enter the group either denying or minimizing. They are evasive about anything involving sex. In a well run group, pressure is exerted on these young men, and they gradually become more honest. Eventually they become leaders in this process, helping other young men to follow in their own footsteps.

CASE EXAMPLE

Antonio S.

Antonio's case is typical. This young man is a low functioning offender who, in fact, attempted penetration on his eight-year-old sister about twenty times. He also acknowledged oral copulation with her. This young man came into the group admitting only fondling. He told a story in which the victim had blackmailed him into committing the offense. She supposedly demanded sex in exchange for not telling his father and stepmother about misdemeanors in other areas of his life.

This young man's story was unusually crude and unsophisticated. The group pointed out the inconsistencies and contradictions in his stories. After about four sessions, he finally admitted what he had done. He broke down into tears saying that he felt like "shit" and was having

141

suicidal impulses. This same session brought out a recurrent fantasy in which a man was hung up by a rope alongside of a nude female. As soon as his penis became erect, the penis was shot off by another man standing a distance away.

This kind of material would have never, in any likelihood, been elicited in individual sessions with this young man. It took long, consistent, and heavy pressure from peers to bring it out. The new data about how the offender really feels both explains his denial and opens him to treatment. The fantasy suggests that he feels fatally tempted to molest again. Without this information, prognosis for treatment would be quite poor. Without group, the information would not be available.

Another area of routine denial involves masturbation. To listen to a group of teenage molesters, one would assume that no adolescent male ever masturbated. Almost without exception, boys come into the group saying they never do. This statement is expected by long-term group members. It often results in outbursts of laughter and comments such as, "That's what I said when I came in here." This kind of pressure often immediately results in an admission that, "perhaps, well, sometimes I do." Eliciting this information is quite important. Masturbation fantasies are revealing and indicative of the nature of a young man's problem. If they are to be explored, the fact of masturbation must be admitted.

Another boy came into group admitting his offense candidly, but denying any masturbation. Steady group pressure resulted in no admission of current masturbation. The young man, however, did gradually acknowledge that he had masturbated in the past. The therapist made a guess that the reason for discontinuance of masturbation was that it was connected with homosexual fantasies. The young man reticently admitted that this had been the case. He was desperately determined not to continue the practice because of its connection in his mind with homosexuality. This again is material that would likely not have emerged without peer pressure in a group setting.

The reasons that adolescent molesters respond better to peer confrontation than to confrontation by a single adult therapist are multiple. There is the simple fact that greater number of individuals expressing disbelief undermines the confidence of the offender in his ability to conceal what he has done. Additionally, there is an age factor. Teenagers are notoriously more responsive to their peers than to adults. They are, in general, anxious for the approval of peers and fearful of their rejection. To see adolescent molesters in group takes advantage of this phenomenon.

So far, the importance of confrontation has been stressed. Quality group treatment offers support as well. Adolescent molesters usually feel that, sexually speaking, they are freaks. This attitude is conditioned by the family environment in which they grew up. Their parents are rarely comfortable discussing sex. When they do, the attitudes they express are rigid and traditional.

It is not only their families that make adolescent molesters feel outside the boundaries of the human race. Normal teenagers are contemptuous of molesters. To be labeled "Chester the Molester" is one of the worst fates that can befall an adolescent. Needless to say, other boys who have molested do not go around talking about it. It is easy for a young offender to feel that he alone has these feelings and problems.

Group treatment provides immediate relief from this sense of isolation. Relief from anxiety is, in and of itself, therapeutic. Anxiety is crippling. It can stop emotional growth and lead to acting out while in a state of panic rather than attempting to think through and work out problems. Treatment cannot really begin until the molester's level of anxiety has been brought down sufficiently so that he can concentrate on therapy. Some degree of anxiety and conflict is necessary for successful treatment of any problem. The crippling anxiety which characterizes the adolescent molester at the onset of treatment is not useful.

The first benefit of group treatment is to create a climate in which the offender can begin to work on his problems. Upon entering the room for his first session, the teenage offender realizes at once that several other young males in the world are in the same boat. An established group will have senior members who have come a long way. They can reassure the new member that progress is possible and that a molesting problem can be overcome.

Both the "old-timers" in a group and the therapist provide models of emotional honesty. This is helpful in discussing the difficult issues which must be dealt with in group. It is the key to getting boys to discuss homosexuality, perhaps the hardest issue ever tackled in an adolescent male group. One or two boys, in most well-functioning groups, can be counted on as catalysts for such discussion.

For a long time, I had an intelligent, articulate offender in one of my outpatient groups. He was genuinely and openly bisexual. He also enjoyed being the rebel and gadfly in the group. One of his great pleasures was to announce his bisexuality to new members almost as soon as they walked into the room. He was always well accepted by group members. Strangely enough, in the homophobic world of adolescent molesters, he became a group leader. As such, he provided an example that emotional honesty does not result in rejection. He also became a living demonstration of the principle that a person can be loved even if he has socially unacceptable feelings.

Here the therapist can easily be trapped between Scylla and Charyldis. On the one hand, if a norm of free expression does not prevail, group discussion will not be meaningful. On the other hand, if child molesting is discussed with no implication that the behavior is negative and destructive, the treatment group could take a turn in the direction of developing a collective attitude that such behavior is acceptable. When a group develops this kind of negative internal value system, the results can undermine the very purpose for which the group was formed. Making a careful distinction between the offender, who is a worthwhile human being, and his acts, which are reprehensible, is a working compromise which allows for a patient's emotional growth without reinforcing his already delinquent and antisocial tendencies.

Discussing the experience of victimization at the hands of an older male is surrounded by as many taboos for teenage males as talking about their own homosexual feelings. Here again, group therapy facilitates discussion. Most groups of adolescent molesters will consist at least 50 percent of boys who have been molested by older males at some point in their life. This fact encourages disclosure. It also lets the young offender know that he is not unique in this experience. Once the issue is opened up, the male victim can explore feelings of rage and shame that are almost universal when boys are sexually exploited by older males.

THE "NUTS AND BOLTS" OF GROUP TREATMENT

So far, this discussion has centered on the theoretical reasons for group treatment. Any clinician looking at this material must wonder, "Now that I've decided to do a group, what do I do next? How do I set up a group, and how do I keep it going successfully?" The most basic questions involve how often the group should meet, and for how long. For outpatient groups, a frequency of once a week has been my standard practice. Once a week has become customary for nonpsychoanalytic outpatient treatment. It is also the frequency that most outpatient molesters tolerate the best. If I try to meet more than once a week with this kind of patient, they run out of things to talk about. True, this is resistance, but resistance also tells us how much a patient can handle. As such, it is something a therapist needs to take into account in treatment planning. Meeting more often than once a week also generates resistance in parents. It raises the cost of treatment as well as the amount of time and energy necessary to transport the adolescent to treatment.

On a more clinical level, a frequency of more than once a week might overload the family system and the adolescent's ability to adjust to it. In many cases, adolescent molesters seem to have more ability to change than their parents. If the child changes too rapidly, it may leave him out of balance with the family system and cause problems in other areas of his life. The pace of treatment needs to be slowed in these cases in order to allow the family to adjust to changes in the offender.

There is room for flexibility in the duration of group sessions. Generally, for older adolescents with a reasonable level of maturity, the group should last about 90 minutes. This allows time to get through resistance and down to serious group work. The last fifteen minutes of the group is often the most productive time of the entire session. With the more immature or younger adolescents, sessions of one hour often are all they will productively use. Very hard working groups or groups above the optimal size should be allowed to go on for two or more hours.

Four to eight members is the optimal size. Reality will create situations where only two or three members may be in a group due to graduations, a slow down in referrals, etc. I believe that these very small groups can be productive if well composed. If at least one, and hopefully all, of the boys in a small group are talkative, it can produce some very nice dynamics. Such groups are much more intimate and informal. They allow more time to be spent on each individual. If, however, the two or three members of a group are withdrawn, depressed, and/or schizoid, it can be a trying and unproductive experience for therapist and patients. When my groups get very small, I consider cutting the amount of time to one hour.

GROUP LEADERSHIP

The kind of group described here requires a professionally trained therapist for its operation. The National Task Force on Sexual Offending (1993) recommends a male/female team to lead the group and favors coleadership of sex offender groups. I believe, however, that there are reasons to question the universal application of this recommendation.

My remarks apply to the kind of outpatient group I am describing here, not a residential group for sophisticated offenders in a correctional type institution. I believe that, for at least a significant part of its duration, the group leadership should be male. There are several reasons for this inclination. The most important is that it will be very difficult to accomplish the kind of work described in earlier chapters with female leadership or female/male coleadership.

A part of the restorative process for boys with problems in male development is to go back and get some of the all male peer group and father/son interactions which either did not occur at the developmentally appropriate time or were not fully used by the boy at the proper time in his life. The presence of a female therapist in such a group will probably prevent it from being the kind of experience advocated by Nicolosi (1991) for males with ego dystonic homosexuality and Dimock (1990) for adult males molested as children. I have come to believe that there is a great deal of value in this kind of group experience for at least the higher functioning outpatient molesters, and that it is worth sacrificing some of the benefits of a female coleader in order to achieve these other goals.

A female coleader generally slows down the process of disclosure. It is much harder for adolescent males to discuss their feelings of sexual inadequacy and perversion with a female present. Exploration of this reluctance often shows that males who are victims of sexual assault feel that their masculinity has been spoiled by what happened to them. To help preserve some sense of masculinity, they need to present a facade of machismo to important females in their life. Hence they strut and posture and fail to get down to business when a female is present in the group.

Even boys who have not been victimized are reluctant to discuss sexual issues with a woman present. They shy away from using street language. They will watch a female leader carefully to see how she is reacting to each sexual remark. After an initial "honeymoon," boys in the group will make sexual remarks deliberately to shock the female therapist. They may ask prying questions about her sexual life. Some may be blatantly seductive. To see that a woman does not collapse in the face of such questioning or attempts at shock has value in itself.

In the 1987 edition of this book, I weighed the advantages and disadvantages of the male/female coleadership team. I came down then on the side of coleadership as the ideal. At that writing, I was coleading a group with a very competent female colleague. This was my highest functioning group. Not long after the publication of the first edition, my female colleague left the group. Shortly after her departure, boys began to disclose things they had been hiding for as much as a year. In a candid discussion of the issue at that time, the group expressed a strong preference for a single male leadership.

Anyone familiar with the 1987 edition will notice that I have put much more emphasis on male issues. Male development and the role of fathers have emerged as key issues in my thinking about why boys become molesters. The rediscovery of the role of the father in the boy's life is a major trend in modern American culture. My changing emphasis on group leadership reflects a shift to a focus on male bonding, fathering, and the male peer group as restorative for boys whose maleness has been damaged. There is always a risk of excess in such a process. I can see significant benefits in having a female coleader in a group. I simply feel that the deficits of a female presence outweigh the benefits for the kind of boys I see and the kind of groups I run.

Although I favor the all male group, it is not without problems. The creation of a totally male peer group can be difficult for boys who are prone to homosexual panic. Boys in an offender group who have been molested by men will relate in complex and difficult ways to the male therapist. Most typically, they have the love-hate relationship that is often found in the relationship between male victims and their molesters. If boys were molested in an aggressive and assaultive way, they might have a real chip on their shoulder about males in general. Boys may project their own homosexual yearnings onto the therapist and feel that he is sexually interested in them. Group therapy, fortunately, dilutes these sexualized transferences. In this atmosphere, it is often possible to help the adolescent resolve his issues of eroticized, and wrathful transference to other males. This, in and of itself, is a major treatment goal. It allows the molester to begin to free himself from what, up to that point, has been a major source of shame and a driving dynamic in his molesting behavior. I have only once had to remove a boy from group because of unresolvable sexualized transferences. This twelve-year-old openly declared himself to be homosexual and propositioned older boys in my waiting room. Usually, the diluted quality of the transference in group allows it to be spread over several members and the leader. This dispersed transference is easier to resolve and usually generates less anxiety than such a transference in individual therapy.

My opting for the all male group has not been without ambivalence. Much is given up when there is no female presence. It allows boys to explore some of their questions about femininity with a female. Most of these boys have been neglected or mistreated in their relationships with adult females. Many have a pervasive hatred and contempt for females. The presence of an empathic female leader also allows for a corrective emotional experience. They will often accept comments and interpretations from a female that they will not accept from a male leader.

A group led by a single female or female coleadership is probably the most difficult of all situations for both leaders and patients. I frankly see no sense in it. It flies in the face of all the recently accumulated data about the importance of the father in male development. It is inconsistent with the view that molesting is a disorder of masculinity best prevented by repairing the damaged masculinity. There are also practical problems. The degree of hostility which some of these young men hold for females is intense. Most feel it is unmasculine to take orders from a female. For these reasons the female therapist has a harder time maintaining order in group. Without caution, very negative dynamics can develop. Molesters who resent females provoke the female therapist. If she responds with hostility and a need to control the group even more, the struggle may turn into a battle of transference and countertransference in which the boys see the efforts of the female therapist to control them as one more assault on their maleness.

GROUP RULES

Rules should be kept to the minimum necessary to preserve order and to allow for freewheeling discussion of emotional and sexual issues. I do not publish a list of rules but deal with issues as they come up. The best way for a leader to maintain order and control is to establish a rapport and then communicate an attitude that demands respect. Adolescent molesters seem hungry for authority lightly wielded by a calm, secure father figure. I rarely have discipline problems in group.

As to what cannot be tolerated, it is mostly the obvious. There should be no fighting in group or outside the group. No intimidation, verbal or otherwise, of group members. No cussing at, or other gross disrespect of, others. I discourage socialization outside the group because on a few occasions, it came to my attention that it might turn into a sexual encounter. I cannot enforce this rule, but warn boys what might happen if they break it. Boys are asked not to come under the influence of alcohol or drugs. They cannot damage the physical plant. For practical reasons, I only allow one boy out of the room at a time to use the restroom. I do not otherwise restrict leaving the room. If trips out of the group are too frequent, it becomes a topic of discussion.

There should be no rules on the nature of the language used in discussion. This may seem obvious to sophisticated therapists. New therapists, however, often ask, "Should I let them use profanity in group?" Profanity is part of the natural language of this population. To prohibit it creates a series of problems. Some adolescent molesters know only street slang with which to discuss sexuality. They simply do not know enough medical jargon to discuss sex in proper terms. To prohibit street language creates a stilted and artificial environment. It erects a barrier between patient and therapist.

It is of vital importance that the male group leader portray an image of competence and that he demand respect. Teenagers will test any adult to see what they will put up with. The tests come with violating major rules, numerous violations of small rules, and direct or indirect insults aimed at the leader. These need to be addressed clinically. When a boy tests by making remarks designed to devalue the leader, it is important to make an appropriate response right away. The proper response is, "I don't treat you that way and you may not treat me that way." This usually stops the testing. If it does not, the teenager should be seen privately and told he will be removed from the group if this continues.

The reason for such firm handling of insults and demeaning remarks is that the male therapist must offer an identification model that the adolescents admire. No one benefits from identification with a devalued person who allows others to walk over him. A male leader also represents adult masculinity to teenagers in group. Since these boys have a major problem in their masculinity, it is crucial that they be offered a positive example of adult masculinity. American teenage males value men who respect themselves. One way self respect is modeled is by not letting the group devalue the leader directly or indirectly. If the leader allows the group to spin out of control and permits the group to implement an agenda of resistance, the group will interpret this as weakness. Nothing useful, and much destructive, will happen if this kind of climate develops in a group.

The group leader needs to create a fine balance in the wielding of authority. He must communicate that he likes the teenagers but will not tolerate nonsense or devaluation. This kind of stance makes it relatively easy to create the proper balance where the leader is in charge, but encourages free expression of feeling and welcomes the boys' coleadership as long as it is responsible.

The countertransference problem here is that some leaders expect to be elevated on a pedestal and to be above criticism. This is an attempt to gratify their own narcissism and control needs. Balance requires that the leader encourage healthy individuation and exploration. Rules apply to the structure of the group, not its contents. Adolescents should be allowed to challenge the opinions of the therapist as long as they do not cross a boundary into devaluation. If the leader creates the right climate and selects boys who are workable via this approach, it is easier to do this than it might seem. If teenage boys respect a male leader, they only occasionally attempt to devalue him. They have a stake in helping the leader maintain his dignity. If this approach works, the therapist becomes one of the teenage boys' major models of what it is to be an adult man. They will test and try to get you to slip up, but they know they too have lost if you fail their tests.

FIGHTS

Occasionally, tension gets very high between certain boys and the risk of a fight develops. At this point, it is necessary to intervene forcefully. A clear statement that a fight is unacceptable and will result in one or both boys being expelled and reported to the probation officer is indicated. Usually, it is possible to spot building tension far in advance and deal with it clinically long before it erupts into violence. In the years I have been conducting groups, I have only had boys hit each other twice.

On one occasion, a thirteen-year-old repeatedly harassed a much larger sixteen-year-old with an explosive personality make-up. I miscalculated and let the incident go too long and the sixteen-year-old gave one powerful shove pushing the younger boy against a wall. He then sat down. On the second occasion, a large boy who with a pattern of bullying others was teasing a younger, passive boy. The older boy made a cutting remark about the other boy's new girlfriend. He must have assumed that his size and the younger boy's reputation for cowardice would allow him to get away with this. The teenage male code of honor requires all but the most cowardly to respond with verbal and/or physical force to such provocation. The younger boy rose quickly from his seat and pushed the older boy over in his chair. The group admired the younger boy for his unexpected courage. They convinced me that the provocation was ample. The incident was not repeated.

GROUP CLIMATE

One of my tactical goals in group is to create a climate much like an informal adolescent peer group. I want maximum freedom to speak on any topic the boys wish to discuss. I hope the discussion will be as natural as if an adult were not present. The purpose of this is to get a free flow of feelings, thoughts, and fantasies. Knowing what is going on in the adolescents' affective life is essential to any effective treatment intervention.

To create the necessary climate of free expression, a number of devices are necessary. In essence, the intent is to help the boys feel that the group is, within the boundaries described in the last section, a friendly and supportive place where they can be spontaneous. The intent of the limited list of rules is to keep as many boys as possible from locking into a transference-laden power struggle with me as the group leader. The absence of a rule on cussing (except at others) sends the message that this group has something in common with less formal assemblages of males.

The feeling of informality is reenforced by the setting of the group. My office is a converted house. The group is held in what used to be the living room. I have preserved the living room quality of this office. When I worked for an agency, I did the group in the kitchen, the only informal room in the building. To promote good feeling, I serve food (donuts and lemonade) regularly. I know this is not health food, but I have had no luck with fruit. These are the kinds of things teenagers would be eating in a peer group they arranged. A second reason for this is that adolescent males are always hungry. I prefer that they concentrate on therapy rather than their hunger. To stress the value of each group member, birthdays are celebrated. For this occasion, pizza is served.

There are several other techniques for creating a free and spontaneous climate in group. Sometimes, group activities are selected by consensus rather than by the leader's choice. Allowing the boys to pick between alternatives is a good way to permit some democracy while being sure some work is done. I also, from time to time, allow members to lead the group for part of the session. Some experience in leading the group is required for graduation. This communicates that I do not want to revel in my authority role, that I want each boy to develop his own leadership capacities, and that I will share leadership with boys who are able to handle it. I believe that letting a boy lead the group also gives him some understanding of the difficulty of the task and hence some empathy for me. Obviously the leader should intervene if a boy takes the group in a negative direction. There are some boys who will need to be told that they are not ready to lead the group.

Generally, these techniques work. They insure the free flow of information that is necessary to find out what is going on within the psyche of adolescent molesters, and what they need in the way of therapeutic intervention. These techniques would not work well with a highly delinquent group. Such adolescents would probably take advantage of the situation. This is one reason that I have stressed that the ability to form a treatment alliance is a key factor in whether a molester is treated with these techniques or with the more standard behavioral-cognitive techniques.

When the flow of referrals results in a higher level of delinquency in a group, I incorporate more elements from the standard model. Delinquency is a matter of degree, another continuum. All molesters are, to some degree, delinquent. Many of the molesters referred for outpatient therapy, and some in residential programs, retain the ability to form a treatment bond with a therapist and work in the manner described here. The greater the degree of delinquency and alienation from adults and authority, the less likely is this approach to work.

The techniques outlined here are also less effective with depressed or withdrawn adolescents. It is important to try to manage group composition so that boys with these problems do not constitute a majority. The depressed or schizoid adolescent seems to benefit in this kind of group as long as the group culture is strong enough to carry him along. Many eventually emerge from their isolation. If that does not happen over time, such a boy may do better with individual treatment at least until he progresses enough to use the group.

GROUP TECHNIQUES

Teenage males are notoriously difficult therapy patients. Those who molest are among the most difficult. They usually come to group full of shame and are reluctant to disclose what they are thinking and feeling. If a therapist tries to run a group for adolescent molesters as a typical, talk-oriented mental health group, little will be said. Over the years, I have devised a number of techniques to elicit a free flow of spontaneous talk as well as the sharing of feelings and fantasies.

Typically, a group session begins with an invitation for anyone to share important developments in their life. If the therapist knows about important issues via the parents, probation officer, etc., this is the time to bring them up. This is a good time to ask if anyone has experienced any sexual feelings which trouble them.

If there is a new boy in group, after the introduction above, the regular group members are asked to share their offense and whether they are victims of molestation themselves. This is not a popular activity. Some boys resist. The best procedure is to point out that the reason to do this is to help the new boy so he knows he is not alone and can get over his anxiety as quickly as possible. The new boy is then asked to share what he has done and whether he is a victim.

The reason to deal so swiftly with the new member's perpetration and victimization is that this is a stage at which the group can easily lose them. New boys are usually a nervous wreck at the beginning of the first session. The idea of coming into a group of strangers and talking about sex is terrifying. Some boys beg not to be put in group and insist that they will do better if they have only individual therapy. By dealing with the most frightening issue almost immediately, the new member's anxiety is almost immediately dissipated. The new boy's statements usually elicit a number of questions from older members. These are generally supportive if the group perceives the boy as having been honest. If not, a kind of cross-examination may follow.

It is important, as a part of the group process, that members know why other boys are there. This includes some details about their offenses and their victimization. It is astounding how this gets buried if the therapist does not take some steps to be sure boys remain aware of each others' key issues. Forgetting why peers are present is a part of the denial process for adolescent molesters. Forgetting about the problems of others is also reflective of a narcissistic preoccupation with self. If allowed to continue, it will undermine the group's ability to form bonds of empathy among the members. This is an aspect of male bonding and is part of the curative process taking place in the group. Forgetting is also part of the denial process which is a typical and pathological way in which molesters try to deal with the shame generated by their behavior. Breaking down denial and preventing its re-emergence is another of the key curative mechanisms in the group process.

It is vital to the curative process of the group that the therapist take steps to be sure that the group does not collectively "forget" why they are present. In part, this is implemented throughout the level system which will be discussed later. There is, however, a more specific way of dealing with this issue. In this initial warm-up stage of the group meeting, the therapist can randomly ask boys to pick two or three group members and tell why they are there and if they are victims.

The invitation to bring up new business, review old business, the introduction of new members, and sometimes a brief review of who is present and for what reason constitutes the warm-up period for the group. In this period, the therapist is very active in getting the group process going. Usually by this time, group members have relaxed and can begin a more spontaneous discussion. This may be in the form of questions or statements to each other or to the therapist. Many of the issues brought up in this section of the group are of a sexual nature. On their own, however, boys usually avoid bringing up deviant issues in themselves. They may, however, bring them up in others. Groups typically have one or more members who are suspected of being gay. This issue may come up at this time. Some management by the therapist is necessary at this point.

Dynamically, groups tend to deal with problematic issues by focusing them on one member and scapegoating the member. This is another of the pathological methods of dealing with one's own problems. It involves both projection and denial and therefore has no healing value. If boys continue to use this kind of defense mechanism as a means of self-restoration, their sexual problems are likely to get worse. When scape-goating begins, the therapist needs to intervene. The process and its goal needs to be identified so the boys know what they are doing. This typically slows it down.

What is typically scapegoated is homosexuality. This fits with the formulations offered earlier about why boys molest. One way of dealing with this in group is to teach the Kinsey Scale to the boys. This scale assumes that homosexual interest is a matter of degree rather than either you are gay or straight. Zero reflects a boy who is totally straight. A six rating would mean a teenager who has absolutely no interest in the opposite sex. As part of group discussion, sometimes boys are asked to place themselves on this scale. Sometimes boys will be asked to rate each other or will ask me to rate each member of the group. I will only do this with the permission of the individual involved in order to respect for the adolescent's privacy and dignity. For the therapist to do this without the boy's consent seems somewhat assaultive to me.

Such a self-assessment is also required for movement through the level system. Using this rating scale forces boys to think about homosexual issues within themselves rather than just projecting the conflict onto others. The scale is one of several means used to get boys to look at their own issues in the area of homosexuality. It has the effect of making this a suitable topic for discussion. Once the issue becomes a matter for more or less relaxed group discussion, group members begin to calm down about homosexuality. Over time, they begin to see that having homosexual feelings, at one time or another, or even being bisexual or gay, is not the end of the world. This can start boys down a path to greater self-acceptance and reduce the intensity of conflicts about ego-dystonic homo-sexuality that have driven some of them to molest.

The process of free-form discussion with occasional therapist interven-tion should be allowed to continue as long as it is productive. It is at the end of this stage when the group is generally into an active, but open and spontaneous interaction that boys should be invited to share any dreams they have. This request belongs here because dreams are among the most difficult material for adolescent molesters to share. They are most likely to do so after they have been in the group session long enough to take some risks.

An important element in the format of adolescent molester groups is a level system. This can be de-emphasized in periods where a lot of good, spontaneous work is being done by the group. It can be dusted off for more focus at times when the group appears to be bogging down. For this kind of group, I have devised a level system consisting of five stages. Level one is an entry level for boys with a high degree of denial and minimal group involvement. Level five is for boys who have mastered most of the group's tasks and are about to leave.

Moving through the levels involves learning a lot about the other boys, their offenses and their victimizations. It requires that they learn about the impact of molesting on victims. They must analyze why they committed their offenses and what will keep them from offending in the future. They must explore their own sexual orientation and interests. They must rate themselves on the Kinsey Scale and much more. This material is introduced gradually as the boys go upward through the level system. Attainment of level five is required for graduation. The level system itself is given to them in a handout and can be found in the appendix at the end of this work.

The use of a level system provides a built-in motivator to work and talk in group. Whenever a boy asks to take an exam for the next level, a wide-ranging group discussion follows since peers must vote on the boy's promotion. It forces boys to be concerned with why others are there. During slow periods in the group's life, it can provide some of the most meaningful discussion in which the group is willing to be engaged.

Mastering the information on this level system is related to the correction of thinking errors that is part of the standard model. I do not believe that this knowledge by itself will stop molesting, but awareness of the cognitive issues required to move through the group levels is an essential part of the treatment of sex offenders. To whatever extent adolescent molesters are acting out of ignorance, mastery of this cognitive material will help. More importantly, the level system forces boys to wrestle with the issues of emotion and relationship which I believe are truly curative.

THE USE OF DREAMS

Adolescent molesters vary greatly in the amount of dreaming they remember and their willingness to share these dreams. Boys in residential programs tend to dream more or be willing to tell more dreams in group than outpatients. When they are willing to share dreams, it is a great aid to treatment. I operate from the proposition that dreams represent a neurobiological process for problem solving along the lines developed by Cartwright (1977, 1978), Winson (1985), and Hobson (1988).

Hobson is a Harvard psychiatrist and neuroscientist. His interest is in the neurophysiology of the brain and how the brain produces and uses dreams. Winson is a professor of neuroscience at Rockefeller University. His interests parallel those of Hobson, but he adds a strong interest in the evolutionary biology of dreaming. Cartwright is a psychologist and dream researcher based at Rush University Presbyterian St. Luke's Hospital. She has devoted her career to sleep laboratory work on dreams. The explanations of the dreaming process these researchers have developed lift it out of the realm of the occult or Freudian dogmatism where it had previously languished. Unfortunately, their work seems little known and less incorporated into psychotherapy.

A detailed review of their work is far beyond the scope of this book. To grossly oversimplify their complex views, they all see dreaming as a process in which a key emotional problem is presented. Once the problem is presented, the brain scans its data bank for solutions to the problem. Typically, what is selected is the way a similar problem has been dealt with in the past. This is why human beings tend to repeat the same dysfunctional behaviors. Viewed in this perspective, dreams offer first a presentation of a key emotional problem with which the patient is confronted and then propose a solution to that problem. What better insight into the inner workings of a patient's psyche could we ask for? Once that knowledge is available, patient and therapist can raise the question as to whether the proposed solution is indeed the best answer. Therapy in this model consists of reprogramming the problem-solving software of the brain to come up with better solutions to emotion-laden problems.

The analysis and use of dreams in group therapy with adolescent molesters can require an immense amount of arcane insight into the nature of dream symbolism, but often the problem and the proposed answer are instantly obvious. A flasher in group used to share very brief dreams about flashing. The interpretation: I have an urge to flash. More subtly, I suspect that the urge to flash is some kind of answer to a problem of asserting himself as a male. The solution implied by this one-sentence dream? Flash! If he told the group, the group always said, "You want to flash." They instinctively identified the proposed solution. If the therapist interprets this sequence, it gives the patient an opportunity to consider consciously the merits of the proposed solution. He can then use his conscious ego to press an "override button" and not implement the proposed solution. Further group discussions can stress the maladaptive nature of this boy's repetitive solution to his masculinity problem, flashing. With time, I believe the software can be reprogrammed. In therapy with patients who are prolific dreamers, new and less pathological solutions to emotional problems begin to emerge in dreams as the treatment process continues.

A young man about to be terminated from a residential program brought in a dream which showed a fear of loss of control and a fear of paranoid psychosis as the principal foci. As a result of his dream, both this young man and his clinicians agreed that his stay in the program needed to be extended. This dream followed a period of outrageously provocative behavior directed at child care staff. These problems emerged when the young man was given a termination date. Bringing the material to group in the form of a dream allowed the issue to be put on the table and to be discussed frankly.

The problem presented was the adolescent's overwhelming anxiety about a premature termination. One of his solutions was to provoke staff so they would reconsider and not allow him to leave because of his "regressive" behavior. The other was to bring this dream to group. A group tuned into this use of dreams could be expected to tell him he was not ready to leave. Acting out to be retained in the program is a pathological resolution of the dilemma. It probably represents this boy's historical way of dealing with a problem, acting out and manipulating others. Bringing the dream to group involves a new way of dealing with a problem, sharing it with others, and letting them help in its resolution.

Most dreams are much more convoluted than the ones examined so far. When complex dream material is presented in group, the therapist should attempt to pick out the one or two important themes upon which to focus. The issue must be timely for the young man. Frequently, dream material is brought which deals with issues that the offender is not ready to face. For example, homosexual content should not be dealt with in the first few sessions. Dreams involving a fear of psychosis are similarly delicate. In this kind of situation, it is advisable to pick a more minor theme in the dream with which the adolescent molester is more able to deal. Eventually, most of these young men should be able to deal with all of the content of their dreams.

One way of being sure that interpretation of a dream is not more than the adolescent can deal with is to ask the dreamer for his own ideas about what the dream means. This is always the best starting place. Early in the process, boys may say they have no idea. Dreamers may be asked to assume that a specific person in the dream is himself or some important figure in their life. Given that information, the therapist can suggest that they attempt to understand the meaning of the dream. After listening to the patient's response, the group is invited to make suggestions about what they think the dream might mean. Over a period of time, some adolescent molesters become excellent analysts of dreams. They frequently pick up material which the therapist has missed. Obviously, some experience is necessary for a group to be able to do this. Boys in my groups have learned it simply by observing and listening.

Complex and convoluted dreams will probably never be thoroughly understood by therapist or group. After listening to the dreamer and the group, the therapist may wish to offer a synthesis of what the dream could mean focusing on the aspects most the dreamer is most ready to use. It is important to stress that the therapist's interpretation is not necessarily the definitive one but one of several impressions being offered for the patient's consideration. This often prevents an argument between therapist and molester about what the dream means. It also allows the young man to back away from content with which he absolutely cannot deal.

Once this process is completed, it is important to listen to the patient's final responses. If the therapist's synthesis leads to new ideas on the part of the patient or elaborations of material already discussed, it is most likely that the patient is able to use the material. Likewise if the interpretation allows the patient to link previously unconnected material, this is a confirmation that the clinician is on the right track. Analyses which help the patient recover previously repressed information are also confirming. Rages, denial, intense anxiety, or argumentation suggest that the patient is not ready to deal with the material. Denial may also mean that the therapist's interpretation is not accurate.

Adolescent molesters sometimes make up dreams to bring to group. This is partly a result of the fact that dreams are an expected part of group routine. It may also be a test to the therapist to see how gullible he is. Such dreams are usually not hard to spot. They are usually too rationally organized and too superficial to be real dream material. A gentle confrontation on the issue of faking is indicated. The reasons for such faking also need to be explored with the patient. One positive aspect of this process is that even a fabricated dream is fantasy material. It can be analyzed as such. It also might be analyzed in terms of the kind of image the molester is trying to put forward by means of conscious manipulation of the treatment process.

The dream presented below is an example of how a well functioning group deals with an extremely complex dream.

CLINICAL ILLUSTRATION

Manuel M.

Manuel is a fifteen-year-old originally treated in a victim group because of a long history of molestation by his own father. In the course of treatment, this young man admitted to molesting his younger brother. Manuel is in a secure residential setting. He makes frequent suggestive remarks and sexual overtures to other boys in the program. There are many paranoid features to his personality makeup.

In group, Manuel presented the following dreams: I am at Disneyland. I go to a plant shop where an old crone gives me a note. The note says this task must be completed within forty-eight hours. It does not identify the task.

When asked for associations, Manuel stated that all he could think of was that the old woman was very evil. He then said he had another dream which he had had recently but had not wanted to share. In this dream he was at Disneyland with his father. The father invited him into a secluded area of the park where he asks "Do you want to have some fun?" The father then pulls out a long tube and a condom. He says, "This is to have fun with." In the next sequence Manuel sees himself walking through Disneyland with the mirror image of himself following him and laughing at him.

Manuel's association to this dream was that he was first molested by his father while at Disneyland. A group member, aware of Manuel's conflicts with his mother, suggested that perhaps the old woman was his mother. The patient blandly denied any anger with his mother. He did, however, recall an additional detail from the dream. He had been driving along in a car. A television image of the old crone from Disneyland kept flashing in front of him.

I suggested to Manuel that perhaps an image of his mother had come to live within him as a part of himself and that this was the source of his self-hatred and self-criticism. Another group member at this point vented his own rage with his mother for betraying and abandoning him. Manuel dropped his bland facade and said, "I hate my mother, that cunt, slut, whore, bitch."

This is a good example of group members working together to help an offender resolve key issues that are brought into the group process by one member's dream. The issues here are multiple: being a victim, a victim of one's father, the sexualization and homosexual conflicts that arise out of victimization, hatred of mother, hatred of women, and the fear of psychotic collapse. The group commentary focuses on the identity of the old woman. As such, the group has collectively decided to deal with the mother issue. Manuel has received strong peer and therapist support for bringing out his most basic conflicts, fears, and wounds.

My interpretation offered at this point focused on the idea that the reason for his rage with his mother might be that Manuel blames her for allowing the father to sexually abuse him for a period of years without intervening. The patient's response to this was to say that the mother comes to the residential facility and pretends that she wants to help. But every time he goes home, she verbally attacks and berates him. He restated his hatred of her. Another agitated group member stated that he also hated his mother because she had divorced his father and then married a tyrannical and abusive stepfather.

This group interchange illustrates the major principles of using dream material in group. Manuel had never previously discussed his feelings about his mother. The dream allowed him to bring this issue up in a very direct way. It also deals with his molestation by his father and the very poor self-image that has resulted both from being molested by his father and rejected by his mother. My interpretations went both to his rage with his mother and his very low self-esteem. There is a covert paranoid quality to this dream material which was not dealt with. Manuel was able to accept his own explorations and my interpretations without adverse reaction. Other group members were able to focus on their own conflicts because of this discussion. I consciously chose not to press this offender to deal with issues he was not strong enough to face at this stage of treatment.

FANTASY AND PROJECTION AS TREATMENT TOOLS

The use of fantasy material in group is also important. Many workers in this field put great emphasis on masturbation fantasies. They are important. They indicate the current sexual aims and objects of the adolescent molester. They also indicate key conflict areas. However, there is probably nothing harder for any patient to discuss than a masturbation fantasy. Adolescent molesters are particularly sensitive in this area since many of their fantasies are antisocial. For this reason, it is often difficult to get them to honestly share masturbation fantasies. What is typically produced is a fantasy of heterosexual intercourse. The next easiest fantasy to share seems to be the mildly sado-masochistic fantasy involving females. This is most commonly manifest in a fantasy of being tied up by a female or tying up the female and having intercourse with her while she is so restrained. Fantasies of sex with other males or with young children are difficult to obtain. The former involves cutting through the young man's homophobia. The latter is often due to fear that any such fantasy will result in longer treatment or further punishment and disapproval.

Adolescent molesters say that they make a deliberate effort to suppress fantasies about other males or young children. I suspect in many cases this is true. In other cases, the fantasies are most likely present but not shared. To get this kind of material, a constant pressure must be put on the young offender. This is why the sharing of fantasies is built into the level system used in group.

Work with drawings can also be a useful tool in group. Boys who say they are interested in drawing can be asked to bring drawings to group for discussion. Occasionally, boys can be asked to draw in the group. A good exercise for boys who have been molested is to ask them to draw themselves as they felt at the time they were molested and as they feel now. A similar exercise can be done by asking them to draw their victim as they believe they felt at the time of the molest and how they feel now.

Drawing is a good technique for bringing out withdrawn boys and for working with the more resistant groups. With a group with several boys who have trouble with talking, the group can be conducted around a large table (or two card tables). The boys can be given drawing material and allowed to draw during discussion or a specific drawing exercise can be given. I once had to place a very nonverbal boy in a large group. He said nothing for weeks. I found out that he loved to draw. His assignment was to draw one picture a week in group and allow the group to discuss it. This got him meaningfully involved in the discussion. His drawings were extremely revealing of his mental state. One is reproduced in Chapter Six. A final note—drawings brought to group or made in group are always to be discussed in terms of their meaning. Drawing is a technique for dealing with the more resistant adolescent. I tend to use it more with younger boys or in periods when group culture is resistant to more a direct verbal approach.

Many adolescent molesters like to write. When they write, it is often an emotional poem or brief, emotion-laden prose. Examples are reproduced in Chapter Six. In some groups boys can be given small personal note-books on which they can write feelings, observations, or just doodle. I require that the notebooks be left at my office so that I can review them. Many boys use these to bring up issues they are afraid to approach more directly. Offenders in residential programs are often asked to keep jour-nals about their sexual feelings and fantasies as well as other emotionally important matters. This material can be brought to group and discussed.

STRUCTURED EXERCISES

Even in the best treatment situations, some adolescent molesters are not able to produce dreams or fantasies spontaneously. Those who are prolific producers of fantasy will, at times, run dry and produce nothing.

During quiet periods in the life of the group, structured exercises can be used to stimulate discussion. Even if a group is working actively, the use of these exercises can be valuable. It should be a routine part of every long-term treatment group. The reason for its inclusion as an essential treatment element is that structured exercises often turn up material that would otherwise not emerge. One form of structured exercise consists of a series of 3 × 5 cards with situations and questions described on each card. These cards can be designed by the clinician to focus the young offender's attention on a variety of issues.

They range from specific situations to general questions allowing a wide range of responses. Here are some samples from the box of 3 × 5 cards I use in my offender groups:

> Select a member of the group to represent your mother. Tell this person what you most like about her and what you most dislike about her.
>
> Name two things that make you very angry.
>
> You are at a family picnic. Also present is an eight-year-old male cousin whom you know has been molested. He asks you to show him how to find the restroom. You do so. Once inside, he asks if he can suck your penis. How do you feel? What do you do?
>
> Go around the group and give two words or ideas which describe each person in the group.
>
> You are walking down the street and you are approached by a homosexual male. How do you feel? What do you say and do?

This sample is by no means exhaustive. It covers the major types of questions included in the structured exercises. Questions like the first are to focus attention on issues about mother and family. The one about the male cousin is there to give some insight into how the offender would handle a high-risk situation. If his response is inadequate, the group can help him deal with it more effectively. Loosely structured questions such as "list two things that make you angry" are included as a kind of fishing trip. They sometimes take the adolescent and group into utterly unexpected territory. The importance of anger in the etiology of sex offending has been discussed elsewhere. This card gives the group an opportunity to see how this particular adolescent deals with anger issues.

The box should include questions about substance abuse to allow for exploration of problems in this area. The exercise involving giving one or two ideas or descriptive statements about each person in the group is an excellent way to explore intra-group relationships. The use of the 3 ×

5 cards is popular with adolescents. It usually results in an animated discussion. Often, the boys ask if they can continue to use the cards after the group has run out of its allotted time.

Many variations of this technique are possible. The therapist can select a card which he presents to a group member for a specific purpose. Cards can also be given out randomly by allowing the young man simply to reach into the box and pull out a card. Another variation is to allow one group member to select a card to present to another member. This latest variation is often productive. Sometimes young offenders perceive problem areas in other members not seen by the therapist. Their selection of cards is a way of translating this perception into group process. A group member may feel more at ease selecting a card and handing it to someone else in the group than he would confronting him directly. Recently, I have experimented with allowing group members to write their own cards for inclusion in the box. This also has been productive.

A dramatic example of new and unexpected material coming from this exercise occurred in a molester group. Tom had been in this group for 18 months. He drew a card which read as follows:

> This group is hiking in the mountains. You come to a fork in the trail. One fork leads down into desert country. It is twenty miles to the nearest road by this route. You are almost out of water and there is none along this trail. The trail is also infested with rattlesnakes. The other fork goes through deep forests. There are many branches of the trail ahead and it would be easy to get lost. The region is inhabited by grizzly bears. It is ten miles to the road ahead by this trail. How do you think your group would make a decision about which trail to use? What role would you take in making the decision?

This exercise was developed to explore leadership patterns within the group. Tom's first response was that he would be terrified in such a situation. He commented on his fear of both bears and snakes. He said that he would not trust his own judgment in this situation at all and would rely on one of the other group members. He commented that this boy really knew how to handle problems and that he would just trust that boy's judgment.

In reality, Tom knows as much about the wilderness as the boy he would follow. Both of these young men are in the same general area in terms of intellectual ability. Tom's response indicates that he is a follower, that he is prone to panic in stressful situations, and that he clings to others in a very dependent way in ambiguous and stressful situations. It also suggests that he decompensates rapidly under stress. His preferred coping mechanism is to cling to someone he perceives as a stronger figure. In all the time this boy had been in group, I had not picked up these personality traits. His accidental selection of this card allowed me to see these issues and to help him begin to deal with them.

Another form of structured exercise is to collect a series of pictures from magazines and other sources. These can be mounted on cardboard and kept in a box. As with the written exercises, pictures are selected to evoke important emotional themes. This exercise can be used in a variety of ways just as can the written exercises. When a boy is presented with a card or selects one on his own, he is asked to tell a story about what he sees. The themes emerging from the story are then discussed by the group. This is not as popular as the written exercises.

GUESTS IN GROUP

It is occasionally useful to bring special speakers into the group. Some therapists are experimenting with confrontations between victims and offenders in group. This can be productive. Every step, however, needs to be taken to protect the feelings of the victim. This kind of confrontation seems best integrated toward the end of treatment when molesters are beginning to work on victim awareness. At this stage, they have developed an ability to empathize with their victims. Ideally, they should have some interests in repairing the damage they have done to others.

On several occasions, I have invited an adult offender to come in for one session and share his experiences with the adolescents. Obviously, an adult offender brought into a group of adolescent molesters must be well on the way to his own rehabilitation. This kind of guest is useful early in the course of the treatment of the young molester. They may regard the comments and prognoses of the therapist as simply so much adult lecturing. Listening to a man who has been further down the same road they are on can be a sobering experience. The adult offender must be at a stage, however, where there is no glamorization of his offense or blaming of the victims.

Another variation on the guest theme is to bring in an adult victim who has been successfully treated and is living a successful life. This is very helpful for boys who are struggling with their own victimization. It gives them a ray of hope. Such adult victims usually speak highly of therapy and its results and can be a powerful source of motivation for juvenile offenders.

If the therapist is working with patients from different ethnic back-grounds, another use of guests is to be recommended. For example, as a white therapist, I do not know a great deal about life in the ghetto. I have been asked to treat a relatively large number of black offenders. At one point, these young men had me convinced that little went on in the ghetto besides a great deal of heterosexual intercourse. Needless to say, I was suspicious, but had no facts with which to back up my hunches. To deal with this issue, I invited a black counselor from a local boy's home to join me for several group sessions. This counselor was a streetwise young man who had grown up in a black community. He was very effective at confronting the distortions with which I had been presented. His presence also seemed to give the young men permission to talk about their fears about their own sexuality.

OTHER ISSUES IN GROUP

A major focus and covert goal of group treatment is to help adolescent molesters change their attitudes about sexual activity and sexual practices. There is an undercurrent of discomfort with all aspects of sexuality in the adolescent molester. Most of the young men referred to me have no sex experience except as victims themselves and as perpetrators with young children. Very few have previous sexual experience with a peer. Of those who claim such experience, I expect they may be covering up to shore up their sense of masculine adequacy. Those who seem to have real sexual experience with peers often describe shallow and exploitative episodes without commitment or caring about the partner. Much of the projective material produced by the younger or less mature boys I see suggests a great deal of fear of females and/or heterosexual intercourse. Their views about homosexuality have been presented throughout this book at length.

The big picture is of a group of boys who seem to be trapped in a situation where they have no outlet for their sexual feelings which are acceptable to their conscience. The best treatment strategy is to help the offender break down his taboos against heterosexuality, intimacy, and commitment. A peer group climate which approves of healthy sexual expression is helpful in getting the adolescent molester to reevaluate his sexual attitudes. The therapist can verbalize as well as model an attitude that consenting sex between adults is okay.

Specific discussion of homosexuality is more tricky. If the therapist appears to be encouraging this sexual orientation, trouble can be expected from many parents, homophobes in the group, and some referral sources. Many boys become angry and suspicious if the therapist takes a stance that seems to be encouraging them to become homosexual. If the boys so label you, the group will probably go no place.

Yet some adolescent molesters are more tilted toward homosexuality than heterosexuality. They need an objective discussion of this issue. Each therapist will have to find his own way to grapple with this issue. My stance is to indicate that if one is truly homosexual, this needs to be accepted. It needs to be pointed out, however, that the presence of homosexual feelings in adolescence does not mean one is homosexual. Adolescent molesters need to know that one does not choose sexual orientation, and that the final outcome is outside of one's conscious control.

It is an unfortunate fact that the majority of adolescent molesters seem to feel that pedophilia is superior to homosexuality if that is the only choice. To the best of his ability the therapist needs to create a group climate in which there is support for adolescents who are homosexual in orientation. Efforts should also be made to create a peer culture that supports the value that pedophilia is the least desirable of all possible outcomes. It is in this area that the male therapist may be able to use the relationship he has developed with the boys and the prestige he has garnered in their eyes through careful cultivation of the therapeutic alliance to teach openly and to be heard insisting that it is pedophilia not homosexuality that is to be the most feared outcome. Boys who end up as pedophiles need to be aware that they will be in chronic conflict with society and may spend much of their lives in jail.

Easier to deal with are issues surrounding various sexual practices. These should be discussed frankly and nonjudgmentally. This shades easily into sex education which should be an important part of group treatment. With the current health crisis, it seems quite appropriate to use a discussion of sexual practices to discuss AIDS and its prevention. This leads into a discussion of other sexually transmitted diseases.

Clinicians working with the adolescent molester should try to help them develop an understanding of how sexuality develops and what constitutes mature sexuality. Most of these young men have no idea that there is a normal period of homosexual interest at puberty. Like most adolescent males, they focus on the purely sensual aspects of sexual contact. With careful work, they can be helped to see that sex is part of a broader pattern of human intimacy and it is at its richest when connected with love and affection for the partner.

Many adolescent molesters have an open or hidden interest in sadomasochism and bondage. At one residential facility, a surprise inspection turned up a huge collection of pornography assembled by the residents in the home. Roughly 90 percent of this pornography dealt with sadomasochism, bondage, and incest. Sadomasochism needs to be discussed in group. The best tactic for discouraging an ultimate sadomasochistic orientation in the adolescent molester seems to be education. Sadomasochism should be presented as something that is inconsistent with a stable, mature, and loving relationship between two individuals.

Sex is only one part of life. No one would dispute that it is an important part, but it is not everything. Because of this truism, no group treating adolescent molesters will deal only with sexual issues. It is impossible to treat a sexual problem by focusing on nothing but sexual issues. Sexuality is enmeshed in a context of a total human being and a total way of life. A cluster of other relevant issues can be identified for discussion in group. Family problems have a place in group. Earlier, the role of family dynamics in the causation of molesting was explored. If these issues contribute to the problem, they must be addressed in group.

As noted earlier, I have become increasingly aware of the role of fear of psychosis as a driving force in the behavior of some adolescent molesters. This issue should be discussed candidly where it is relevant. I have been surprised at the willingness of adolescent molesters to discuss psychotic experiences such as hallucinations and paranoid feelings. Often this is a "sleeper" issue that no one working with the boy is aware of or is addressing. Discussion in group can help address the problem directly. It can also allow the clinician to make others aware of the problem so the offender can get help focused on this issue. This is part of the package of focusing on the whole patient rather than just the specifically sexual aspects of the adolescent's personality.

Sometimes, it is important to discuss such issues as jobs and school problems with boys in group. This shows an interest in the adolescent molester as a total human being rather than as a sexual problem to society. Helping an adolescent to be successful by focusing on success issues such as jobs and education also states that the group and leader want the adolescent to grow into a successful male adult. This is essentially an empowerment strategy. Most American males relate power and maleness. Boys who feel they have a future in which they may be productive and responsibly powerful will develop a more secure masculinity, a masculinity less likely to be interested in molesting children.

RESIDENTIAL GROUPS

When adolescent molesters can be treated by the approach outlined here, the basic principles of group apply in residential as well as outpatient settings. There are some differences which need to be noted. In general, adolescent molesters in residential treatment will be more disturbed. They will have more serious offenses and more serious personality problems including antisocial personality, borderline personality, and frank psychosis. There will be a higher percentage of boys, even in the placements for the less severe sex offenders, who will benefit more from the standard model than from what is offered here. Yet, if an adolescent molester can benefit from a transforming therapy as opposed to a supportive one, he should be offered the therapy with the potential for full resolution of his problems even if he is in residential treatment.

I have done groups with adolescent molesters in a wide range of residential facilities. I have always found a number of boys who are able to work with this approach. In fairness, I have never worked in the facilities that deal with the most serious of the offenders such as the California Youth Authority. My suggestion to large residential facilities that treat a range of pathology in sex offenders is that they establish some groups along this psychodynamic model and others within the standard model. That way the needs of both groups could be met. Something to consider would be making the psychodynamic group an advanced group and graduate suitable candidates into it after a period of diagnostic study in a standard model group.

I have actually been gratified by the opportunity to work in a residential treatment facility. This setting offers an opportunity for more intensive group therapy. The boys actually live with each other and know each other much better than outpatients. They tell on each other which brings all kinds of issues into group that would be hidden by outpatients. It is in the residential setting that the issue of homosexuality and homosexual attractions between group members really come to the fore. Sometimes the boys become sexually involved with each other. The greater interaction, more mutual observation, and the potentiality for sexual contact allow an opportunity to explore some of the most critical dynamics in a safe setting.

The residential facility has the opportunity to offer treatment twice a week or more, vastly speeding up the process. The boy in placement has been removed from his home. There is no longer an issue of destroying the family equilibrium by inducing too rapid a change in the molester. If homosexual panic or transient psychotic states are induced by the greater frequency and intensity of treatment, the residential setting offers a network of clinicians and trained staff to help manage these eventualities.

Chapter Ten

INDIVIDUAL AND FAMILY THERAPY

The previous chapter was devoted to group therapy. Nothing in that chapter should be interpreted to mean that group is the only treatment necessary for the perpetrator. In this chapter, a number of other modalities and treatment issues will be examined. For most adolescent sex offenders, some kind of treatment needs to be extended to their family. If this is not done, the young molester's chances of recovery are significantly reduced. Unfortunately, some families flatly refuse to be involved in the treatment of their child. Others are so toxic and destructive that the adolescent must be protected from them.

An example of this latter situation is the family of a boy in a residential treatment program. His schizophrenic father had left New York after giving up what he felt was a mission to rescue that city from the clutches of the devil. Early on, the father indicated a wish to be involved in the boy's treatment. He came increasingly to ruminate and perseverate on his son's sexual assaults upon his sisters. During one family session, he became so agitated that he started to pace up and down in the interview room and to threaten his son with physical attack. Other staff had to be called into the room to quiet him. After this session, he made phone calls to the residential facility threatening the boy's life.

This is an extreme case, but it is not unique in the issues it raises. This is a toxic family beyond repair. The young man's task is to emancipate himself from it. Family therapy is essential where the perpetrator's victim or victims live in the family home and there is a goal of eventual reconciliation with the molester. Under no circumstances should such reconciliation be attempted without family therapy.

Any clinician practicing in this area will occasionally get a referral of a case where an offender has been left in the home with his victim. These are usually young offenders whom law enforcement chooses not to prosecute. Here again, family therapy is absolutely essential. These cases pose a very high risk of reoffense because of the ready availability of the victim. As a casework procedure, it would be better to at least temporarily separate the victim and the offender. This, however, is a decision sometimes made without clinical consultation. The therapist is presented with a *fait accompli.* The clinician's only choice in this situation is to treat or not to treat. My own feeling is that some treatment is better than no treatment. Clinicians working under these conditions should advise all concerned parties that the prognosis is guarded as long as the offender remains in the home.

Why is family treatment so important? There is a variety of reasons. In an earlier chapter, we looked at ways in which the family system shapes the offending behavior of the adolescent. This is particularly true where the victim is a member of the family or is otherwise closely associated with the family. Another reason is that when the parents are not involved in treatment, they can be a source of resistance and sabotage.

Often, parents have a stake in the child's offending behavior. This is to be suspected when one or both of the parents have been sexually victimized themselves. They may unconsciously put their children into high-risk situations. An example is the case of James. James was in treatment for sodomizing a brother and a nephew, both age 9. His parents were reluctant to involve themselves in family therapy. When seen for a family session at the insistence of the therapist, they brought up a concern as to whether James should be allowed to go on vacation with a 10-year-old male friend. The boy's parents had offered to include James as a part of the family's summer outing. There are only two possible readings of this data: incredible stupidity on the part of the parents, or an unconscious need to put their son in a situation where he is likely to reoffend. As a result of the family session, the vacation plans were canceled and the friendship with the ten-year-old boy was terminated.

Even in less dangerous situations, when parents are not seen, serious distortions in their perceptions of the therapist and therapy can arise. Adolescent offenders frequently minimize the therapeutic content of their treatment. They give the impression to their parents that nothing is really happening, or they emphasize aspects of the treatment they know will antagonize the parents. With religious parents, they may stress that cussing is allowed in group or that sexual issues are frankly discussed. This is sometimes part of a deliberate effort to maneuver their parents into pulling them out of treatment. Parents of offenders have a kind of natural inclination to feel that the problem is better brushed under the rug anyway. They need the contact with the therapist in order to form some kind of working alliance and to keep their children in treatment.

Even where treatment is court ordered and parents cannot remove their son, they can undo treatment's effectiveness by devaluing the treatment process.

On a more positive note, there is much that the adolescent molester needs from his parents. This is best obtained through family therapy. In order to develop a nonperverse sexuality, young men need permission from their parents to explore in this area and to work out their own personal synthesis of the nondestructive aspects of sexuality that they will integrate into their lives.

A good illustration of this comes from a nonoffender case. An eleven-year-old boy was in treatment for behavioral problems, passive-aggressive behavior, and underachievement at school. His mother was a strong and domineering figure. His stepfather was an aggressive borderline personality given to loud verbal disapproval of any sexual interests or activity on the patient's part. This young man, Tom, had been sexually stimulated by a fondling episode with his grandfather and by observing his teenage sister engaged in oral copulation with her boyfriend. In a regular family session with his therapist, the boy went to a bookshelf and pulled out a simple book the therapist had used to explain basic sexual facts to him. He asked his mother to go over the book with him. He used the book very cautiously to bring up the subject of masturbation. The mother was uncomfortable, but with guidance was able to tell her son that masturbation is okay and a normal sexual practice. The young man left the session considerably relieved.

What applies to the masturbation anxieties of a nonoffending eleven-year-old applies many times over to the sexual anxieties of the adolescent molester. Such issues as masturbation, oral and genital sex, homosexuality and bisexuality are emotion-laden issues for these young men. It is helpful, perhaps essential, in making their own synthesis that they know where their parents stand on these issues. If parental approval can be obtained for whatever synthesis the young offender works out, it will speed up the molester's resolution of his sexual conflicts.

The teenage perpetrator needs to put together an emotionally meaningful synthesis, including his sexual orientation, what sexual practices are acceptable to him, and under what circumstances. If such a synthesis is not made, there is a considerable risk that the adolescent molester will drift in the direction of pedophilia. Parental endorsement of at least the teenager's right to make his own synthesis and define his own sexual values facilitates this process. Family therapy is the best arena for the working out of these issues.

Another area of concern which can be dealt with in family therapy is parental overreaction to the adolescent's sexual interest and activity. Teenage molesters tend to come from families with sexual conflicts, repression, and inhibition. Sometimes, this is due to deeply held religious values. Other times, it is due to the parents' own sexual training and background. In most cases, sex was shrouded in secrecy and prohibition prior to the young man's offense. After the offense, there is often an hysterical overreaction. This overreaction can include such intense supervision that the minor has no opportunity for interaction with appropriate potential sexual partners. Many parents prohibit their offending adolescents from dating or other healthy contact with females their own age. They sometimes equate all sex with molestation. Parents need help in understanding what is a normal, healthy adolescent sexual interest, and what is a potentially risky situation.

In these days of health maintenance organizations and preferred provider organizations, many clinicians will be presented with a request that family treatment be provided by someone other than themselves. This is because the family has coverage which will pay for such care but only by other designated professionals. There will be other instances in which the primary therapist is too busy to take on the responsibility of family treatment and must refer elsewhere. The principal need in this kind of situation is for close cooperation between the two therapists involved. As has been illustrated before, both the adolescent molester and his parents are manipulative. Splitting the treatment easily allows the playing off of one therapist against the other. Frequent consultation and communication is necessary to reduce this risk.

Specific techniques of family therapy vary widely. It is beyond the scope of this book to evaluate different systems of family treatment or to single out any one specific approach that is more effective than others with the adolescent molester. It does seem important, however, to review a few procedural issues here. The ideal in family therapy is to see all the members, at least for initial diagnostic sessions. This can pose a problem where the victim is part of the family. Some victims are not ready to face their molester. Hopefully, any victim will also be in treatment. Inclusion of the victim in a family session should be worked out in consultation with the victim's own therapist. In such cases, priority needs to be given to the treatment needs of the victim.

Assuming that the victim is not part of the immediate family, an initial diagnostic session including the entire family should be held. In my experience, very young children do not tolerate family therapy sessions for long and probably should not be routinely included except for some specific and carefully diagnosed reason. Most of the issues the molester needs to work out can be dealt with in conjoint sessions with the offender and his parents. If the victim lives with the parents, sooner or later he/she must be included in the family therapy process. Other siblings should be brought in as indicated by family dynamics. Family therapy always seems to evoke more resistance than individual or group. The most frequent focus for this resistance is the father or stepfather who refuses to be involved at all. Such individuals should be contacted directly and invited to participate. If the father figure will not involve himself, the therapist is left with the choice to work with the mother and/or siblings only or to offer nothing approximating family therapy. In such a situation, I would opt for the course of treating the family members who are willing.

In the ideal situation, both parents and appropriate siblings will all be involved. Here there is the best opportunity to resolve family issues which contributed to the perpetrator's offense. Teenage molesters often occupy the scapegoat role in their families. In these situations, the family needs help in changing its dysfunctional system of roles. Family treatment is also an opportunity to examine the sexual values and to make necessary changes.

Earlier in this chapter, families so toxic that they could not be treated were discussed. Here the offender must emancipate from his family and prepare for independent living. This kind of case is most frequent in residential settings. The most dysfunctional families seem to dump the adolescent molester when his offense is discovered. Once in placement, boys who have been rejected by their family develop an intense desire to reunite with them. All adolescents appear to yearn for parenting. Male adolescent molesters in placement seem to particularly yearn for mothering. Even in the face of years of rejection, they cling to the hope that if they just do the right thing, say the right thing, or get the right help, they can be reunited with their mother.

In such cases, it is futile to prohibit contact and tell the young man that contact with his mother or father is destructive to him. The technique of facilitating emotional separation from a hopeless family situation will vary somewhat between outpatient and residential contexts.

Helping an adolescent molester emancipate from a parent or parents with whom he lives is a difficult and slow task. The therapist needs to be very careful not to make critical remarks about the parent. These simply backfire. Any criticism to be made must come from the adolescent. The clinician can be supportive if and when such material emerges but should not be its initiator.

In residential settings, the issue is more sharply drawn. Two situations are typical. In one, the parents are remote and aloof. They are either totally unwilling to be involved or schedule appointments which they infrequently keep. The other is the situation where a parent has a pathological need to reclaim a child who has been taken from their custody and ordered into residential treatment. These parents want desperately to be involved but for all the wrong reasons.

In Chapter Five, a mother was discussed who, during a family session, insisted that her son's sibling victims sit on his lap. She also left him to baby-sit with these siblings during a home visit. When this woman was finally told by her son that contact with her was too painful and that he wanted no more, she went irately to the probation officer and demanded that her son be transported to her home for visits against his own wishes and against the recommendations of the clinical team at the residential facility in which he was placed. The issue here appears to be largely one of control and a need to deal with her issues by acting them out with her son.

This young man was able to realize that he needed to emancipate from his mother as a direct result of family sessions and visitation. This allowed him to experience and deal with his mother as a real figure. Had the placement or the probation officer prohibited visiting or discouraged family therapy, the young man would have probably turned his mother into an embodiment of his fantasy of the ideal, all-giving, all-loving parent. He would have blamed the authority figures in his life for keeping him from this wonderful fantasy being. This would have seriously damaged his relationship with his therapists. He would also have been likely to resume a pathological relationship with his mother when he left placement. This eventuality would probably have led to reoffense.

There are risks in allowing an adolescent to see his destructive parents as they really are. It can lead to feelings of rootlessness and rejection. In this type of case, carefully planned family therapy can help the young offender see for himself the toxic nature of his parent and make a rational decision about how he can best cope with such a parent.

INDIVIDUAL TREATMENT

Adolescent molesters vary widely in their ability to use individual treatment. I have softened my view about the role of individual therapy since the publication of the 1987 edition. Several years of additional experience have convinced me that most adolescent molesters will make some use of individual sessions. For some, they are essential to any real resolution of their underlying problems. In general, they should be part of all comprehensive treatment plans. Group treatment must remain the cornerstone of the treatment of this population, but a good group will inevitably stir up issues that will need more attention than they can get in group. These issues need to be processed in individual therapy.

In some cases, individual therapy may consist of little more than processing material from the group. Other molesters will make much more extensive and intensive use of their individual sessions. This will vary according to personality make-up. The planning of individual therapy requires a focus on the individual and his strengths and needs. There can and should be great flexibility in planning individual therapy for adolescent molesters. Frequency of treatment can be varied according to the ability of the offender to use his sessions. Some offenders should be seen weekly or more often for individual treatment. Others might be seen every two weeks, once a month, or as needed. What is important is that the clinician remain aware of the emotional needs of his patients and implement a treatment plan appropriate to those needs.

A basic decision about the nature of the treatment plan needs to be made at the time of intake. Most molesters should be routinely placed in group. The very anxious, schizoid, or depressed may need to be seen individually first in order to work on the most urgent issues. In this period, it may also be possible to establish enough rapport to incorporate the boy into the group after a few individual sessions. The individual sessions should continue if the adolescent is using them.

Some boys will state a preference for group and a reluctance to be involved in individual therapy. This usually occurs a little way into treatment. The first reaction to the mention of group is near panic. I calmly ask boys to try group before they reject it. Usually they agree. Once boys are placed in group, some will decide they do not want individual sessions. Generally, I respect this and make it plain that they can have individual therapy if and when they are ready for it. It is rarely profitable to force a patient into individual sessions. As some boys progress in the group it becomes clear that they are anxious for individual sessions. Some ask explicitly for them. Others bring in so many issues that it becomes obvious that group alone will not allow the time and intensity of relationship necessary to solve the problems. These boys belong in individual therapy usually with a once-a-week frequency. Some make excellent use of the experience as did Brian.

Brian

Brian was referred to me at age 15 after he molested a very young female cousin. He disclosed at intake that he had been molested since age eight by males old enough to be his father. At the onset of treatment he was strongly homoerotic and regaled the group with eroticized accounts of his victimization. He identified himself on the Kinsey Scale as a three (bisexual), but he seemed to me closer to the homosexual pole of this continuum. He specifically requested individual as well as group sessions.

Brian spent the better part of two years in individual treatment with me. At first he seemed to be consciously testing me to see if I was corrupt like the other fathers who had seduced him. He dressed exhibitionistically and posed suggestively in his chair. He repeatedly suggested I take him on trips or become otherwise involved in his personal life. I did visit him when he was hospitalized for a medical problem, but turned down all other offers to see him outside the office. I made a point of sitting across a desk from him. I chose for a variety of reasons not to discuss his seductiveness directly with him. I ignored it while encouraging his increasing number of forays into relationships with girls his age. His seductiveness with me steadily decreased. He worked on dreams, family problems, and his victimization over many months. Toward the end of his treatment he developed a sexually active and committed dating relationship with a girl he brought to the office to meet me. In group, he began to describe himself as a two on the Kinsey Scale (heterosexual preference with some homosexual inclinations). He showed no anxiety about occasional sexual attractions to male peers.

In these latter states of his treatment, his seductive behavior toward me vanished. The relationship felt to me like father-son. He increasingly consulted me on his relationship with his girlfriend (mostly its nonsexual aspects), career issues, how to deal with his difficult mother and other similar father-son type issues. He was very aggressive in defending me from verbal attack or devaluation in group.

Brian had been raised from birth by a single mother. He was probably molested when he reached out for a father to facilitate his male development. He got himself into a byway of highly eroticized relationships with older men which probably would have resulted in exclusive homosexuality or molesting little girls as a compensatory mechanism. He needed a father who could not be corrupted and found it in me. This adolescent seems to have been fixated at the pre-oedipal stage described by Blos (1985) in which the boy relates in an idealizing, passive, and eroticized manner to the father. This is a necessary stage in identification with the father and the development of maleness. It is a time in which boys are vulnerable to molestation by father figures. Most fathers do not betray this and instinctively do what I did in Brian's case. Brian seemed to instinctively know what he needed and used me to get it.

Brian is the exception, rather than the rule, with the teenage male victim. More commonly, adolescent male victims enter the treatment relationship, not with seductiveness, but with anxiety and distrust, or even suspicion and hostility bordering on paranoia. I make a number of subtle adjustments to defuse these potentially destructive concerns. They are all rooted in the same fear, that the male therapist will molest them as have other once-trusted men.

There are a number of ways to reduce these kinds of fears to manageable proportions. One boy is so paranoid of my intentions that I see him only conjointly with his mother. Generally, it is wise to conduct interviews with this kind of victim with a barrier of a desk or table between you and the patient. An office with lots of windows and nearby people is also reassuring. Within the first few sessions, it is usually possible and desirable to discuss the boy's fear of the therapist. Frankly acknowledging the trust issue is appropriate. The therapist should not expect immediate trust and should communicate this to the patient. He should also clearly state that although he does not expect immediate trust, he will conduct himself in such a way that the patient will eventually see that the therapist will not molest him. Staying on your side of the desk, avoiding touch, and encouraging age-appropriate sexual interaction with peers will all send the message that you have no sexual designs on the patient.

There are some victimized boys who cannot work with a man at all and should be referred to a female therapist. In these cases, the patient can work on female and mother issues first. If at all possible, these boys should eventually return to finish up with a male therapist for reasons elaborated elsewhere. In some cases this might be facilitated by some conjoint sessions with the female and male therapist prior to transferring the case.

The response of boys that I have treated individually ranges from extremely guarded to outrightly enthusiastic. There are some cases where the boy wants to come and is coming voluntarily, but the therapist must initiate almost all conversation. With these adolescents, you have to ask lots of questions, listen carefully to the answers, and follow up clues and hints on what is presented. Very often, it is necessary to start with material other than the explicitly sexual.

Very few adolescent molesters are as forthcoming with clinical material and as responsive to individual therapy as Brian, but a well run group will stir up issues in even the more resistant molesters that go very deep. For those who are able, it is vital that they be able to explore these issues with an empathic adult in individual therapy.

Many of the boys have serious issues involving their mother. Issues about father, homosexuality, deviant arousal to children, and transferences to group leaders are stirred up in group and can usually be followed-up in individual therapy. There are caveats here, however. Just because group stirs up an issue does not mean that all molesters will be willing or able to explore it in individual therapy. Conversely, if there is no group to stir up issues, many adolescent molesters will say little in individual therapy that relates to their sexual problems.

The need to individualize the treatment plan should be stressed. There are some problematic offenders for whom the parameters of individual therapy must be modified. The molester who has a major antisocial component in his personality make-up will often attempt to misuse his sessions. Typically, delinquents use individual sessions to pursue agendas, create some impression they want the therapist to have, or simply enjoy tricking a gullible clinician. This does not *a priori* exclude individual sessions, but the therapist must be aware of the potential pitfalls and insist that the adolescent work on meaningful issues.

Individual treatment can pick up and elaborate on themes which arise in group or family therapy. If a molester must emancipate from a destructive parent, he will need individualized help and support to do so. If reconciliation with the family is the goal, the patient will need an opportunity to explore his feelings individually as well as in family therapy.

Individual crises are another area difficult to deal with in group. Adolescent molesters are often self-centered and unwilling or able to give the time or the quality of help a teenager may need with a crisis situation. Here, individual sessions are a must. Jack's case offers an example of an individual crisis demanding more than group attention.

Jack M.

Jack is a sixteen-year-old molester referred for treatment after fondling a young girl he was baby-sitting. His mother was a disturbed individual who constantly projected blame for her own problems onto other family members and outsiders. When Jack became involved in molestation, the family went into crisis. The mother acted as if he had destroyed an otherwise smoothly functioning family. In actuality, the family had a history of crises and problems going back for years. They also had a history of finding a scapegoat for each of these traumas. From the time of his conviction in the juvenile court, Jack's mother maintained that he had ruined the family, first by disgracing it and then by using their scarce financial resources for lawyers, juvenile hall fees, and therapy bills. Working herself into an increasing hysteria, the mother finally left the home.

Jack's reaction was a mixture of guilt and anger. He was first seen with his father. After this family meeting, it was agreed that he would have a series of individual sessions as a supplement to group therapy. He used these sessions to focus on his intense ambivalence about his mother. It is unlikely that he could have dealt with this issue in a once-a-week outpatient group. Jack's problems with his mother were also discussed in group. Other members associated their own problems with their parents to Jack's problem. This was productive for the group as well as for Jack. The group, however, simply had neither the time nor the patience to help Jack in the full resolution of his problem with his mother. Individual sessions were essential in this situation.

Certain other situations absolutely require individual as well as group treatment. Offenders with borderline personality structure and those struggling with psychoses are one such category. So are boys for whom homicide or suicide are an issue. Some such cases may also require hospitalization and medication. Psychiatric evaluation and consultation is essential in these situations. Unfortunately, these severe and critical issues are encountered all too frequently in working with adolescent molesters in residential settings.

Nathaniel F. illustrates the basic principles and difficulties posed by this kind of molester. About halfway through a weekly group session, Nathaniel, a relatively new member of his outpatient offender group handed me the following note:

> I think that life sucks. School is a place for fucking cocksuckers. I would love to blow up the fucking school. I feel like killing anyone I dislike. So leave me alone or you die. Sometimes I feel like a devil ready to attack. Everybody I know is on my ass about grades. Well, fuck them. They don't know shit. I had

one of my teachers tell me I am a devil. I thought to myself and I decided she should be dead. She's a fucking Jehovah Witness. They suck.

This young man had been asked to write about his feelings because of his previous withdrawn behavior in the group. I read the note to the group and invited discussion. This discussion led the young man who wrote the note to share that he was experiencing dreams in which he was murdering his own and other families. He also shared that he had been considering suicide.

With Nathaniel's cooperation, a family meeting was scheduled. He shared his feelings with his parents. The family was a subscriber to a local preferred provider organization. For financial reasons, they preferred to seek individual treatment and psychiatric evaluation through their insurance plan. The psychiatrist to whom they were referred decided that this young man's remarks might reflect adolescent turmoil stimulated by the group. He declined to provide individual treatment or medication. He suggested continued group treatment and a new referral to him if the pathological material persisted. I maintained my feeling that additional treatment was needed, but could not overcome a mixture of family and professional resistance. Nathaniel seems clearly to be the kind of offender who needs much more than group therapy.

Some boys will need to be seen individually because there is no community group into which they might fit. Fred is an example.

Fred

Fred had fondled and orally copulated a niece and nephew, aged three and four. These allegations were found true, and Fred was sent to a residential facility which had no special program for adolescent molesters. After serving his time, he was sent to the home of his grandmother who brought him to treatment as a molest victim. He had been molested over a period of years by a male relative.

On interview, Fred's affect was flat. Much of the content of his thought was paranoid in nature. He talked about being picked upon and harassed by blacks and Mexicans. He appeared to have no insight into his problems or judgment about how to deal with his life situation. The therapist decided he simply would not fit into any available group.

This kind of adolescent is accepted by very few of his peers. They are quickly identified as "weirdos" or "space cases" and *de facto* excluded from the group. His racially based fears would make it hard to place him in a group with nonwhite males. The therapist agreed to see this young man individually. Treatment focus was to be on his victimization and his psychiatric problems, not his offending behavior. His therapist tried to work him into a group on an occasional basis as a supplement to his individual treatment. This was never successful.

There are some cases which are clearly not suitable for group treatment. Other adolescent molesters fall into a gray area where they can receive some benefit from individual therapy but also need group treatment.

George

George was treated for a considerable period of time in an outpatient group. His parents were members of an HMO and could not find an individual therapist they wanted to work with in spite of the group therapist's request that they do so. This young man's father had died a lingering death of chronic disease. When the mother and father separated, George chose to go with the father in order to care for him. When the father died, he returned to the mother. He remained chronically depressed from the time of his father's death.

He had participated with an older stepbrother in molesting an eight-year-old sister. His offense had consisted of fondling, masturbating in front of the victim, and some limited attempts at vaginal penetration. He discussed these issues freely in the group sessions. Then he clammed up and said very little. In group he began to make bitter comments about other members. Aside from these remarks, he withdrew from group interaction.

The therapist finally insisted that this young man be in individual treatment. He was taken out of the group with the understanding that this was a temporary withdrawal. George was able to work very productively on his unresolved problems with his father and to return to the group treatment. Once back in the group, he was able to resume work on his sexual conflicts and molesting behavior.

George's individual treatment had been with the same therapist that conducted the group. The period of individual treatment allowed him to develop a strong therapeutic alliance which had not really developed in the course of group treatment. One of the reasons for his successful readjustment to the group was his ability to use his relationship with the therapist in order to feel comfortable in a group setting where he had previously been extremely uncomfortable.

PARENT GROUPS

Large agencies receiving many referrals of patients with problems in the area of sexual abuse frequently use the parent group as a treatment vehicle. A large referral base is necessary to use this approach with adolescent sex offenders. Typically, a high percentage of parents of these offenders refuse to be meaningfully involved in their treatment. For this reason, many therapists working in the field have no possibility of establishing such a group.

The advantages of a parent group are multiple. They allow parents to focus on problems common to all families where molestation has occurred. Such groups can also engage in problem solving as to how to best help their offending teenagers. The parent peer group offers an excellent vehicle for putting pressure on unreasonable parents to change behaviors and attitudes which are destructive to their son's welfare. It is possible to bring much greater pressure to bear on parents in a group than it is in either family or individual sessions.

RESISTANCE

Regardless of what treatment modality is used, there will be resistance. The offender's resistance comes from a variety of sources. On the surface, it is embarrassing to discuss one's sexual misdemeanors. Going beyond that, molesters are usually conflicted about sex and find the area embarrassing to discuss. Their repeated and insistent denial of masturbation is just one illustration of this evasion and reluctance.

The resistance of the adolescent molester is, in many aspects, the same as any resistance in psychotherapy. Patients have a deep stake in their own psychopathology. Personality patterns and defenses are involved in response to whatever environmental and family pressures a child experiences as he or she grows up. These patterns and defenses are often seen by the patient as essential to psychological survival. This is particularly true in cases where there is a borderline personality disorder. Borderline personality patterns are common among adolescent molesters. When the therapist attacks the defense that is seen as life preserving, he can indeed expect resistance.

Resistance takes all of the usual forms. Conscious withholding and suppressing, repression, evasion, and denial. In some cases, resistance is so strong that the offender simply plays a game in order to get out of treatment. This is particularly true in residential settings. Some young men placed for sex offenses have candidly told me that their only goal is to get out of the program and they will do anything clinical staff asks of them in order to do so. When asked to define a behavior they wish to change, they are speechless.

Residential programs are liable to an especially nasty form of resistance. Echo Glen Children's Center is an Oregon facility that treats adolescent molesters. They seem to be unusually conscientious. They discovered that adolescents in their program were making up stories of their own abuse or additional victims of their own criminality in order to curry favor with treatment staff and speed their departure from the program. All these dramatic disclosures seem to convince some clinicians that the perpetrator is now being totally honest and is on the road to true recovery. Details of this are published by Green and Kahn (1989). This kind of resistance seems to become a hazard when program pressure is high and the molesters' incentives to leave the program strong.

Parental resistance is also characteristic. As noted earlier, parents often have a stake in their adolescent's pathology. From the perspective of family therapy, the offender is doing something to preserve the family system or the sanity and emotional equilibrium of one or more of its key members. Such families cannot be expected to come cooperatively into treatment. Some families attempt to shelter their offenders from the consequences of their crimes. They hire expensive lawyers and participate fully in their adolescent's denial of his misdeeds. Other families need to scapegoat the offender and completely exclude him from family life. Either type of parental resistance makes treatment difficult. In some cases, such resistance renders treatment futile.

Chapter Eleven

COUNTERTRANSFERENCE ISSUES

We may treat neurotics any way we like.
They treat themselves with transferences.
SIGMUND FREUD

This is one of the wiser things said by Sigmund Freud. Translated out of psychoanalytic jargon, it simply says that human beings try to solve their intrapsychic problems by interacting in meaningful ways with other human beings. Given the way our personalities form, we all seek out those who remind us of key figures in our past and to correct what went wrong with them in a new series of interactions. Since therapists, case managers, child care staff, and others working with adolescent sex offenders are human beings too, we all will do this. It can be a problem, or it can actually enhance our ability to work with young males who molest.

Freud spoke in a technical way of transference and countertransference. They are really the same human phenomenon. Countertransference is simply transference when it occurs in a therapist. It once had a bad name. Therapists who had it needed to be analyzed so it would go away. The more modern view is that it cannot and should not go away. It should be domesticated in the service of our work. This means that it should be listened to and used. Only if it causes us trouble or interferes with our ability to work with others should it be considered a problem.

To Freudians, transference meant relating to someone in the present just as if they were a key figure from the past. It is used here in a broader sense. Here it means what Freud said as well as any and all emotional reactions we have to our patients. Taming countertransference means being aware of our emotional reactions to patients and what they mean to us as human beings. It means confronting the often scary words and projections of adolescent molesters and not becoming ineffective, inca-

186

pacitated by our own emotional response, or joining the adolescent in some form of subtle or not-so-subtle acting out.

Adolescent molesters are often deeply troubled individuals. Sometimes what they say or feel is profoundly troubling to us. It is hard to know how to respond tactically when confronted with some of this kind of material. It is perhaps even more difficult to modulate our own emotional responses when we are confronted with the kind of troubled, ambivalent material reproduced below:

> I wish my mom loved me like I loved her. We would be a more and better life. I wish that I could kill my mom so I could have a better life. My feelings inside of me is tonight my mom will know why I want to kill her. She will feel inside of her that I hate her and I want to kill her. But I still love her very much. Inside of me I feel hurt and not wanted by anyone.

What kind of feeling does this evoke in a therapist attempting to work with this young man? If it evokes none, that in itself is a form of countertransference. If the clinician tries to set aside his or her defenses and listen, the material is both frightening and a key to this boy's treatment. Clearly, his basic issues involve mothering. He has been terribly hurt, and his response is homicidal rage. Without treatment, he is likely to be a serious danger to women and female children. The ambivalence here is so intense as to suggest psychosis. No treatment will have any effect if the therapist's countertransference is to deny the meaning of material or, worse yet, fear or hate the patient for what he has revealed. This writing may seem extreme in its intensity. Indeed, it is among the more pathological material I have collected over the years. On the other hand, where a therapist will permit free expression, this kind of communication flows all too often from the pens of adolescent molesters. It takes psychic strength and self-awareness to deal with such issues and such patients.

All people who work with adolescent molesters in any capacity are vulnerable to potentially destructive countertransference reactions. Those who see adolescents in residential facilities are probably confronted with the greatest challenges. This is because treatment here is more frequent and intense. Generally, therapists seeing adolescents in such settings have far more power over their lives than those who see them as outpatients. For these reasons, those treating adolescent molesters in residential settings will find themselves more frequently forced to deal with often difficult countertransference issues. But the difference between the countertransference issues of outpatient vs. inpatient settings is one of degree. Everything discussed here can and does happen with outpatients and inpatients. It is just usually more obvious in residential settings.

Nor are the issues limited to therapists. Case managers, such as social workers based in child protection agencies and probation officers, are also vulnerable in the face of such issues. Child care workers in residential settings are very vulnerable. They generally have minimal training and they have to live 24 hours a day with adolescent molesters.

Teenage perpetrators are a population guaranteed to elicit an emotional response in most other people. They bring into focus two emotion-laden conflict areas: power and sexuality. They present us with issues that are usually either avoided or regarded with disgust in our society. Their very offense demands that we talk about sex. Many of us are not comfortable doing so. Taking it a step further, the adolescent molester's problem insists that we explore sexual activity between younger children and adolescents. The molester's act violates a strong social taboo. He invades the innocence of childhood with the sexuality of adolescence. Most people react with anger and disgust to such an invasion.

The molester's victims often respond by becoming sexualized. This shatters our culture's cherished illusion that prepubescent children are not capable of being sexual. If this were not bad enough, the molester sometimes uses force upon his victim, a small and innocent child. Sometimes, the children are seriously hurt. A two-year-old victim of one of my patients was nearly killed. Finally, the clinically sophisticated are aware that the depredations of the adolescent molester do severe and lasting damage to their victims. None of these issues make it easy to establish the climate of mutual respect that is an essential element of any treatment process.

So far, we have only looked at the externals of the adolescent molester's behavior. For the professional who goes further and attempts to enter and understand the psychic life of the adolescent offender, countertransference issues loom larger. The dreams and fantasies of the teenage offender are full of violence and sadomasochism. Many offenders have a precarious hold on reality. Their dreams will reflect their fear of becoming insane.

Most adolescent molesters are delinquent young men. They are likely to blame the very victims with whom we, the professionals, empathize. Their callousness toward their victims can be appalling. When a molester is really candid, he may do such things as telling his group that he saw nothing wrong with forcing his younger brother to orally copulate him. We have also seen examples of the violent fantasies the adolescent molester produces in the course of treatment. Patients who deal with violence, sadomasochism, fear of insanity, and antisocial attacks on others invite strong negative emotional reactions from professionals who work with them.

Adolescents in general, and adolescent molesters in particular, challenge those attempting to treat them in another vital area: power and control. It is a truism that adolescent molesters are angry young men. Their hostility will come out in the treatment process. Many are grandiose. There is often an aura of omnipotence in their approach to others. The helping person's expected roles of interpretation and confrontation often provoke rage and sometimes verbal attacks upon the therapist or other professional. Confronted with such patients, the most frequent countertransference response is, "I'll show you whose in charge here," or, "You will pay for such hostility to me."

In residential groups, boys may get together in between group therapy sessions and agree on strategies to avoid certain issues. If they know the therapist well, they may set traps for him by offering manufactured clinical material to see if they get the response they have predicted. In candid discussions, adolescent molesters will tell you that they play such games, and that they use their often insightful knowledge of the therapist to produce for him/her the material desired for advancement in whatever program they are in. This is always a risk in dealing with any delinquent population. If the staff dealing with these problems responds in kind, that is with countertransference, they usually become locked into a cycle of punishment and retaliation with the boys in treatment. This is, in effect, the death of treatment. To do this job well, it is important to master our countertransference and realize that treatment takes place alongside the ongoing conning process which is typical of the adolescent molester as well as other delinquents. This is a case where, "If you can't stand the heat, get out of the kitchen." The proper response is to know yourself so that you cannot be easily fooled, and to have a good enough relationship with at least some of the boys that they will tell you what is going on. You then firmly, but not hostilely, confront the manipulator with the fact that you are aware of what is going on and that you expect more emotional honesty in the future.

On a deeper, and more honest, level lies other troubling material with which therapists in particular must deal. One of the puzzles of this population is that their fantasies appear to be far more violent than their acts. In a permissive group setting, some of these fantasies about the therapist emerge clearly. Murderous rage and sexual seductiveness directed at the therapist were discussed in the section on transference. The professional confronted with these issues will almost certainly have an emotional reaction to them. The poem below was given by Daniel to his group therapist. Daniel was an intensely angry young man. He had been repeatedly and brutally molested by an older brother. He had a lot of anxiety that he might be homosexual. Dealing with this issue in group enraged him. The writing below seems to tell the therapist how he feels about him.

> "Sweet dreams," said Popeye.
> "How is life?"
> "Fuck you!"
> "No, really, how is life?"
> "Fuck you!"
> "You seem sweet today."
> "Your mama."
>
> Come to see me in the light.
> Drug and dreams make me feel all right.
> Fuck society. Fuck life.
> Go to hell. I'll fuck your wife.
> You sexual faggot. kill, kill, kill.
> Loving pussy. Sweet, wet, and lovely.

This kind of communication cannot help but make the therapist uncomfortable. It says that the patient hates you, wants to kill you and rape your wife in the process. The source of the rage was probably the homosexual issues that were dealt with in group. For a therapist this is a "dammed if you do, dammed if you don't" kind of situation. If you do not deal with these issues, some boys will never get better. If you do, there is a risk of evoking this kind of reaction. This offender left treatment against the advice of program staff. He never attempted to act in any violent way against this therapist or other staff. One of the lessons to internalize is that if you do this kind of work, you may be killed a thousand times in the fantasies of the more disturbed molesters, but you will probably make it to retirement.

Adolescent offenders only occasionally make threats as pointed as the poem above. More common is the attack on the therapist's narcissistic need to be important to the adolescent in treatment. Many will make remarks which seem intended to hurt the therapist's feelings. For example, one boy in a group exercise was invited to give two ideas about each member of the group. When he came to the therapist, his ideas were that the therapist was a recovering alcoholic and looked like a goat.

Another case in point was a boy who had been in treatment for 18 months when confronted by the therapist with his grandiosity and contempt for others. Frank was enraged by the comment. The therapist's response to his angry tirade was that he would pay a high price for those personality traits in the future. This triggered more argument and denial. The therapist, wishing to ease out of the confrontation, suggested that the young man simply take note of the price he was paying five-years hence and report back to the therapist. The patient's response was that he would not even remember the therapist in five-years since the therapist was unimportant in his life.

This kind of hostility, criticism, and attack on the therapist's narcissistic sensitivities is to be expected by therapists working with adolescent molesters. They will often emerge if the adolescent offender is given permission to express his feelings freely in a therapeutic context. These kind of issues emerge in the course of treatment of many kinds of patients, not just molesters. The difference with adolescent molesters is that they are probably more angry and more provocative than most outpatients seen by clinicians in general practice. A professional can avoid dealing with this material by prohibiting its expression, or by subtly (or not so subtly) punishing them for such utterances. In most cases, this would be counterproductive. It would probably also be rooted in a countertransference need to control as opposed to treat.

There is a very fine distinction to be made here. Expression of genuine feeling is always desired in treatment. Yet, sometimes, what on the surface appears to be such a feeling is really a maneuver to throw the adult off balance and get control of the situation. An expression of real feelings should be explored, understood, and if pathological, resolved. Sometimes the adolescent patient becomes locked into an irresolvable negative transference to therapist. He does seem to truly hate the therapist. The feeling is real, and no treatment effort seems to resolve it. In such a situation, the therapist or other adult should ask himself, "Who owns this problem? Am I doing something here that is creating this, or is the problem purely in the patient?" A peer or professional consultation on this kind of issue is highly desirable. If there is a treatment team, it should be discussed there.

If the problem lies in the adult, he or she clearly needs to correct it. If it lies largely in the adolescent, such a pervasive negative transference may not be resolvable. Where the bulk of the problem is with the patient, the adolescent is likely to be psychotic, borderline, or antisocial in personality make-up. After reasonable efforts toward resolution, such a patient should be transferred for a fresh start with someone else. Some such adolescents are simply not treatable. A helping person who allows sustained attacks on their person need is probably acting out their own masochism. Even if the need to attack is the patient's, the need to permit this to go on over time is a countertransference problem in the adult.

Up to this point, focus has been on those issues raised by adolescent offenders which evoke a strong emotional response in most adults working with them. The problem becomes more intense when the professional has unresolved conflicts which interact pathologically with the problem of the adolescent molester. Some professionals who work with offenders fall into the well-known categories of rescuers or persecutors. Rescuers (aka enablers) overidentify with patients and then try to "help" them by assisting them in doing the kind of dysfunctional things they have always done. Where staff identify in this way with adolescent molesters, serious and potentially destructive countertransference is at work.

Persecutors take an opposite stance. They identify in the molester something they hate in themselves or in some key figure in their life with whom they cannot deal directly. They then take their hatred out on the patient or client. An example is a probation officer who told the director of a residential facility that she always looked at the pictures of her own small children before going to juvenile hall to interview an adolescent molester in order to get herself in the right frame of mind. In her interviews with teenage perpetrators, she made her contempt and need to punish them quite clear. Clearly, the need she was meeting here was not society's need to prevent and treat, but hers to control and punish a molester who symbolized someone who had hurt her.

At the other extreme of countertransference are the rescuers. A case manager told a perpetrator with a serious record of offenses that he was being treated too severely in a structured residential program. He promised to remove the young man, against the staff's advice, and to return him to the family where he had molested his younger sister. The mother in this family was a hopeless alcoholic who totally rejected her son. It is actually hard to tell whether this individual is a rescuer or a persecutor since his proposed plan of action seems to have elements of both. What is likely here is profound ambivalence about the issues posed to the case manager by the offender. On the surface, he is being kind and supportive, yet his actions constitute, in actual fact, a set-up which will probably be disastrous to the perpetrator as well as the victim. Here, as so often with enablers, intense hostility seems to be disguised in the form of inappropriate rescuing. The more charitable explanation is stupidity and/or naiveté. Whatever the explanation, everyone would be better off if this case manager dealt with his countertransference.

There are a number of unresolved problems in the professional that can undermine their ability to deal with the adolescent molester. A classically difficult situation is the therapist who is a victim. Such a person clearly needs to have resolved his own victimization before attempting to treat adolescent molesters. Similarly, professionals with conflicts about homosexuality, sadomasochism, or fears about their own hold on reality will have serious difficulty dealing with this population. The risk is that the professional with unresolved conflicts in these areas will try to deal with them through countertransference just as the patient tries to deal with his conflicts through transference.

Adolescents in general, and many teenage molesters in particular, are very intuitive about the unresolved problems of others. The professional is not likely to be able to hide his unresolved conflicts from this population. If he is unconscious of these problems, as is often the case, he is vulnerable to manipulation by those he/she is supposed to help. Once this process is set in motion, the adolescent in treatment and those responsible for helping him can get involved in some very destructive games.

The other problematic pattern among those who do not deal with their countertransference is to develop negative countertransference to the adolescents with whom they are working. If the helping person is a victim of abuse, adolescent perpetrators are logical candidates to symbolically represent whoever molested them. The transaction then becomes to control and punish the molesters just as they wish to punish and control the person who assaulted them.

Victim status is not necessary to set this kind of countertransference in motion. Treatment staff may see the patients' anger, drive for control, or their sadism. Depending on their issues, they may identify with these traits or be enraged because they have been damaged by important people in their lives who have these problems. Whatever the specifics, until the helping person becomes more self-aware, they will project their problems onto the clientele and then become involved in games which undermine both client and helper.

SEXUALIZED COUNTERTRANSFERENCES

Sexualized countertransferences are a problem no one likes to talk about. Given the fact that adolescent molesters are often highly sexualized, sexual issues are likely to be mobilized in any staff that have a vulnerability in this area. This problem will be at its greatest in residential programs because of their more intensive nature. Here, staff have more power over the boys. They interact more frequently, and some of the staff either live with or spend long hours with the clientele. Here again, the residential vs. inpatient difference is only one of degree. Those dealing with outpatient molesters will sometimes have to deal with sexualized transferences from the boys and sexualized countertransferences in themselves.

Victims of sexual abuse will have a particular problem. Victims seem to have a countertransference-driven need to work in this field. This is fine if their issues have been resolved. It is a serious problem where the victim is seeking cure through countertransference. It is not just sex abuse victims on the staff who will get involved in these countertransferences. So will staff of both sexes who have issues about sexual attraction to adolescents. Some of the boys in treatment have been male prostitutes, many more are sexualized, and all are manipulative. A significant percentage will behave seductively with both sexes. This is often more about power and revenge than about sex. Part of the game is often to lure staff into inappropriate activity and then tell on them.

An illustration comes from the case of a member of the treatment staff at a residential facility. No historical data was available, but this individual was probably molested as a child. Her interactions with many of the offenders in the home were highly seductive. She sought out a young offender who had a history of prostitution with older females. She became involved in long, intimate discussions with the boy. She gave him special treatment when she was on duty. She intervened to protect him when he got in trouble with staff or peers. This young molester had a lot more self-awareness than the staff member. He flirted with her, knowing full well what both of them were doing. He told his therapist that his specific intent was to seduce the woman and then use her misbehavior to blackmail and control her.

Therapists with vulnerability will get no help from adolescent molesters. Female therapists and staff can be the target of special provocations from adolescent sex offenders. In a coleading situation, boys will, with some prodding, usually admit to sexual fantasies about the female therapist. They will also sometimes state that they would enjoy a sexual relationship with the female therapist. In one group, two boys playfully competed for the affection of the female coleader. One boy's approach was subtle, including gently touching her knee, smiling, and making mildly suggestive remarks. The other boy, hopefully in jest, started to unbuckle his belt and take down his zipper when restrained by the therapist.

Nor are male staff exempt from this kind of thing. Many adult males have unresolved issues about sexual attraction to other males or specifically to adolescent or younger males. For obvious reasons, such men are drawn to work with adolescent molesters, especially in residential settings. Frequently, the problem is one of a latent attraction to the boys not something fully recognized by the individual himself. In the intimacy of living with boys and supervising their daily life, male staff may begin to lose their ability to repress this problem. The boys are usually acutely aware of it. Some use it to seduce and control, just as they would with a female. Among child care staff, this often plays out with the adult deciding that he alone can solve the perpetrator's problems. This leads to efforts to get a foster care license or to adopt the boy. Sometimes, such individuals can convince case managers (enablers?) that this is a good idea. In my career, I have seen several such arrangements. In all cases where I could get follow-up data, the adult had made some sort of sexual overture to the adolescent before their relationship was terminated. Once again, a molester's treatment has been derailed by countertransference issues in those who are supposed to be providing treatment.

LESSER COUNTERTRANSFERENCES

There are more general and less pathological problems which interfere with the professional's ability to treat the adolescent offender. Most of us have a need to be liked and appreciated by our clientele. This can interfere with our ability to take the firm or confrontive stance often necessary with this population. This is not just a matter of a personal problem in the professional. It may be something that has been emphasized in his training. Training for traditional psychotherapy has generally underscored the need for empathy, understanding, and support, rather than for confrontation and structure. There is clearly a place for empathy, understanding, and support in treating the adolescent molester. There is also a vital need for structure and carefully considered confrontation.

Two other issues run counter to the thrust of the training of most professionals. One is the lack of confidentiality appropriate in treating adolescent molesters. This is particularly essential in outpatient settings. An adolescent offender in the community is always at some risk of reoffending. The therapist must be free to work with other professionals to keep this from happening. In residential settings, there is a need to share clinical information with other professionals including representatives of the criminal justice system.

USING AND MANAGING COUNTERTRANSFERENCE

We have looked at many of the problems of countertransference in the treatment of the adolescent offender. Some kind of emotional response to this population is inevitable. It is not, however, inevitably a problem. Countertransference has an important clinical use. Assuming the therapist does not have significant unresolved problems, countertransference is a valuable diagnostic tool. It is one of the mechanisms by which our own unconscious gets in touch with the unconscious of the adolescent molester. The kind of visceral reactions we have to a young perpetrator may tell us as much about his psyche as our own. We need to pay attention to these clues. They need to be sifted carefully in terms of whether our perceptions are a truly accurate response to our patient's unconscious or a response to our own inner needs.

If we truly know ourselves, and we perceive a boy as controlling and manipulative, that is an important clue about the nature of our patient. If we feel a boy's underlying psychosis, we can explore that issue clinically. That opens a door to an area of treatment that no one has previously explored. It may make the boy feel truly understood and therefore more amenable to our other efforts and more accepting of necessary confrontations. If a male clinician senses seductiveness, it is a clue to possibly undisclosed victimizations, unresolved father issues, and/or conflicts about homosexuality. Sometimes, it is what we perceive about others via our humanness, rather than our official training, that allows us to be truly helpful.

Several concepts seem useful in managing and utilizing countertransference. First of all, the professional needs to be aware that it is inevitable because they are human. If the problem is our own and minor, we can get help from coleaders or from professional peers. For serious, unresolved problems, the ideal solution, of course, is therapy for the professional. I doubt that anyone with serious unresolved problems which intertwine with those of the molester population can continue working effectively in this field for very long. Typically, such individuals end up in the various traps examined earlier in this chapter.

Appendix A

SAMPLE LEVEL SYSTEM GROUPS

REASON FOR A LEVEL SYSTEM

In my experience in working with boys who have had sexual problems, I have found that it is extremely difficult for them to discuss these problems. Most boys hope that by not talking or thinking about the problem, it will go away. Many boys are also deeply ashamed of what they have done. If the problem could be solved by ignoring it, I would be the first to recommend doing that. Ignoring the problem, however, is one of the best ways to ensure that it will occur again. For this reason, I have set up a level system to help boys to talk about their problems in the group. This system is designed to help, not to hurt or humiliate.

Level One: Level one is an entry level. Boys at this level play down their offense or do not talk about being molested if that has happened to them. They may make excuses or blame others if they have molested younger children. At this level, boys have little or no understanding of why they committed their offense. Often, they do not wish to talk about it and refuse to answer questions in group. They evade participating in the group and do not talk unless asked to do so by the leaders.

Level Two: To be placed on this level, one must be able to define deviant arousal. They must also know something about the offenses committed by other boys in the group. At this level, boys will begin to discuss their offenses openly. They will talk freely without being questioned. They will ask questions of group leaders and members. They will also start to explore the role of their own feelings in their offense. At this level, boys will begin to share dreams and fantasies. They will also begin to question unreasonable ideas such as blaming victims for what happened or minimizing offenses.

Level Three: Certain behavior in group is required in order to be considered for this level. These behaviors include: (1) Involving oneself in group discussion without specific request by the leader, (2) Not disrupting or diverting the group from productive discussion, (3) Expressing anger and disagreement with peers and leaders when one feels it, (4) Not just trying to figure out what the therapist wants to hear and saying that, (5) Bringing to group issues, dreams, and fantasies that you want to work on. *Once on this level, a client must continue these behaviors in order to stay here. They will be placed back on level two if you stop doing these things.*

One must be able to define and discuss deviant arousal in order to be considered for this level. They must also know the offenses committed by at least a majority of other boys in the group. They must also have some idea about the age and sex of

199

their victims. At this level, boys who have been sexually victimized will begin to discuss this. They must be sharing their sexual fears with the group. They will be willing to discuss any homosexual feelings or fears that they may have. They will be sharing sexual fantasies or impulses they are having for younger children.

To be considered for this level, group members must have begun to explore the role their relationship with their mother and their father played in causing them to molest a younger child. They must give the group some idea of what it means to be a man and how one shows that in day-to-day life.

Level Four: Basic requirements are: continue to behave in group as required for level III. One must define deviant arousal and explain how it is related to their offense. Members will be asked to describe the offenses committed by several other boys in the group. They should be able to talk about using sex responsibly in your life and how that fits in with being a man. If one is a victim of sexual abuse, they must talk about how that has effected them. Has it had any effect on their sense of being a man?

At this level, a boy is deepening his understanding of why he committed his offense. They will need to give the group a detailed explanation of what they did with their victim. They must have spent some time exploring how their relationship with their mother and father affected their molesting behavior. Is there anything particular in their relationship with their father that contributed to their sexual problems?

The client must now be able to talk about the effect molestation has on both male and female victims. They need to be able to tell the group what sexualization means.

To qualify for this level, one must have begun to think about their own sexual identity and orientation. Are they sexually interested in females, males, or to some degree both? Do they still have an interest in younger children? They need to tell the group what sadism is. They must tell the group again what they think is responsible sexuality for a boy their age and what they think it will be when they are a man.

Level Five: Basic requirements: (1) Know what deviant arousal is. (2) Continue to behave in group as described for level III. (3) They must have led the group at least once before asking to be placed on this level. (4) Know the offenses and other basic facts about most or all other group members. They will need to understand the damage that victimization has done to younger children with whom they have been sexually involved. They need to be specific about how being molested effects both boys and girls. What difference does it make if a victim is forced into sex or tricked into it?

If they were molested, how did it affect them? Clients need to give the group a detailed account of what happened to them when they were molested and how it affected them.

At this stage, group members must be able to offer a clear and convincing explanation of why they committed a sex offense. This explanation must include the role of being molested if they are a victim. It must also address the role played by their relationship with both parents in creating the circumstances that led them to become a molester. They must also know how an effort to protect their sense of maleness figured into their problem. The contribution of anger and the need to control also need to be considered in their explanation. Clients need to tell the group what sadism is and whether they feel it was involved in their sex offense.

Level five also requires that a group member has used all of the information he has gathered so far to come up with a solution to his molesting problem. They must be able to tell the group clearly what will stop you from molesting again. They must demonstrate to the leaders and to the group that they have worked out some kind of outlet for their sexual feelings which is realistic and legal. This will include a statement about where they stand sexually: Are they heterosexual, bisexual, or homosexual? Or still confused? Do they still have a sexual interest in children? Clients must also show the group that they know what kind of pressure might cause them to molest in the future, and how they will guard against and deal with that pressure. They must have a good answer to the question: Why won't you molest again?

At this level, a boy should be, to the best of his abilities, a coleader in the group. To qualify for this level, he must at least talk freely, ask questions of others, and help the leader get discussion going during quiet times in the group.

Setting of Levels: Boys will be placed on levels in the group during a group discussion. When a boy feels he is ready for a specific level, he may ask to be questioned by the leaders and the group to see if he is ready for that level. Each member of the group will be asked to state his opinion about whether the boy has earned a new level. The final decision about placement on a level will be made by the group leader. Boys may also be lowered on levels if they violate basic group rules or if they slip backwards after attaining a new level.

ANNOTATED BIBLIOGRAPHY

Abel, G. G., & Blanchard, E. B. (1974). The role of fantasy in the treatment of sexual deviation. *Archives of General Psychiatry,* 30, 467–475.

> Elaborates on McGuire et al. (1965). This hypothesis says that sexual deviation arises when subjects masturbate to deviant fantasies. The fantasies themselves probably arise out of earlier traumatic or deviant sexual experiences. This idea has been immensely influential in the sex offender field.

Abel, G. G., Becker, J. V., Cunningham-Rathner, J., Rouleau, J., Kaplan, M., & Reich, J. (1984). *Treatment Manual: The Treatment of Child Molesters.* Tuscaloosa, AL: Emory University Clinic, Department of Psychiatry.

> Elaborates on McGuire et al. (1965). This hypothesis says that sexual deviation arises when subjects masturbate to deviant fantasies. The fantasies themselves probably arise out of earlier traumatic or deviant sexual experiences. This idea has been immensely influential in the sex offender field.

Abel, G. G., Mittelman, M., & Becker, J. V. (1985). Sex offenders: Results of assessment and recommendations for treatment. In: H. Ben-Aron, S. Hucker, & C. Webster (Eds.), *Clinical Criminology: Current Concepts.* Toronto, Canada: M&M Graphics.

Abel, G. G., Becker, J. V., Mittelman, M., Cunningham-Hathner, J., Rouleau, J., & Murphy, W. B. (1987). Self reported crimes of nonincarcerated paraphiliacs. *Journal of Interpersonal Violence,* 2, 1, 3–23.

> Well-known study suggesting that over fifty sex crimes are committed for each one that is reported.

Abel, G. G., Osborn, C. A., & Twigg, D. A. (1993). Sexual assault through the life span: adult offenders with juvenile histories. In H. E. Barbaree, W. L. Marshall, & S. M. Hudson (Eds.), *The Juvenile Sex Offender.* New York: The Guilford Press.

Adams, H. E., Motsinger, P., McAnulty, R. D. (1992). Voluntary control of penile tumescence among homosexual subjects. *Archives of Sexual Behavior,* 1, 17–31.

Barbaree, H. E., & Cortoni, R. R. (1993). Treatment of the juvenile sex offender within the criminal justice and mental health systems. In H. E. Barbaree, W. L. Marshall, & S. M. Hudson (Eds.), *The Juvenile Sex Offender.* New York: The Guilford Press.

Barbaree, H. E., Hudson, S. M., & Seto, M. C. (1993). Sexual assault in society: The role of the juvenile offender. In H. E. Barbaree, W. L. Marshall, & S. M. Hudson (Eds.), *The Juvenile Sex Offender.* New York: The Guilford Press.

Barbaree, H. E., Marshall, W. L., & Hudson, S. M. (Eds.). (1993). *The Juvenile Sex Offender.* New York: The Guilford Press.

Barker, J. G., & Howell, R. J. (1992). The plethysmograph: A review of recent literature. *Bulletin of the American Academy of Psychiatry and Law,* 20,1, 13–25.

Barnard, G., Fuller, K., Robbins, & Shaw, T. (1989). *The Child Molester.* New York: Brunner-Mazel.

This book deals with the adult molester, but provides information useful in understanding and treating the adolescent. It embodies a basically psychiatric approach to the problem. It provides some useful balance to the behavioral-cognitive approach now dominant in the field. It contains a brief but informative section on hormonal treatment of the offender.

Bateson, P. P. G. (1978a). Sexual imprinting and optimal outbreeding. *Nature,* 273, 259–260.

Bateson, P. P. G. (1978b). Early experience and sexual preferences. In J. B. Hutchison (Ed.), *Biological Determinants of Sexual Behavior.* New York: John Wiley.

Bateson, P. P. G. (1981). Ontogeny of behavior. *British Medical Bulletin,* 37, 2, 159–164.

Bateson, P. P. G. (1983a). The interpretation of sensitive periods. In A. Oliverio & M. Zapella (Eds.), *The Behavior of Human Infants* (pp. 57–70). New York: Plenum.

Beck, A. T., & Young, J. E. (1985). Depression. In *Clinical Handbook of Psychological Disorders.* New York: The Guilford Press.

Becker, J. V., Cunningham-Rathner, J., & Kaplan, M. S. (1986). Adolescent sexual offenders: Demographics, criminal and sexual histories, and recommendations for reducing future offenses. *Journal of Interpersonal Violence,* 1, 431–445.

Contains a review of several research studies as well as research on 67 adolescent male offenders studied by the authors. It contains separate data for molesters and rapists.

Becker, J. V., Kaplan, M. S., Cunningham-Hathner, J., & Kavoussi, R. (1986). Characteristics of adolescent incest sexual perpetrators: Preliminary findings. *Journal of Family Violence,* 1, 85–97.

Becker, J. V. (1988a). Adolescent sex offenders. *Behavior Therapist,* 11, 185–187.

Becker, J. V. (1988b). The effects of child sexual abuse on adolescent sexual offenders. In G. E. Wyatt & A. G. J. Powell (Eds.), *Lasting Effects of Child Sexual Abuse.* Newbury Park, CA: Sage.

19 percent incidence of victimization among adolescent perpetrators. Atypical population?

Becker, J. V., Kaplan, M. S., Tenke, C. W., & Tartaglini, A. (1991). The incidence of depressive symptomatology in juvenile sex offenders with a history of abuse. *Child Abuse and Neglect,* 15, 4, 531–536.

Becker, J. V., Hunter, J. R. (1992). Evaluation of treatment outcome for adult perpetrators of child sexual abuse. *Criminal Justice and Behavior,* 1, 1, 74–92.

Becker, J. V., & Kaplan, M. S. (1993). Cognitive-behavioral treatment of the juvenile sex offender. In H. E. Barbaree, W. L. Marshall, & S. M. Hudson (Eds.), *The Juvenile Sex Offender* (pp. 531–536). New York: The Guilford Press.

Beech, H. R., Watts, F., & Poole, A. P. (1971). Classical conditioning of a sexual deviation: A preliminary note. *Behavior Therapy,* 2, 400–402.

Bell, R., & Weinberg, M. (1978). *Homosexualities.* New York: Simon and Schuster.

Explores sociological diversity of homosexual population. Turns up lowest incidence of victims cited by Urquiza and Keating.

Bell, A., Weinberg, M., & Hammersmith, S. K. (1981). *Sexual Preference: Its Development in Men and Women.* Bloomington, IN: University Press.

Argues against any psychological determinants for homosexuality.

Blanck, G., & Blanck, R. (1979). *Ego Psychology II.* New York: Columbia University Press.

Blos, P. (1975). The concept of acting out in relation to the adolescent process. In A. Esman (Ed.), *The Psychology of Adolescence.* New York: International Universities Press.

A classic paper on adolescent acting out.

Blos, P. (1985). *Son and father.* New York: The Free Press.

A very good psychodynamic exploration of the role of father in male development.

Bettelheim, B. (1955). *Symbolic Wounds, Puberty Rites and the Envious Male.* New York: Collier Books.

Turns the table on penis envy.

Breer, W. (1992). *The Diagnosis and Treatment of the Young Male Victim of Sexual Abuse.* Springfield, IL: Charles C Thomas.

Browne, E. J., Flanagan, T. J., & McLeod, M. (Eds.). (1984). *Sourcebook of criminal justice statistics: 1983.* Washington, DC: Bureau of Justice Statistics.

Data on female offenders.

Burgess, A. W., Groth, A. N., Holmstrom, L. L., & Sgroi, S. M. (1978). *Sexual Assault of Children and Adolescents.* Lexington, MA: D.C. Heath and Co.

Bourduin, C. M., Henggeler, S. W., Blaske, D. M., & Stein, R. J. (1990). Multisystemic Treatment of Adolescent Sexual Offenders. *International Journal of Offender Therapy and Comparative Criminology, 34,* 2, 105–113.

Cartwright, R. D. (1977). *Night Life, Exploration of Dreaming.* New Jersey: Prentice-Hall.

Cartwright, R. D. (1978). *A Primer on Sleep and Dreaming.* Reading, MA: Addison Wesley.

Castonguay, L. G., Proulx, J., Aubut, J., McKibben, A., & Campbell, M. (1993). Sexual preference assessment of sexual aggressors: Predictors of penile response magnitude. *Archives of Sexual Behavior, 4,* 325–334.

Coates, S. (1990). Ontogenesis of boyhood gender identity disorder. *Journal of the American Academy of Psychoanalysis, 18,* 414–438.

Coates, S., Friedman, R. C., & Wolfe, L. (1991). The etiology of boyhood gender identity disorder: A model for integrating temperament development and psychodynamics. *Psychoanalytic Dialogues, 1,* 481–523.

Cook, M., & Howells, K. (Eds.). (1981). *Adult Sexual Interest in Children.* New York: Academic Press.

Daldin, H. (1988). The fate of the sexually abused child. *Clinical Social Work Journal, 16,* 1.

This author presents an overview of psychoanalytic thinking about the impact of sexual victimization on children. Identification with the aggressor and repetition compulsion are identified as principle responses. The creation of a predisposition to borderline personality organization and other severe psychopathology is also discussed. Although it deals ostensibly with victims, the comments on identification with the aggressor and repetition compulsion provide an explanation of how some victims may turn into offenders.

Davis, G., & Leitenberg, H. (1987). Adolescent sex offenders. *Psychological Bulletin*, 3, 10, 417–427.

Doshay, L. J. (1943). *The Boy Sex Offender and His Later Career*. New York: Grune and Stratton.

Dwyer, M. S., & Myers, S. (1990). Sex offender treatment: A six month to ten year follow-up study. *Annals of Sex Research*, 3, 305–318.

Eccles, A., Marshall, W. L., & Barbaree, H. E. (1994). Differentiating rapists and non-offenders using the rape index. *Behavior Research and Therapy*, 32, 5, 539–546.

Erickson, M. F. (1991). How often do abused children become child abusers? *Harvard Mental Health Letter*. Boston, MA: President and Fellows of Harvard College.

Exner, J. E. (1979). *The Rorschach, A Comprehensive System*. New York: John Wiley and Sons.

Fehrenbach, P. A., Smith, W., Monastersky, C., & Deisher, R. W. (1986). Adolescent sexual offenders: Offender and offense characteristics. *American Journal of Orthopsychiatry*, 56, 225–233.

University of Washington study of 300 sex offenders. Much descriptive data, but does not distinguish between rapists and molesters.

Feldman, M. P., & MacCulloch, N. J. (1971). *Homosexual Behavior: Theory and Assessment*. Oxford: Pergamon.

These writers belong to the same school as Storms, seeing the development of sexual orientation as a predominantly pubertal phenomenon guided by the principles of learning theory. The first intensely erotic experience, reinforced by orgasm, plays a vital role in fixing sexual orientation. If this first experience is homosexual, and it is followed by unpleasant heterosexual experiences, the likelihood of an adult homosexual orientation is great. Developing homosexual orientation is reinforced by fantasy about sex with males. It is entrenched more deeply by masturbation and orgasm. These ideas could easily be extrapolated into an explanation of the origins of pedophilia.

Finkelhor, D. (1979). *Sexually Victimized Children*. New York: The Free Press.

Finkelhor, D., & Araji, S. (1986). Explanations of pedophilia: A four factor model. *Journal of Sex Research*, 22, 2.

This is one of the best theoretical treatments of the causes and classification of the pedophilias. The authors emphasize that this is a multiply-determined behavior. Areas of causation are explored. Some subdivisions of the pedophile population are also proposed.

Fisher, G., & Howell, L. M. (1970). Psychological needs of homosexual pedophiles. *Diseases of the Nervous System*, 3, 623–625.

Characterizes male victims as predisposed to abuse.

Fogel, G. I., Lane, F., & Liebert, R. (Eds.). (1986). *The Psychology of Men.* New York: Basic Books.

A psychoanalytically-oriented work. I found the introduction and chapter eight on the history of homosexuality well written and useful. Several other chapters suffer the twin defects of dogmatism and poor writing style that characterize many psychoanalytic works.

Ford, K. C. S., & Beach, F. R. (1951). *Patterns of Sexual Behavior.* New York: Perennial Library.

A survey of the anthropological literature on sexuality in a wide sample of world cultures. Documents some culturally approved behaviors occurring in other cultures which would be sex offenses in ours.

Freeman-Longo, R. E. (1986). The impact of sexual victimization on males. *Child Abuse and Neglect,* 10, 411–414.

Freud, S. (1953). *The Interpretation of Dreams.* New York: Basic Books.

Freund, K. (1977). Psychophysiological assessment of change in erotic preference. *Behavior Research and Therapy,* 15, 297–301.

Freund, K., Watson, R., & Dickey, R. (1988). *Does Sexual Abuse in Childhood Cause Pedophilia?* Joint Study of the Dept. of Behavioral Sexology and the Forensic Division, Clarke Institute of Psychiatry, Toronto, Canada.

Freund, K., & Watson, R. J. (1992). The proportions of heterosexual and homosexual pedophiles among sex offenders against children: An exploratory study. *Journal of Sex and Marital Therapy,* 18, 1, 33–34.

Friedrich, W. N., Beilke, R. L., & Urquiza, A. J. (1988). Behavior problems in young sexually abused boys. *Journal of Interpersonal Violence,* 3, 1, 21–28.

Comparison study of 112 sexually abused boys with a control group.

Frisbie, L. D. (1965). Treated sex offenders who reverted to sexually deviant behavior. *Federal Probation,* 29, 52–57.

Furby, L., Weinrott, M., & Blackshaw, L. (1989). Sex offender recidivism: a review. *Psychological Bulletin,* 105, 1, 3–30.

This is a major study which is very critical of the recidivism research in the sex offender field. The research is faulted for not subdividing sex offenders into subtypes or dealing meaningfully with the issue of unreported offenses. A major conclusion is that, as of this writing (1989), there is no scientific evidence that sex offender treatment is effective. The article deals with adult sex offenders.

Gebhardt, P., Gagnon, J., Pomperoy, W. P., & Christianson, C. V. (1956). *Sex Offenders: An Analysis of Types.* New York: Harper and Row.

Gerber, P. N. (1990). Victims becoming offenders: A study of ambiguities. In M. Hunter (Ed.), *The Sexually Abused Male, Vol. 1.* Lexington, MA: Lexington Books.

Gilgun, J. F. (1990). Factors mediating the effects of childhood maltreatment. In M. Hunter (Ed.), *The Sexually Abused Male.* Lexington, MA: Lexington Books.

Goldberg, R. (Ed.). (1984). *Heinz Kohut: How Does Analysis Cure.* Chicago & London: University of Chicago Press.

Goldberg, R. (1985). *Progress in Self Psychology.* New York: The Guilford Press.

Gomes-Schwartz, B. (1984). Juvenile sexual offenders. In *Sexually exploited children: Service and research project.* Washington, DC: U.S. Department of Justice.

Green, A., & Kahn, M. T. (1989, January). The malingering adolescent sex offender. *Interchange. Cooperative Newsletter of the Adolescent Perpetrator Network.*

Reviews phenomenon of adolescent sex offenders making up additional offenses and victimizations in order to extract various benefits from staff and program.

Grossman, L. S., Cavanaugh, J. L., & Haywood, T. W. (1992). Deviant sexual responsiveness on penile plethysmography using visual stimuli: Alleged child molesters vs. normal control subjects. *Journal of Nervous and Mental Disorders,* 180, 3, 207–208.

Groth, A. N. (1977). The adolescent sexual offender and his prey. *International Journal of Offender Therapy and Comparative Criminology,* 21, 249–254.

Groth, A. N., Burgess, A. W., Birnbaum, H. J., & Gary, T. S. (1978). A study of the child molester: Myths and realities. *LAE Journal of the American Criminal Justice Association,* 41, 1.

Groth, A. N., & Loredo, C. M. (1981). Juvenile sex offenders: Guidelines for assessment. *International Journal of Offender Therapy and Comparative Criminology,* 25, 1, 31–39.

Groth, A. N., Hobson, W. F., & Gary, T. S. (1982). The child molester: Clinical observations. In J. Conte & D. A. Shore (Eds.), *Social Work and Child Sexual Abuse.* New York: Haworth.

Groth's well-known fixated and regressed offender typology is presented here.

Group for the Advancement of Psychiatry (1977). *Psychiatry and Sex Psychopath Legislation: The 30s to the 80s,* 18, 90. New York: Group for the Advancement of Psychiatry.

This book deals with adult offenders. It reviews the appropriateness of various treatment modalities, such as traditional psychotherapy, behavior modification, and aversive techniques. Its conclusion recommends the repeal of sexual psychopath legislation under which adult offenders have been prosecuted and incarcerated for treatment.

Hall, G. C. N., Maiuro, R. D., Vitaliano, P. P., & Proctor, W. C. (1986). The utility of the MMPI with men who have sexually assaulted children. *Journal of Consulting and Clinical Psychology,* 54, 493–496.

Herdt, G. H. (1981). *Guardians of the Flutes.* New York: McGraw-Hill.

This is a study of male initiation rites in a society discovered by the west only in the 1930s. The rites seemed to be aimed at strengthening masculine identity in a society where it is likely to be weak for complex cultural reasons. The procedures are shocking, but they underline many of the themes about the development and importance of maleness to men put forth in this book. I reviewed this data extensively in my 1992 book. I believe familiarity with Herdt's work is essential for anyone who wants to understand the nature of maleness.

Hindman, J. (1988). New insight into adult and juvenile sex offenders. *Community Safety Quarterly,* 1, 4, 1.

Hobson, J. A. (1977). *The Dreaming Brain.* New York: Basic Books.

Howells, K. (1981). Adult sexual interest in children: Considerations relevant to theories of etiology. In M. Cook & K. Howells (Eds.), *Adult Sexual Interest in Children.* London: Academic Press.

Develops situational vs. preferential typology of offenders.

Hsu, L. K. G., & Starzynski, J. (1990). Adolescent rapists and adolescent child sexual assaulters. *International Journal of Offender Therapy and Comparative Criminology.* 34, 1, 23–30.

A study of fifteen adolescent rapists and seventeen adolescent child sexual assaulters. The child sexual assaulters sound like molesters. This study finds the child sexual assaulters to be younger and less violent. The authors imply that molesting at a young age may progress into rape with increasing age and experience. The population was drawn from court referrals to a psychiatric clinic.

Hunter, J. A., Goodwin, O. W., & Becker, J. V. (1994). The relationship between phallometrically measured deviant sexual arousal and clinical characteristics in juvenile sex offenders. *Behavior Research and Therapy,* 32, 5, 533–538.

Hunter, J. R., Jr., Childers, S. E., Gerald, R., & Esmaili, H. (1990). An examination of variables differentiating clinical subtypes of incestuous child molesters. *International Journal of Offender Therapy and Comparative Criminology,* 34, 2, 95–104.

This study compares MMPI data with known clinical facts about the offenders. It supports the belief that child molesters are not a heterogeneous population and that treatment prognosis and treatment selection should vary according to clinical subtypes. The two variables associated with the greatest pathology, as measured by the MMPI, were a history of victimization in the offender and a pattern of molesting with greater frequency. The authors urge further exploration of a history of physical abuse as a dynamic factor.

Hunter, J. R., & Santos, D. R. (1991). The use of specialized cognitive-behavioral therapies in the treatment of adolescent sexual offenders. *International Journal of Offender Therapy and Comparative Criminology,* 34, 3, 239–247.

This study looks at twelve adolescents who have molested younger males and fifteen who have molested younger females. (Seven of the sample have molested both sexes and are included in each set of data, so the actual N for the study is 20). Penile plethysmograph responses are taken to deviant and heterosexual stimuli to form a baseline. After treatment, a new measurement is made. One population shows a 33 percent drop in erectile response to deviant stimuli and the other a 39 percent decrease. The included charts indicate that what is being measured is the degree of erection, not presence or absence of response. For example, the female victim group reduced degree of tumescence from about 75 percent to slightly less than 50 percent.

Johnson, R. E. (1987). Mother's versus father's role in causing delinquency. *Adolescence,* 12, 305–315.

Johnson, R. I., & Shrier, D. (1985). Sexual victimization of boys. *Journal of Adolescent Health Care,* 6, 372–376.

> Statistical data showing 58 percent of sexually abused boys self-identify as nonheterosexual vs. 10 percent of controls.

Johnson, R. I., & Shrier, D. (1987). Past sexual victimization by females of male patients in an adolescent medicine clinic population. *American Journal of Psychiatry,* 144, 5, 650–652.

> 20 percent of boys molested by females self identify as nonheterosexual. 57 percent of boys molested by males self identify as nonheterosexual. Only 4 percent of controls identify as nonheterosexual.

Kavoussi, R. J., Kaplan, M., Becker, J. V. (1988). Psychiatric diagnoses in adolescent sex offenders. *Journal of the American Academy of Adolescent Psychiatry,* 27, 241–242.

Kelly, R. J. (1982). Behavioral reorientation of pedophiliacs: Can it be done? *Clinical Psychology Review,* 2, 387–408.

Kempton, T., & Forehand, R. (1992). Juvenile sex offenders: similar to, or different from, other incarcerated delinquent offenders. *Behavioral Research and Therapy,* 30, 5, 533–536.

Kernberg, O. (1985). *Borderline Conditions and Pathological Narcissism.* New York: Jason Aronson.

Knight, R. A., Rosenberg, R. A., & Schneider, B. A. (1985). Classification of sexual offenders: Perspectives, methods, and validation. In H. W. Burgess (Ed.), *Rape and Sexual Assault.* New York: Garland.

> Comments on heterogeneity of adolescent offender population.

Knight, R. A., & Prentky, R. A. (1990). Classifying sexual offenders. In W. L. Marshall, D. B. Laws, & H. E. Barbaree (Eds.), *Handbook Of Sexual Assault.* New York: Plenum.

Knight, R. A., & Prentky, R. A. (1993). Exploring characteristics for classifying juvenile sex offenders. In H. E. Barbaree, W. L. Marshall, & S. M. Hudson (Eds.), *The Juvenile Sex Offender.* New York: The Guilford Press.

Knopp, F. H. (1982). *Remedial intervention in adolescent sex offenses: Nine program descriptions.* Syracuse, NY: Safer Society Press.

Kohut, H. (1971). *The Analysis of the Self.* London: International Universities Press.

Kohut, H. (1984). *How Does Analysis Cure?* Chicago, University of Chicago Press.

Kroth, J. A. (1979). *Child Sexual Abuse: Analysis of a Family Therapy Approach.* Springfield, IL: Charles C Thomas.

Lachar, B. (1974). *The MMPI: Clinical Assessment and Automated Interpretation.* Los Angeles, CA: Western Psychological Services.

Lane, S. (1991). Special offender populations. In G. Ryan & S. Lane (Eds.), *Juvenile Sex Offending.* Lexington, MA: Lexington Books.

Langevin, R. (1985). *Erotic Preference, Gender Identity, and Aggression in Men: New Research Studies.* Hillsdale, NJ: Lawrence Erlbaum Associates.

> This is an anthology composed of research studies in the areas suggested by the title. Its conclusions attack many of the commonly held beliefs about these

issues. Many of the studies are of small populations. Some compare sex offenders only with a control group of other criminals, making the findings more tenuous than the editor suggests in his conclusion.

Langevin, R., Hucker, S., Handy, L., Purins, J., Russon, R., & Hook, H. (1985). Erotic preference and aggression in pedophilia: A comparison of heterosexual, homosexual, and bisexual types. In R. Langevin (Ed.), *Erotic Preference, Gender Identity, and Aggression in Men: New Research Studies.* Hillsdale, NJ: Lawrence Erlbaum Associates.

An interesting group of several research studies. The most interesting finding is that control group men respond erotically to children as young as six years of age in laboratory phallometric testing. The control group consists of a small sample of 16 men who are inmates charged largely with fraud and theft.

Langs, R. (1995). Psychoanalysis and the science of evolution. *American Journal of Psychotherapy,* 49, 1.

Lanyon, R. I. (1986). Theory and treatment in child molestation. *Journal of Consulting and Clinical Psychology,* 54, 2, 176–191.

Reviews literature on classification, etiology, and treatment of molesters. Comes down on the side of the behavioral view and of behavioral and family treatment modalities. Urges the subdivision of the offender population into molesters and rapists for research purposes.

LeVay, S. (1991). A difference in hypothalamic structure between heterosexual and homosexual men. *Science,* 253, 5023, 1034–1037.

This paper is cited by some as proof that homosexuality is a genetically transmitted condition. In actuality, the results are still in dispute, since the study involved a very small sample of brains of homosexual men who had died of AIDS.

Lewis, D. O., Shankok, S. S., & Pincus, J. H. (1979). Juvenile male sexual assaulters. *American Journal of Psychiatry,* 136, 1194–1196.

Longo, R. E., & McFadin, B. (1981). Sexually inappropriate behavior: Development of the sexual offender. *Law and Order,* 29, 21–23.

Longo, R. E. (1982). Sexual learning and experience among adolescent sexual offenders. *International Journal of Offender Therapy and Comparative Criminology,* 26, 235–241.

Longo, R. E., & Groth, A. N. (1983). Juvenile sexual offenses in the histories of adult rapists and child molesters. *International Journal of Offender Therapy and Comparative Criminology,* 27, 150–155.

McConaghy, N. (1970). Penile response conditioning and its relationship to aversion therapy in homosexuals. *Behavior Therapy,* 1, 213–221.

McCraw, A. K., & Pegg-McNab, J. (1989). Rorschach comparisons of male juvenile sex offenders and nonsex offenders. *Journal of Personality Assessment,* 53, 3, 546–553.

McGrath, R. J. (1991). Sex offender risk assessment and disposition planning: Review of empirical and clinical findings. *International Journal of Offender Therapy and Comparative Criminology,* 35, 4, 328–350.

An excellent review of factors leading to the likelihood of recidivism in adult sex offenders.

McGuire, R. J., Carlisle, J. M., & Young, B. G. (1965). Sexual deviations as conditioned behavior: a hypothesis. *Behavior Research and Therapy*, 2, 185–190.

An important formulation of the view that sexual attraction to and preference for children is instilled when a perpetrator-to-be masturbates to deviant fantasies about children.

Marshall, W. L., & Barbaree, H. E. (1990). An integrated theory of the etiology of sexual offending. In W. L. Marshall, D. R. Laws, & H. E. Barbaree (Eds.), *Handbook of Sexual Assault: Issues, Theories and Treatment of the Offender.* New York: Plenum Press.

Marshall, W. L., & Barbaree, H. E. (1990b). Outcome of comprehensive cognitive-behavioral treatment programs. In W. L. Marshall, D. R. Laws, & H. E. Barbaree (Eds.), *Handbook of Sexual Assault: Issues, Theories and Treatment of the Offender.* New York: Plenum Press.

Marshall, W. L., Jones, R., Ward, T., Johnson, P., & Barbaree, H. E. (1991). Treatment outcome with sex offenders. *Clinical Psychology Review,* 11.

Marshall, W. L., & Eccles, A. (1993). Pavlovian conditioning processes in adolescent sex offenders. In H. E. Barbaree, W. L. Marshall, & S. M. Hudson (Eds.), *The Juvenile Sex Offender.* New York: The Guilford Press.

Marshall, W. L., Hudson, S. M., & Hodkinson, S. (1993). The importance of attachment bonds in development of juvenile sex offending. In H. E. Barbaree, W. L. Marshall, & S. M. Hudson (Eds.), *The Juvenile Sex Offender.* New York: The Guilford Press.

Mohr, J. W., Turner, R. E., & Jerry, M. B. (1964). *Pedophilia and Exhibitionism.* Toronto, Canada: University of Toronto Press.

Money, J. (1965). Psychosexual differentiation. In *Sex Research: New Developments.* New York: Holt, Rinehart & Winston.

Data on critical periods occurring early in human development and irreversibly shaping gender orientation and identity.

Money, J. (1968). Discussion of the hormonal inhibition of libido in male sex offenders. In R. Michael (Ed.), *Endocrinology and human behavior.* London: Oxford University Press.

Money, J. (1970). Use of androgen-depleting hormone in the treatment of male sex offenders. *Journal of Sex Research,* 6, 165–172.

Money, J. (1972). The therapeutic use of androgen-depleting hormone. *International Psychiatric Clinics,* 8, 165–174.

Money, J. (1990). Forensic sexology: Paraphilic serial rape (biastophilia) and lust murder (erotophonophilia). *American Journal of Psychotherapy,* 4, 1.

Included here because the author argues that paraphilias and perversions are a brain disease best treated by chemotherapy. The article is mostly a summary prepared for use by a defense attorney in a specific case.

Muster, N. J. (1992). Treating the adolescent victim turned offender. *Adolescence,* 27, 106, 441–450.

> Describes adolescent sex offender treatment as focusing on confrontation and lacking in empathy. Surveys therapists working in the sex abuse field. Those in correctional settings prefer the confrontational mode. The majority, in outpatient settings, did not.

National Task Force on Juvenile Sexual Offending (1988). Preliminary report from the National Task Force on Juvenile Sexual Offending. *Juvenile and Family Court Journal,* 39, 2, 1–67.

National Task Force on Juvenile Sex Offending (1993). The revised report from the National Task Force on Juvenile Sex Offending, of The National Adolescent Perpetrator Network. *Juvenile and Family Court Journal,* 44, 4.

Nicolosi, J. (1991). *Reparative Therapy of Male Homosexuality.* New Jersey: Jason Aronson.

O'Brien, M. J. (1989). *Characteristics of Male Adolescent Sibling Incest Offenders: Preliminary Findings.* Orwell, Vermont: Safer Society Press.

O'Brien, M., & Bera, W. (1986). Adolescent sexual offenders: A descriptive typology. *A Newsletter of the National Family Life Education Network,* 1, 1–5.

O'Donohue, W., & Letourneau, E. (1993). A brief group treatment for the modification of denial in child sexual abusers: Outcome and follow-up. *Child Abuse and Neglect,* 17, 2, 299–304.

Paz, O. (1961). *The Labyrinth of Solitude.* New York: Grove Press.

Proulx, J., Aubut, J., McKibben, A., & Cote, M. (1994). Penile responses of rapists and nonrapists to rape stimuli involving physical violence or humiliation. *Archives of Sexual Behavior,* 3, 295–310.

Quincy, V. L., & Earls, M. (1990). The modification of sexual preferences. In W. L. Marshall, D. R. Laws, & H. E. Barbaree (Eds.), *Handbook of Sexual Assault: Issues, Theories and Treatment of the Offender.* New York: Plenum Press.

Rachman, S. (1966). Sexual fetishisms: An experimental analogue. *Psychological Record,* 16, 293–296.

> This and the following work lay the foundation for behavioral thinking about sex offenders and for assumptions about their proper treatment for years to come.

Rachman, S., & Hodgson, R. J. (1966). Experimentally induced "sexual fetishism:" Replication and development. *Psychological Record,* 18, 25–27.

Robertson, J. M. (1990). Group counseling and the high risk offender. *Federal Probation,* 54, 48–51.

> Found that 73 percent of a population of adult homosexual pedophiles had been sexually molested as children.

Ross, J., & Loss, P. (1991). Assessment of the juvenile sex offender. In G. Ryan & S. Lane (Eds.), *Juvenile Sex Offending.* Lexington, MA: Lexington Books.

Rossman, P. (1980). The pederasts. In L. G. Schulz (Ed.), *The Sexual Victimology of Youth.* Springfield, IL: Charles C Thomas.

Classifies pederasts. Describes victims as from problem-ridden families, hungry for affection, money, gifts, excitement, and with previous homosexual contact.

Rubinstein, M., Yeager, C. R., Goodstein, C., & Lewis, D. O. (1993). Sexually assaultive male juveniles: A follow-up. *American Journal of Psychiatry*, 150, 2, 262–265.

Ryan, G., & Lane, S. (Eds.). (1991). *Juvenile Sex Offending*. Lexington, MA: Lexington Books.

Ryan, G., Lane, S., Davis, J., & Isaac, C. (1987). Juvenile sex offenders: Development and correction. *Child Abuse and Neglect*, 11, 3, 385–395.

Salter, A. C. (1980). *Treating Child Sex Offenders and Victims*. Newbury Park, CA: Sage Publications.

This book deals with the treatment of both offenders and victims. It provides an excellent summary of the behavioral-cognitive approach to treating offenders. It has an extensive bibliography of the research literature. The title implies that the work deals with child sex offenders, but this does not seem to be the case. The treatments outlined are the standard ones used with adult offenders. No specific reference is made to the special treatment needs of children or adolescents who offend.

Sandberg, D. N. (Ed.). (1989). *The Child Abuse-Delinquency Connection*. Lexington, MA: Lexington Books.

Sanders, M., Bain, J., & Langevin, R. (1985). Peripheral sex hormones, homosexuality and gender identity. In R. Langevin (Ed.), *Erotic Preference, Gender Identity, and Aggression in Men: New Research Studies*. Hillsdale, NJ: Lawrence Erlbaum Associates.

This is a research study on the question identified in the title. It finds no connection between hormones, homosexuality, and gender identity. In reviewing other studies of this issue, the authors conclude that the better designed studies have produced similar results.

Saunders, E. B., & Awad, G. A. (1988). Assessment, management, and treatment planning for male adolescent sexual offenders. *American Journal of Orthopsychiatry*, 58, 4, 571–579.

Schram, D. D., & Malloy, C. D. (1992). *Juvenile Sex Offenders: A Follow-up Study of Reoffense Behavior*. Seattle, WA: Urban Policy Research.

Five-year follow-up study of 197 offenders treated in a residential program. Twelve percent recidivism on sex offenses. Much higher recidivism for nonsexual offenses.

Sefarbi, R. (1990). Admitters and deniers among adolescent sex offenders and their families: A preliminary study. *The American Journal of Orthopsychiatry*, 60, 3, 460–465.

Seghorn, T. K., Prentky, R. A., & Boucher, R. J. (1987). Childhood sexual abuse in the lives of sexually aggressive offenders. *Journal of the American Academy of Child and Adolescent Psychiatry*, 26, 2, 262–267.

Good data comparing rapists and molesters. Large sample of prisoners well-known to these researchers. Data from case records and extensive interaction with inmates.

Sermabeikian, P. G., & Martinez, D. (1994). Treatment of adolescent sexual offenders: Theory-based practice. *Child Abuse and Neglect,* 10, 11, 969–975.

Shapiro, S., & Doniniak, G. (1990). Common psychological defenses seen in the treatment of sexually abused adolescents. *American Journal of Psychotherapy,* 44, 1.

Discusses seductive mannerisms copied from the perpetrator as a form of reaction formation or denial of anxiety aroused by the trauma. Stresses the need to take on defenses slowly so that they are not overwhelmed. This of necessity requires long-term treatment.

Shaw, J. A., Campo-Bowen, A. E., Applegate, B., Perez, D., Antoine, L. B., Hart, E. L., Lahey, B. B., Testa, R. J., & Devaney, A. (1993). Young boys who commit serious sexual offenses: Demographics, psychometrics, and phenomenology. *Bulletin of the American Academy of Psychiatry and Law,* 21, 4, 399–408.

A psychiatrically oriented description and analysis of the young offender population in terms of DSM–III criteria and underlying psychodynamics.

Shoor, M., Speed, M. H., & Bartelt, C. (1966). Syndrome of the adolescent child molester. *American Journal of Psychiatry,* 122, 783–789.

Simon, W. T., & Schouten, P. G. (1993). The plethysmograph reconsidered: Comments on Barker and Howell. *Bulletin of the American Academy of Psychiatry and Law,* 21, 4, 505–512.

Sizonenko, P. C. (1978). Endocrinology in preadolescents and adolescents. *American Journal of Diseases of Children,* 132, 704–712.

Adolescent males experience an increase in testosterone levels of up to four times prepubertal levels.

Smets, A. C., & Cebula, C. M. (1987). A group treatment program for adolescent sex offenders: Five steps toward resolution. *Child Abuse and Neglect,* 11, 247–254.

Smith, W. R., Monastersky, C., & Deisher, R. M. (1987). MMPI-based personality types among juvenile sexual offenders. *Journal of Clinical Psychology,* 43, 4, 422–430.

Spence, J., & Helmreich, R. (1978). *Masculinity and Femininity.* Austin, TX & London: University of Texas Press.

A research study with the traditional questionnaire method applied to a sample of college students. The prose is difficult, but the authors conclude that their sample suggests that males and females identify a series of traits that they label as masculine and feminine. In other words, this population is characterized by a series of somewhat variable stereotypes about what is masculine and what is feminine.

Stoller, R. (1968). *Sex and Gender.* New York: Science House.

Stoller in an analytically-oriented psychiatrist working at the gender identity clinic at UCLA. This work offers many insights into the process of gender identity formation, the various classifications of gender identity, and the treatment of conflicts arising out of gender identity issues.

Stoller, R. (1985). *Observing the Erotic Imagination.* New Haven, CT & London: Yale University Press.

This work contains a definition of perversion as a form of erotic fantasy or activity which features hostility toward the object or toward the self. Hurting and humiliation are key features of the perverse act or fantasy. The work also includes some fascinating data on male issues in a New Guinea culture. Stoller uses this exploration of sexuality to write a devastating criticism of learning theory and an equally devastating criticism of writing and research within psychoanalysis.

Storms, M. D. (1981). A theory of erotic orientation development. *Psychological Review,* 88, 340–53.

This article develops the thesis that homosexual orientations (and, by implication, other sexual orientations) arise at the time of puberty, rather than early childhood. Normal bonds between same-sex peers and sexual experimentation between such peers provide the matrix. Some individuals have stronger sex drives during this period and thus eroticize these experiences to a greater extent than others, leading to a lifelong homosexual orientation.

Struve, J. (1990). Dancing with the patriarchy: The politics of sexual abuse. In M. Hunter (Ed.), *The Sexually Abused Male.* Lexington, MA: Lexington Books.

Summit, R. (1988). Hidden victims, hidden pain. In G. E. Wyatt & G. J. Powell (Eds.), *Lasting Effects of Child Sexual Abuse.* Beverly Hills, CA: Sage.

Summit is an important spokesman for those who believe that sexual abuse is pandemic and ignored or covered-up by society. He is a strong believer in the importance and common occurrence of repressed memories.

Swan, R. (1985). The child as an active participant in sexual abuse. *Clinical Social Work Journal,* 14, 1, 62–77.

Tartar, R. E., Hegedus, R. M., Alterman, A. I., & Katz-Garris, L. (1983). Cognitive capacities of juvenile, nonviolent and sexual offenders. *Journal of Nervous and Mental Disease,* 171, 9, 564–567.

Tracy, F., Donnelly, H., & Morgenbesser, L. D. (1983). Program evaluation: Recidivism research involving sex offenders. In J. G. Greer & I. R. Stuart (Eds.), *The Sexual Aggressor: Current Perspectives on Treatment* (pp. 198–213). New York: Van Nostrand Reinhold.

Truscott, D. (1993). Adolescent offenders: comparison for sexual, violent, and property offenses. *Psychological Reports,* 73, 2, 657–658.

MMPI study. Groups found not to differ, but sex offenders were twice as likely as other groups to have a history of sexual abuse.

Ulman, R. B., & Paul, H. (1989). Self-psychological theory and approach to treating substance abuse disorders: The "intersubjective absorption" hypothesis. In R. Goldberg (Ed.), *Dimensions of Self Experience.* Hillsdale, NJ: The Analytic Press.

U.S. Department of Justice (1988). *An Administrators Overview: Questions and Answers on Issues Related to the Incarcerated Male Sex Offender.* Washington, D.C.: Government Printing Office.

Data on recidivism with and without treatment.

U.S. Department of Justice, Federal Bureau of Investigation (1977–1980). *Uniform Crime Reports.* Washington, D.C.: Government Printing Office.

Urquiza, A. L. (1988). *The Effects of Childhood Sexual Abuse in an Adult Male Population.* Doctoral Dissertation, University of Washington, Seattle.

Urquiza, A. L., and Keating, L. M. (1990). The prevalence of sexual victimization of males. In M. Hunter (Ed.), *The Sexually Abused Male, Vol. 1.* Lexington, MA: Lexington Books.

Reviews previous studies of the incidence of sexual abuse of males. The authors' own method of study has yielded a much higher incidence (17.3%) than the other studies. Urquiza and Keating argue that their methods are the best and probably yield the most accurate results.

Vander Mey, B. J. (1988). The sexual victimization of male children: A review of previous research. *Child Abuse and Neglect,* 123, 671–672.

Van Ness, S. R. (1984). Rape as instrumental violence: A study of youth offenders. *Journal of Offender Counseling, Services, and Rehabilitation,* 9, 161–170.

Whitam, F. L., & Mathy, R. M. (1986). *Male Homosexuality in Four Societies.* Praeger: New York.

White, J. W., & Koss, M. P. (1993). Adolescent sexual aggression within heterosexual relationships: prevalence, characteristics, and causes. In H. E. Barbaree, W. L. Marshall, & S. M. Hudson (Eds.), *The Juvenile Sex Offender.* New York: The Guilford Press.

White, R. L. (1985). *The First Three Years of Life.* New York: Prentice-Hall.

Widom, C., & Ames, M. A. (1994). Criminal consequences of childhood sexual victimization. *Child Abuse and Neglect,* 18, 4, 303–318.

Winson, J. (1985). *Brain and Psyche.* New York: Anchor Press.

Yates, A. (1978). *Sex Without Shame: Encouraging the Child's Healthy Sexual Development.* New York: William Morrow.

Presents a wide variety of case material illustrating sexual practices and attitudes in different social and cultural contexts.

Yates, A. (1982). Children eroticized by incest. *American Journal of Psychiatry,* 139, 482–485.

Yochelson, S., & Samenow, S. (1976). *The Criminal Personality.* New York: Jason Aronson.

Although not formally dealing with adolescent molesters, this book is widely read and cited by clinicians in the field.

Young, A. (1992). Sex-offender treatment likened to child abuse. *The Arizona Republic,* June 14.

Young, A. (1992). Sex-test device halted for boy. *The Arizona Republic,* June 24.

INDEX

A

Abel 1984, 9
Abel and Becker 1985, 14
Abel, Osborne, and Twigg 1993, 19
Abuse cycle, 59, 133
Adams et al. 1992, 119
Addictions, 59
Adolescence
  sexual orientation issues in, 71
  significance in sexual development, 134
  adolescent molesters as victims, 7, 10, 133
  adolescent molesters, clinical literature, 13
African-American culture, 70
African-Americans, 12, 18
  masculinity issues among, 12
Ageton 1983, 8
Aggression, 118
Aggression in males, 57
Ambitions and ideals
  in self psychology, 54
  role of in male development, 55
Ambivalence, 75
  about perpetrators, 75, 76
Amir 1971, 10
Anger, 102, 199
  role of in sex offenses, 132
Anger management, 132
Anthropological literature
  on male development, 63
Antisocial personality, 60
  among sex offenders, 16
Anxiety, 58, 59, 60, 143
  assessment, 108, 120
Attachment, 30–31 (*see also* Bonding)
Attacks
  on therapist, 192
Authority
  use of in group, 149–50
Awad, Saunders, & Levine 1979, 35

B

Bandura, 37
Barbaree and Eccles 1990, 30
Barbaree and Marshall 1993, 33
Barbaree, Hudson, and Seto, 10, 17
Barker and Howell, 118
Bateson, 35
Becker, Cunningham, Raffner, and Kaplan 1986, 35
Becker, Judith, 10, 15, 16, 18, 22, 25, 46, 64, 131
Beech, Watts, and Poole, 14
Behavioral-cognitive theorists, 14
  behavioral-cognitive therapy vs. psychodynamic therapy, 139–140
Behavioral-cognitive treatment, 15
  effectiveness of, 24–25, 30
Bettelheim 1955, 49
Biological determinism, 64
Biological theories, 31–36
  of human sexuality, 33
Blaming victims, 199
Blanchard, 28–29
Blanck, Gertrude and Reuben, 49, 62
Blos, Peter, 49–53, 62
Bonding, 30–31
  borderline personality, among adolescent molesters, 61–62
Breer, 63
Browne et al. 1984, 7

C

Card sorts, 111
Cartwright, Rosalind, 104
Castonguay et al., 118
Castration, 63
Classical analysis, 48–50
Cognitive distortions, 15, 130

217